Mohawk Region Waterfall Guide

From the Capital District
to Cooperstown & Syracuse

The Mohawk & Schoharie Valleys, Helderbergs,
and Leatherstocking Country

Russell Dunn

D1430440

BLACK·DOME

Published by

Black Dome Press Corp.
1011 Route 296, Hensonville, New York 12439
www.blackdomepress.com
Tel: (518) 734-6357

First Edition Paperback 2007
Copyright © 2007 by C. Russell Dunn

ISBN-13: 978-1-883789-54-1
ISBN-10: 1-883789-54-0

Library of Congress Cataloging-in-Publication Data

Dunn, Russell.

  Mohawk Region Waterfall guide : from the Capital district to Cooperstown & Syracuse the Mohawk & Schoharie Valleys, Helderbergs, and Leatherstocking Country / Russell Dunn.

    p. cm.

  Includes bibliographical references and index.

  ISBN-13: 978-1-883789-54-1
  ISBN-10: 1-883789-54-0

1. Hiking—New York (State)—Mohawk River Valley—Guidebooks. 2. Waterfalls—New York (State)—Mohawk River Valley—Guidebooks. 3. Mohawk River Valley (N.Y.)—Guidebooks. I. Title.

  GV199.42.N652D86 2007

  796.5109747'6—dc22

                                                    2007019698

Outdoor recreational activities are by their very nature potentially hazardous and contain risk. See "Caution: Safety Tips," page 18.

Maps created with TOPO! software © 2006 National Geographic Maps. To learn more visit: http://www.nationalgeographic.com/topo

Cover photograph: *Outlet Falls after Floyd* by Dietrich Gehring, dietrichgehring.com.

Design: Toelke Associates

Printed in the USA

10   9   8   7   6   5   4   3   2   1

To Adam R. Dunn—

white-water enthusiast, musician,

drummer, and graphic designer.

The fact that he is my son

is simply a bonus.

Table of

Contents

Foreword

While reading one of Russell Dunn's earlier books, *Adirondack Waterfall Guide*, it occurred to me that the author was helping to create a new type of outdoor enthusiast—someone who, instead of "bagging mountain summits" (a phrase Dunn uses in the current book), would spend their time "bagging" waterfalls. Sure enough—in the preface to *Mohawk Region Waterfall Guide* there is a whole section on "Waterfall Networking." It describes the work these new enthusiasts have been doing—cataloguing waterfalls, rating waterfalls, creating Web sites with information and photographs of waterfalls, etc. There is even a section in the preface advising enthusiasts how to find additional waterfalls on their own.

The book is a multi-facetted resource. It describes the regional geologic setting for the waterfalls—how they came into being many thousands of years ago, and how they are still changing. It provides information about the history and local lore surrounding many of the waterfalls. When appropriate, the book also describes other nearby features of interest to make your trip even more interesting.

The directions to the waterfalls, at least for the ones I have visited, are all very clear. As editor of the *Helderberg Escarpment Planning Guide*, I consider myself somewhat of an expert on natural resources in the Helderbergs. So I am embarrassed to say that Mr. Dunn's book even provides directions to a waterfall by Long Road, only a few miles from my home, that I had never visited.

Finally, the book includes extensive endnotes and a large bibliography. The endnotes should not be ignored; in addition to listing sources, many of them provide more in-depth information about topics.

Mohawk Region Waterfall Guide is a book that will help to make the region a better and healthier place to live and to work. Creative people, the kind of people we need in "Tech Valley," migrate to communities with great, accessible natural resources. It is one of several important amenities they consider. This has long been a focus of the Mohawk-Hudson Land Conservancy as we create new preserves and design new trails. Along with scenic overlooks, waterfalls are a premiere destination for a new trail. And here is a whole book about waterfalls.

In addition to providing places for healthy recreation, the Conservancy works to improve water quality. It does so by protecting watersheds with conservation agreements and by creating preserves around important water resources.

What better place to observe the quality of water than at a waterfall where the water cascades over rocks, picking up oxygen, and "coins of foamy white" are minted in the pool at the base of the falls. At a waterfall you can observe many of the aquatic creatures that biologists use to judge the health of a stream. Trout, for example, are an important indicator of water quality. Although waterfalls tend to block their passage upstream, if water quality is adequate trout can often be found in the deep pools of oxygenated water at the base of waterfalls (but they are hard to see because of the foam and ripples).

This book includes a short section on waterfall conservation. The Conservancy is doing its best to help. It recently acquired a 135-acre preserve on the Bozenkill Road that will help to rectify the problem of accessibility to waterfalls along the Bozen Kill. The property includes two creeks—Wolf Creek and an unnamed tributary of the Bozen Kill. Together, the creeks have over six waterfalls. This new preserve will be named Wolf Creek Falls Preserve and should be open to the public soon after this book is published; check the Conservancy Web site, www.mohawkhudson.org, for the latest information.

While conservation is a sure way to make waterfalls accessible to the public; it is expensive to acquire and steward land just for that purpose. Landowners should be encouraged to let people hike on their property along acceptable routes to visit waterfalls. While landowners may rightfully be concerned about people trekking near their homes, they should not be overly concerned about liability. The Long Path uses New York State General Obligations Law, § 9-103, to encourage landowners to open their land to hiking. The law provides extensive liability protection for landowners who, without fee, let hikers enter their property. Under the law, landowners have "no duty to keep [their] premises safe" for hiking. However, the law "does not limit the liability ... for willful or malicious failure to guard, or warn against, a dangerous condition, use, structure or activity."

The Conservancy also recently acquired two conservation agreements along Hoffman's Fault in Glenville, Schenectady County. This fault was the cause of the ancient waterfall on the Mohawk at Hoffmans that is described in *Mohawk Region Waterfall Guide*. The waterfall made it necessary for early Native Americans to leave the river at that point and continue by land along the Primitive Path. The conservation agreements protect sections of the fault, an important archeological site, part of the Primitive Path, and a section of Chaughtanoonda Creek close to where it empties into the Mohawk.

To know a waterfall is to love a waterfall. Thank you Mr. Dunn; in this book you have created a wonderful resource for people who live in or visit the Mohawk region. *Mohawk Region Waterfall Guide* will give boundless enjoyment as you make it your companion on visits to the waterfalls described in its pages. So, be healthy and spiritually refreshed—go visit a waterfall.

Daniel A. Driscoll, Ph.D.
Knox, New York
May 2007

Dan Driscoll is a board member, past president, and chair of Land Preservation & Stewardship for the Mohawk-Hudson Land Conservancy. He is also on the board of the Huyck Preserve, the Patroon Land Foundation (which produces food for the local food bank) and the Onesquethaw Coeymans Watershed Counsel.

Preface

Mohawk Region Waterfalls

Humans have been enthralled by waterfalls since the beginning of time. The first in New York State to gaze upon the splendor of waterfalls tumbling down into the valleys from great heights were, of course, the Native Americans. They perceived waterfalls as centers of spirituality—places where nature was revealed at its most sublime and awesome. Streams emanated from the Great Spirit and brought water to nourish the land and surrounding forests. Streams created the waterways through which the dense wilderness could be traveled and explored. By periodically flooding, streams ensured that the fertility of the land would be sustained and endlessly renewed.

And streams produced waterfalls—sometimes cataracts of enormous size and power. Native Americans were drawn to these magnificent waterfalls for a variety of reasons. The Mohawks frequently courted one another at waterfalls (as they did at Canajoharie Falls), much like Americans do today at Niagara Falls, the honeymoon capital of the world. Waterfalls may have provided a unique backdrop for special events and ceremonies such as the inauguration of a new chief or the marriage of a tribal couple. Waterfalls may even have been visited by chiefs and shamans on vision quests.

Waterfalls have also had their darker side. In "The Legend of Bash Bish Falls" an unfaithful Indian maiden is strapped in a canoe and sent over the top of the falls to meet her end (see *Hudson Valley Waterfall Guide*, Chapter 64).[1] If looking to inflict maximum terror as well as terrible punishment, then the equally deadly, but quick plunge of a spear or blow from a tomahawk may not provide sufficient satisfaction to the revenge-seeker. What could prove more terrifying than to dispatch the unfaithful lover by lashing her to a canoe and sending her over the top of a tumultuous waterfall? And, since water is universally associated with purification, death by waterfall would represent the ultimate washing away of sin.

There are several stories and legends of frontiersmen hiding behind waterfalls to avoid capture by their enemies. Deep chasms with their rushing streams, tumbling cascades, rocky walls, and ricocheting echoes produce areas of wild pandemonium. Such distractions may have been sufficient to throw off pursuers. The exploits of Timothy Murphy at Bouck Falls in Panther Gorge (see chapter on Bouck Falls), for instance, is a case in point, although the tale is likely more fanciful than factual.

In James Fenimore Cooper's historical novel *The Last of the Mohicans,* Hawkeye and his companions temporarily elude a pursuing war party of Hurons by hiding out in Cooper's Cave at the base of Glens Falls. In the spring 2004 issue of *Glens Falls Magazine,* an article compared the Glens Falls of today with that of Cooper's novel, and pointed out the unlikelihood that the real Glens Falls could have provided sufficient cover.[2] Still, it's the story that counts, and Cooper's is a good one.

Waterfalls provided Native Americans living in the Mohawk Valley with a sense of security, for the Mohawks could be reasonably certain that no large ship could threaten them by advancing west up the Mohawk River past seventy-foot-high Cohoes Falls, nor east past forty-two feet of drops and rapids at Little Falls. In reality, this slowed but didn't stop European expansion into Native American territory, for even a good-sized bateau could be carried over demanding terrain and across significant distances by a determined group of men, as the Sullivan-Clinton Campaign illustrated (see chapter on Cemetery Falls).

Aside from water craft, the primary modes of transportation in the Mohawk and Schoharie valleys were by foot, horseback, and wagon. Paths were gradually worn down and widened into roads over time. Routes 5, 5S, and 20, all paralleling the Mohawk River, developed in this fashion and were instrumental in spurring on the rapid advance of populations throughout the region. This was equally true for Route 30 in the Schoharie Valley. Waterfalls were sometimes used as reference points on early maps, enabling travelers to navigate the wilderness terrain from one point to another via easily recognizable landmarks.

While Native Americans viewed waterfalls aesthetically, seeing them as wild, unfettered forces of nature to be revered and celebrated, Europeans viewed them with an eye towards industry. By the late 1600s, waterfalls and dams (artificial waterfalls) were being used to power vertical saws, grinders, bellows, buzz saws, presses, and a variety of other tools, thus freeing humans (and large domesticated animals such as oxen, mules, and horses) from some of the burdens of hard labor.

The early mills and waterwheels were crude at best, but with greater craftsmanship came significant technological advances. Within a short length of time, mills started converting from under-shot waterwheels to more massive and powerful overshot water-wheels, which were capable of extracting enormous amounts of energy from falling waters. Later, waterwheels were replaced by tur-bines and generators.

As more highways and roadways were constructed and con-stantly upgraded, the number of travelers passing through the region increased dramatically. In 1825 the rate of travel accelerated even further with the opening of the Erie Canal. The canal connected the Hudson River at Waterford to Lake Erie in western New York State. Now it was possible for goods and travelers to be transported at lower cost, greater speed, and in relative ease and comfort. No lon-ger were travelers exposed to interminable bumpy roads and dust mingled with horse dung.

But it was inevitable that the speed, efficiency, and comfort of transportation would be ratcheted up even further as the Indus-trial Revolution shifted into high gear and entered into the era of the railroad. These Herculean iron horses were capable of transport-ing goods and people in even greater numbers and at even greater speeds than ever before possible. Further, railroads were not bound by fixed waterways imposed by nature, but could go wherever tracks were laid. Once the railroads became firmly established, the fate of the Erie Canal was sealed, for it simply could not compete with this new transportation technology.

The Industrial Revolution created a large middle class who were freed from many of the repetitive tasks of daily life and thus had more leisure time. Victorian sensibilities spurred on the wealthy and middle class to leave the hot, teeming cities in the summer for the natural beauty of the Catskills and Adirondacks, where they could vacation in mountain houses and elegant hotels.

In the Mohawk and Schoharie valleys there were fewer opportunities to cash in on the new tourism industry since neither area could boast any mountains of appreciable height. Most of the towns and communities in the valleys had formed around industry and commerce. Tourism was essentially a secondary consideration. But there were some exceptions. Sharon Springs, on the southern rim of the Mohawk Valley, and to a lesser extent Richfield Springs, fur-

Butter Milk Falls, Little Falls, N.Y.

Every town along the Mohawk River has its own secret glen. Postcard circa 1910.

ther west, became a Mecca for the leisure class who sought out the mineral springs and baths for health cures or who simply desired a respite from city life. In its prime, Sharon Springs closely rivaled Saratoga Springs and might have achieved even greater prominence were it not for Saratoga Springs' association with gambling and horse racing, and eventual state sponsorship.

Sharon Springs does, however, boast one thing that Saratoga Springs cannot—its own waterfall, a natural beauty called Dugway Falls. What's more, the waters that pass over Dugway Falls are from the same sources as the mineral springs and baths whose waters were once believed to possess healing powers. This makes Dugway Falls, along with Mineral Spring Falls in the southern Hudson Valley (see *Hudson Valley Waterfall Guide*), one of the few regional waterfalls to be sought out for its curative, medicinal powers.

By the late 1800s, most of the great forests of the Catskills, Adirondacks, and Hudson River Valley were sadly depleted from over-harvesting by the countless mills that depended on them as a source of energy and for the lumber and bark they provided. Simultaneously, fossil fuels were harnessed, and coal, oil, and natural gas became plentiful and easily available. Mills and factories were no longer waterfall and dam-dependent; they could now be built wherever natural resources and waterways were available. By the turn of the century, most industries had abandoned the waterfalls that once drove their waterwheels, leaving behind deserted and dilapidated buildings that were broken down into bits of mortar, brick, and glass as the erosive powers of wind, rain, snow, ice, and unchecked vegetation took their toll.

For this reason, many of the waterfalls described in this guidebook have returned to a semi-natural, post-industrial state. Even so, vestiges of bricks, mortar, pipes, and machinery can be seen lying scattered about. Regrettably, some historically significant waterfalls have been privatized and are no longer accessible. Others have been pirated by houses built next to them. Some privately owned waterfalls have been included in this book with the caveat "historical." This is to ensure that their unique histories are recognized while private property rights are respected. They cannot be accessed directly without permission from the landowners.

The Allure of Waterfalls

Waterfalls are the embodiment of poetry in motion—forever dancing and leaping as we look upon them with wondrous eyes. No matter how often we watch their cascading waters, the pattern never repeats itself. When you stare at a waterfall, you are looking at eternity falling before your eyes.

With the advent of summer, waterfalls are soft and serene; babbling, gurgling, and tumbling over impassive ledges of moss-covered rock. Hikers stretch out on flat rocks below or on nearby ledges and are lulled into a state of peaceful somnambulism.

In fall, waterfalls turn into strutting peacocks, wrapped up and swirling in the glorious colors of autumn. They become kaleidoscopic, changing throughout the day as sunlight illuminates the multicolored leaves around them.

In winter, waterfalls become stoical and inert as the world plummets into the depths of winter and turns white and frosty. Encased in an armor of ice and snow, they wait patiently for the sun to return and to melt away their icy mantle.

And in spring, waterfalls are rekindled, bursting into life again, loud and boisterous, summoning all within earshot.

This is the eternal cycle that waterfalls repeat every year in the northeastern United States—a cycle of endless death and rebirth.

It is in our nature to love waterfalls in all of their moods. Perhaps it is even hardwired into our genes, for it is from water that we can ultimately trace the origin of life, many millions of years ago.

In the Beginning

Many of the waterfalls in eastern New York State were set into motion at the end of the last ice age, approximately 10,000 years ago, as the Earth warmed and mile-high glaciers began their northward retreat. Land that had been previously smothered by the weight of billions of tons of ice suddenly rebounded and, now unburdened, burst forth with forests and living creatures.

In their wake the glaciers left behind overflowing lakes and raging rivers that soon carved out deep valley systems. In the Mohawk

"SHOOTING" THE RAPIDS AT KESHENA FALLS

Cascades attract paddlers like a magnet. Postcard circa 1930.

Valley a number of mighty waterfalls were created by the Iro-Mohawk River (the ancestor to today's Mohawk River), but those have since vanished, leaving behind only Cohoes Falls. Fortunately there are numerous tributaries to the Mohawk River (as well as Schoharie Creek and the Black River), and it is to these tributaries that we must turn if waterfalls are to be found.

Unfortunately, for all their might and majesty, waterfalls are short-lived from a geological standpoint. The bigger the waterfall and the greater its volume of water, the more quickly will it self-destruct. Niagara Falls, for example, has migrated seven miles upstream since its geological clock began ticking at the end of the last ice age. Rainbow Falls at Ausable Chasm (a more regional example) has retreated one and a half miles up the Ausable River. When you look down into the Niagara Gorge or Ausable Chasm, then, bear in mind that every inch of distance represents a corresponding interval of geological time.

Big waterfalls, geologically speaking, are like hummingbirds—wondrously fast moving, but regrettably short-lived.

When Is a Waterfall a Waterfall?

The word "waterfall" is an umbrella term for cascade, fall, falls, catadupe (an obsolete term), foss (a Scottish term), cataract, drop, chute, or water slide. A waterfall can be categorized according to its size, height, broadness, power, shape, volume, verticality, proximity to the bedrock, whether it fans out at the top or bottom, etc. Does any of this really matter or help you better understand or appreciate what you are viewing? Perhaps—if you enjoy labeling and quantifying what you see. If this is the case, then you are clearly a waterfall enthusiast.

Chances are that most people can better agree when a waterfall isn't a waterfall—for instance, when a stream is simply racing downhill, even steeply, without any discernible drops or plunges. Even then, if the streambed is bedrock instead of gravel, it may look something like a series of long, low cascades.

Perhaps subjectivity must decide in the end. If *you* call it a waterfall, then it is one.

Waterfall Networking

If you love waterfalls, then consider yourself in good company—there are thousands of others just like you. Here's how to find them:

The Internet can be helpful. A number of Web sites have the sole purpose of promoting waterfalls. Several have been established in the Northeast; more will undoubtedly follow in time. The ones that I'm most familiar with are:

Waterfalls of the Northeast: www.northeastwaterfalls.com/links.php
  (Dean Goss)
Michele's Waterfall Page: www.MichelesWorld.net/waterfalls
  (Michele)
Ruth's Waterfalls: www.naturalhighs.net/waterfalls (Ruth)
Waterfalls of New York State: www.angelfire.com/ny4/waterfalls
Eastern Waterfall Guide: www.aria-database.com/waterfalls/
  falls-search.html (Robert Glaubitz)
Western New York Waterfall Survey:
  www.geocities.com/Yosemite/Rapids/8910
  (Scott Ensminger)
Waterfalls of the New England Region:
  www.ecet.vtu.edu/ ~ pchapin/water (Peter Chapin)

Waterfalls of Connecticut: www.ctwaterfalls.com (David Ellis)
Waterfalls of Massachusetts: www.berkshirephotos.com
    (Jan & Christy Butler)
Waterfalls of New England: newenglandwaterfalls.com/
    (Greg Parsons & Kate Wilson)
Waterfalls of Pennsylvania: waterfalls.nature.st/Pennsylvania/
    index.html (Gary Letcher)
www.usfalls.com/falls.php?idnum = 171 (Joseph Bushee, Jr.)

Attempts are currently underway to identify and catalogue all known waterfalls in specific geographic areas both in this region and worldwide. In 1991, Scott A. Ensminger began compiling a dossier of waterfalls of western New York State and, as of October 2006, had expanded his list to include 986 waterfalls. His criteria are that a waterfall must have a minimum vertical drop of five feet, with a stream that is water-bearing all year round. (See *Western New York Waterfall Survey*, www.geocities.com/Yosemite/Rapids/8910/.)

    Other individuals have taken a stab at the enormous task of compiling waterfalls lists. In the late 1990s, Steve Young, a botanist with the New York Natural Heritage Program, compiled a lengthy roster of New York State waterfalls by county based upon leads he had obtained from books, old postcards, topographical maps, Delorme's *NYS Atlas & Gazetteer*, old maps, and so on. But this only scratched the surface.

    Several counties have since made concerted efforts to catalogue waterfalls within their borders. The Rensselaer-Taconic Land Conservancy, for instance, has put together a fairly comprehensive list of waterfalls in Rensselaer County, and continues to upgrade the list as new discoveries are made.

    Dean Goss and his Pacific Coast counterpart, Bryan Swan, are presently attempting to create a worldwide database of all waterfalls exceeding three hundred feet in height, or with a water flow of over 5,000 cfs combined with a height of at least twenty feet.

    And, to top it off, a retired actuary and statistician, Richard Beisel, Jr., has developed a way of categorizing waterfalls so that each one can be given a numerical rating. It's called the International Waterfall Classification System and has been enthusiastically embraced by many waterfall enthusiasts (www.waterfallclassification.com). Beisel's goal is to create a methodology by which waterfalls can be quantified and standardized.

"Why network with other waterfall enthusiasts?" you might ask. The main attraction is that it presents the opportunity to develop leads to discovering waterfalls and gorges that might otherwise remain beyond your knowledge. It is also an opportunity to connect with other enthusiasts and, if they live close enough, to do an outing together. There is something to be said for the old adage of "safety in numbers."

Some hiking clubs and organizations now offer treks expressly to waterfalls. This has not always been the case. In the past, waterfalls were often just a stopping point (or side exhibit) along the way to the main destination—a mountain summit, lake, or overlook. Today, hiking groups like the ADK (Adirondack Mountain Club), AMC (Appalachian Mountain Club), Mohawk Hiking Club, Catskill Hiking Club, Taconic Hiking Club, New York-New Jersey Trail Conference, and others take hikers specifically to waterfalls, which have now become a destination in their own right.

My wife, Barbara Delaney, and I have played an active role in promoting waterfalls as hiking destinations. On the last weekend of every April, we help organize and lead a waterfall weekend at Trails End Inn (Innkeeper@trailsendinn.com) in the High Peaks region of the Adirondacks. We kick the weekend off with a meal on Friday night at the Ausable Inn in Keene Valley, and then spend the next two days trekking to some of the eastern Adirondack's most magnificent waterfalls. All of this came about following an article I wrote for the May/June 1998 issue of *Adirondac* (an Adirondack Mountain Club publication) called "Hiking the Waterfall Trail."[3] Up until then, the many waterfalls along the East Branch of the Ausable River were merely passing curiosities for hikers who were intent on bagging mountain summits. These falls were passed by quickly in the quest to get into the interior of the High Peaks. "Hiking the Waterfall Trail" changed all of that. Suddenly the many spectacular waterfalls along the East Branch, including Pyramid Falls, Wedge Brook Falls, Beaver Meadow Falls, Rainbow Falls, and multiple cascades along Gill Brook became destinations that were worthy of attention, and hiking clubs began leading groups in to see them, proving that the written word can, and does, have an impact on the way we perceive the world around us.

Finding Waterfalls on Your Own

There are more waterfalls in eastern New York State than can be included in any guidebook. A large number of falls cannot be properly documented because they are located on private property and are inaccessible without trespassing. There was a time, and not too long ago, when landowners were less concerned about hikers crossing their lands to visit a waterfall, but times have changed. We live in a litigious society. Landowners simply cannot afford to take the chance that they may be sued by people who are unwilling to take responsibility for their own actions.

Some waterfalls are inherently dangerous. Canajoharie Falls, postcard circa 1940.

Other waterfalls are in deep woods and require an extensive bushwhack to access. These waterfalls also cannot be written up in a guidebook intended for the general public without risking the possibility of a hiker getting lost. There are also a few waterfalls on public lands that have achieved such notoriety for the dangers associated with them and for the lethal accidents that have occurred that hikers are aggressively dissuaded from visiting them. T-Lake Falls in the Adirondacks is a case in point.

Finally, there are waterfalls that will likely remain obscure simply because they are known only to a few closed-mouth woodsmen or hunters who don't want their "secret" woodland haunts teeming with people.

If you are interested in "discovering" waterfalls on your own, the first step is to purchase a topographic (topo) map of the area that you are interested in and use it as a rough guide. Topo maps use contour lines to reveal elevation. The more compressed the contour lines, the steeper the grade. There are books that explain how to read topo maps and how to apply that information. This is a good skill to learn and is called "orienteering."

But even if you head out with topo map and compass in hand and end up finding no waterfalls, you will still have had a good adventure, for half of the fun is simply getting out and enjoying nature.

Waterfall Conservation

Waterfalls are rapidly disappearing from public view as land is divided, subdivided, and increasingly privatized. Advertisements regularly appear in newspapers offering a piece of property that contains its own waterfall. Who could resist such an enticement—to be able to build your dream house right next to a choice waterfall?

Fortunately, New York State Department of Environmental Conservation, Scenic Hudson, Inc., the Adirondack Council, Parks & Trails Network, hiking clubs (including the Mohawk Hiking Club), land conservancies (such as the Mohawk-Hudson Land Conservancy), the Open Space Institute, private organizations, and individuals are working to create parks and preserves so that land with natural beauty can be kept pristine forever. Often waterfalls are centerpieces of such land acquisitions. Decades ago, New York State came to the realization that natural resources such as the Adirondacks and Catskills, as well as the Mohawk and Hudson valleys, attract tourists, and increased tourism translates into increased revenue for the state.

For now, we must appreciate those waterfalls that are accessible to the public and be grateful to the many landowners and the many private and public conservation organizations that have made public access possible.

Accessing Waterfalls: Degree of Difficulty

The waterfalls described in this book are generally more readily accessible and involve a less demanding hike to reach than the ones contained in *Adirondack Waterfall Guide: New York's Cool Cascades* or *Catskill Region Waterfall Guide: Cool Cascades of the Catskills & Shawangunks*, which explore the mountainous regions of New York. Therefore, most treks in this book will fall into an "easy" to "moderate" category. The longest hike contained herein involves the multiple trails described in the Plotter Kill Preserve

Easy—Less than 1.5 miles each way, with mostly even terrain and minimal elevation change
Moderate—Up to 2.5 miles one way, with mixed terrain and some elevation change
Difficult—Significant elevation change and mixed terrain, possibly including some rock scrambling; over 2.5 miles each way

Waterfalls listed as "historic" (in parentheses) are not currently open to the public. These waterfalls are included for the sake of historical completeness.

How to Get There

By carefully following the directions in this book, you should have no difficulty locating the trailheads and the waterfalls. Still, it would be prudent to purchase a *New York State Atlas & Gazetteer* if you do not already own one. The *Atlas & Gazetteer* contains a series of large-scale topo maps that show you in broad detail the general area where you will be hiking. If you are approaching from a different direction than the one given in this book, the *Atlas & Gazetteer* will help you to improvise and find your own way to the trailhead. It will also allow you to plot out your own course for getting from one waterfall site to the next.

If you are interested in more specific and more detailed geological information, then a topo map of the particular area you are interested in will show you the landscape and how the waterfall relates to the surrounding area.

Many of the waterfalls in this book are formed on tributaries that descend into a river valley, making it difficult to get lost, but if you do find yourself momentarily disoriented, simply follow the creek downstream to the nearest main road.

Photographing Waterfalls

The mechanics of photographing waterfalls can be very complicated, and there is much literature written on the subject. Waterfalls have mercurial personalities, changing according to atmospheric conditions and the season of the year. In spring they are thunderous and awe-inspiring, tornadoes of white, brought to life by winter's snowmelt. Photos taken in spring will capture waterfalls in all their might and boundless energy. Little bedrock will be visible—just white water barely contained in overflowing streambeds. The images can be almost overpowering. In early spring, with no foliage to obscure views, you can take shots that might otherwise be impossible when the trees burst forth with life again. If the waterfall is large enough, a cloud of mist created by the spray can rise up, causing the image to blur. This could work for you if the spray captures the sunlight and produces a rainbow, or against you if the spray causes the waterfall to appear hazy and indistinct.

In summer, waterfalls turn languid as less water flows over them. Green is the color that predominates, produced by forest life and verdant moss on rocks. Considerably more bedrock will show. In fact, at particularly dry times in the summer, the bedrock may be mostly what you see. You may want to time a summer visit to coincide with the end of a rainstorm. The combination of the white from the water, the green from the flora, and the darker colors of the bedrock allows for great photographs.

In the autumn, waterfalls are framed by the forest's burst of glorious colors and, with the growing season now over (which soaks up billions of gallons of water in the ground that might otherwise seep into the stream), there is generally more water flowing than in summer. It is a wonderful time to take photographs, and usually there are no annoying, biting insects to disturb you.

In winter, many smaller or less vibrant waterfalls become indistinguishable from the cliff faces that surround them. Bigger waterfalls often create thick layers of ice that attract ice-climbers. If a waterfall is a plunge falls, it will produce a huge inverted cone of ice at its base. Photos taken of waterfalls in the winter tend to be monochromatic, with white predominating. Even the trees tend to look gray and ashen, with the exception, of course, of evergreens, which generally are not found next to most of the waterfalls in this book. The most striking winter photographs of waterfalls include a colorfully garbed person standing next to the fall or looking across to it. If you are lucky, an ice-climber hacking his way up the mammoth icicle may add an element of color and tension to your photo.

Whatever the season, the quality of the sunlight is extremely important. Bright sunlight will produce maximum contrast, meaning that if the waterfall is properly exposed, the surrounding bedrock may look dark and uninteresting, and if the bedrock is properly exposed, then the waterfall may be grossly overexposed and look like a smear of white. Although the human eye can readily adjust to extreme differences of contrast between brightness and darkness, the camera lens can not. Dazzling bright sunlight is not necessarily the ideal illumination for picture taking. Sunny days do have their good points as well as their bad, however. When the sun is at the proper position in the sky, it can illuminate the deepest gorge and bring out details that would otherwise be lost on a cloudy day.

A cloudy, dreary, heavily overcast day may not be ideal, either, for little light will penetrate into the depths of a gorge surrounded by a canopy of trees.

The optimal condition is a hazy, dimly lit day, when the sun isn't beaming directly down. This will provide proper illumination, but without extreme contrast. The bedrock, trees, and waterfall will all be about equally exposed.

Does it help to have a fancy camera to photograph a waterfall? Sure it does. But you can take an excellent waterfall photo with a simple point-and-shoot camera. Expensive cameras are only necessary if you intend to produce professional quality photographs.

The most dramatic view of a waterfall is generally from its base and taken from some distance back (the distance back being dependent upon the height of the waterfall and its width). It's helpful to have someone standing near the base of the waterfall to provide a sense of scale and dimension that would otherwise be lacking.

In some cases, however, it will not be possible to approach a waterfall from its base without appreciable effort or danger. Some waterfalls, for instance, are encased in deep gorges with towering side walls. Canajoharie Falls on Canajoharie Creek is an excellent example. In these situations, unless you can follow the creek upstream to the base of the waterfall, you must satisfy yourself with pictures taken from the top.

In many instances it is possible to get excellent pictures from the side of the gorge. In rarer cases, where the stream turns perpendicularly at the base of the falls, you can get wonderful head-on shots of the waterfall from the top of the opposing bank.

The opportunities are virtually unlimited as long as you use your imagination. My wife and I take stereographic pictures, which means that we try to include an attractive or interesting foreground, such as wildflowers or interesting rock formations, when composing the shot.

One last tip, obvious but important: always remember to bring along extra film (or extra memory cards) and batteries!

Acknowledgments

To Warren Broderick, Roland Vineyard, Carol Darling, Linda Vincent, and Wayne Hilleston—thank you all for your contributions. As always, special thanks go to Bob Drew, premier postcard collector in the Capital Region, whose knowledge of geography is virtually limitless, as is his generosity as a postcard collaborator. Thanks to Charley Kested for drawing my attention to several waterfalls along the Long Path, and to Jim Besha for opening my eyes to the possible harmonious coexistence of waterfalls and power plants.

I am grateful to Curtis Seaburg, proprietor of the Alcove Store, for providing historical background on the area next to his store. I am especially indebted to Chuck Porter for his valuable input on the geology of the Mohawk Valley. Thank you to Wayne Wright, Associate Director of the Library at the New York State Historical Association, and to Win McIntyre and Cate LaBarre, for their help in locating Otsego County waterfalls.

Special thanks go to all the historical societies, land conservancies, private benefactors, local, county, and state governments, and all others who serve to protect and preserve New York State's priceless waterfall wonders.

I am especially grateful to Daniel A. Driscoll for his wonderful foreword, and to Dietrich Gehring for his outstanding front cover photo of Outlet Falls taken in the aftermath of Hurricane Floyd. All postcard illustrations are from my collection.

As always, bringing a book to completion is a team effort and one that could not be done without: the aid of proofreaders Matina Billias and Natalie Mortensen; my ever-diligent editor and wordsman, Steve Hoare, who makes sure I sound good; graphic designers Ron Toelke and Barbara Kempler-Toelke who brought this book to life; and, of course, my ever-energetic, youthful publisher, Debbie Allen, who strives for perfection and sometimes comes close to it through the books she publishes.

Most of all I am especially grateful to my wife, Barbara Delaney, who accompanied me on nearly all of the hikes described in this book.

Caution: Safety Tips

Nature is inherently wild and unpredictable, so play it safe and don't be reckless. Outdoor recreational activities are by their very nature potentially hazardous and contain risk. All participants in such activities must assume the responsibility for their own actions and safety. No book can replace good judgment. The outdoors is forever changing. The author and publisher cannot be held responsible for inaccuracies, errors, or omissions, or for any changes in the details of this publication, or for the consequences of any reliance on the information contained herein, or for the safety of people in the outdoors.

Remember that the destination is *not* the waterfall or the mountain summit. The destination is home; get back there safely.

Safety Tips Specifically for Waterfalls

1. Always stay well back from the top of a waterfall. Some waterfalls have gracefully curved lips at the top, which means that if you start to slip forward, there is nothing to stop you from continuing over the brink and tumbling to the bottom. Think of how the pitcher plant traps unwary insects and you will have a clear picture of how this mechanism works. The fact that the bedrock near the top of a waterfall is often wet or slimy further increases the likelihood of losing traction and inadvertently riding the waterfall down to a most unpleasant outcome.

2. Never jump or dive off ledges above a waterfall, no matter how inviting the pool of water below looks. You may lose your footing as you make the leap and end up landing on the rocks instead of in the water, or you may collide with unseen objects such as boulders and submerged logs below the waterline. Remember that conditions can change overnight. You cannot rely on the fact that the pool may have been clear of objects or debris the last time you visited the falls.

3. Never swim in a pool of water at the top of a cascade. There's always the possibility that the force of the stream may flush you out of the pool and eject you over the top of the fall. Keep in

mind that rocks are usually worn smooth at the waterfall's summit, which means that there will be nothing to grab hold of to save yourself if you get caught up in the current.

4. Never throw rocks over the top of a waterfall. You never know if someone might be below, even if you just looked over the top.

5. Never try to climb up the face or the sides of a waterfall. Waterfalls are often formed out of sedimentary rocks like shale and slate, which don't provide reliable supports for footholds and handholds. Waterfalls also send up sprays of water that can keep the surrounding rocks damp and slippery.

6. If you decide to cool off in a swimming hole at the base of a waterfall, be sure to enter the water slowly and carefully to avoid injuring yourself on obstructions such as submerged tree limbs and boulders.

7. Enjoy waterfalls by viewing them from the base, whenever possible. This provides the best views, the greatest safety, and the most optimum photo shoot.

8. Never drink water from streams, brooks, and waterfalls, no matter how clean the water may look. Giardiasis is often the result of drinking untreated water.

9. If you are visiting a waterfall in the winter, be on the lookout for blocks of ice above you that could break off and come tumbling down.

10. If you follow a creek upstream to a waterfall, you cannot get lost as long as you follow the creek back downstream to your starting point.

General Hiking Safety Tips

1. Always hike with two or more companions. That way, if someone is hurt, one person can stay with the victim while the other goes for help.

2. Make it a practice to always take along a day pack complete with emergency supplies, compass, whistle, flashlight, dry matches, raingear, high-energy food, extra clothes, duct tape, lots of water (at least twenty-four ounces per person), insect repellent, emergency medical kit, and sun block.

3. Your skin is the largest organ in your body. To protect it, wear sunblock whenever you're exposed to sunlight for extended periods of time, especially in the summer, and insect repellents when you know that you are going into an area where there are mosquitoes or blackflies. Remember that you can get burned even on a cloudy day. Wearing a hat with a wide brim is always helpful to keep out the sun. Wear long pants and a long-sleeved shirt to further protect yourself from both the sun and biting insects. One substitute for repellents is to take a lead from horses and bring along a "swisher"—a leafy branch that you can wave in front of and around yourself to keep the air free of biting insects.

4. Wear ankle-high boots—always! Boots provide traction, gripping power, and ankle support that sneakers and shoes do not.

5. Be aware of the risk of hypothermia, and stay dry. Keep in mind that the temperature doesn't have to be near freezing for you to become too cold. If you become accidentally immersed in water in the spring, fall, or winter, return to your car immediately unless the air temperature is above 70 degrees. Also be cognizant of the dangers of overheating (hyperthermia) and always drink plenty of water when the weather is hot and muggy. Stay in the shade whenever possible, and use the stream near a waterfall to cool off in if you begin to overheat.

6. To be on the safe side, stay out of the woods during hunting season. If you do venture into the woods while hunters are about, wear an orange-colored vest and make periodic loud noises to draw attention to the fact that you are a human, and not a wild animal.

7. Always stand back from the base of a tall waterfall. Someone at the top might unthinkingly toss a rock over the edge.

8. Stay on trails whenever possible to avoid the chance of becoming disoriented and lost, and to avoid causing damage to the environment (particularly where there might be rare plants and mosses off-trail). Do not consider bushwhacking through the woods unless you are an experienced hiker, you have a compass with you and you know how to use it, you are prepared to spend several days in the woods if necessary, and you are with a group of similarly prepared hikers.

Always know where you are. Guidebooks, topographic maps, and compasses are essential if you venture out into the wilderness. A GPS unit is also worth bringing along. Nothing, however, is a substitute for good judgment and basic common sense.

9. Be flexible and adaptive to a wilderness environment that can change abruptly. Trails described in this book can become altered by blowdown, beaver dams flooding the adjacent land, or even forest fires.

10. Always let someone know where you are going, when you will return, and what to do if you have not shown up by the designated time.

11. Avoid any creature that is acting erratically. If any animal should advance towards you and cannot be deterred, assume that it is either rabid or predatory.

12. If you encounter a problem, do not panic. Unless it is critical that you react immediately and decisively, it is best to stop for a moment and think through what your options are. This is particularly true if you suddenly find yourself lost or disoriented.

Old Mill and Falls, Gilboa. Postcard circa 1910.

13. Leave early in the morning if your hike requires covering a lot of ground. Plan accordingly and allow for plenty of time if the hike is in the winter, when footing may not be easy and nighttime arrives hours earlier than it does in the summer.

14. Avoid cornering any wild animal as you approach a waterfall in a gorge. The animal's only path of retreat may be right through where you are standing!

Follow these tips and you will maximize your chances for having an enjoyable and safe time visiting waterfalls.

Special Precautions for Children and Pets

This subject takes us back to the underlying premise that waterfalls must always be respected and viewed as wild, unbridled natural wonders. Waterfalls can kill, but you have to be terribly negligent to become a victim.

No one really knows for sure just how many people have died at Niagara Falls over the last three centuries, for many deaths have occurred without witnesses. We do know, however, that by the end of the nineteenth century, Niagara Falls had not only become the honeymoon capital of the world, but its suicide capital as well (this dubious honor was only brought to an end when the Golden Gate Bridge in San Francisco, California, was erected). Cataracts such as T-Lake Falls in the Adirondacks, Bash Bish Falls in the Taconics, Kaaterskill Falls in the Catskills, Hamilton Falls in southern Vermont, and Canajoharie Falls in the Mohawk Valley, all have a sizable number of casualties and deaths associated with them—generally because youths engage in horseplay, do reckless stunts, get too close to the top of the waterfall, or choose to tempt fate by rock climbing where they shouldn't.

When approaching the top of a large waterfall, keep young children carefully supervised and dogs leashed at all times. If you hike directly to the bottom of the waterfall, which is what we recommend, then only general precautions are required

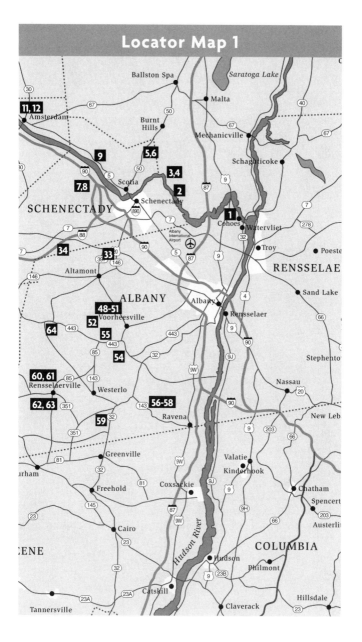

Ballston Spa

Saratoga Lake

30

11, 12
Amsterdam

67

Malta

50

Burnt
Hills

40

67

Mechanicville

67

9

5,6

Schaghticoke

30

90

5

50

Scotia

3,4

9

7,8

2

87

SCHENECTADY

890

Schenectady

1

7

Cohoes

Watervliet

278

Albany
International
Airport

7

34

88

90

5

32

Troy

Poeste

7

33

39

30

146

87

9

RENSSELAE

146

Altamont

4

Sand Lake

ALBANY

Albany

66

48-51

Rensselaer

52
Voorheesville

9

64

443

90

55

443

9J

Stephento

85

54

32

60, 61

85

143

Nassau

Rensselaerville

20

62, 63

351

Westerlo

56-58

90

59

32

143

New Leb

351

Ravena

9

203

66

81

Greenville

9W

Valatie

rham

32

Kinderhook

Freehold

81

Coxsackie

9J

Chatham

9

Spencert

145

9H

66

203

23

Cairo

23

Austerli

COLUMBIA

CENE

32

9W

Hudson River

Hudson

Philmont

9

23B

23A

Catskill

9

Hillsdale

Tannersville

23A

Claverack

23

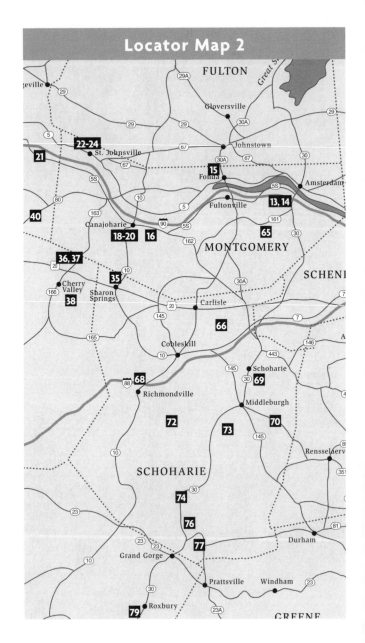

Locator Map 2

FULTON

geville — 29

Gloversville

29A

29

29

30A

29

5

22-24

Johnstown

21

St. Johnsville

67

30A

67

30

67

30A

5S

15

Fonda

Amsterdam

5S

80

10

163

5

Fultonville

13, 14

40

Canajoharie

90

5S

161

18-20 16

162

65

30

36, 37

MONTGOMERY

20

10

SCHEN

35

30A

Cherry Valley

166

Sharon Springs

Carlisle

7

38

20

7

145

66

146

165

Cobleskill

443

10

145

Schoharie

88

30

69

68

Richmondville

Middleburgh

72

73

70

145

Rensselaerv

10

351

SCHOHARIE

74

30

23

76

81

23

23

77

Durham

10

Grand Gorge

30

Prattsville

Windham

23

79

Roxbury

23A

GREENE

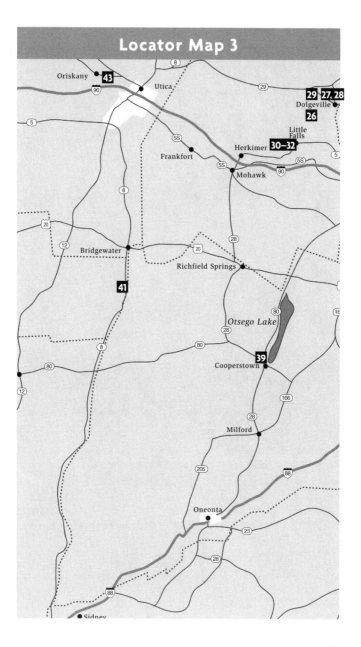

Locator Map 3

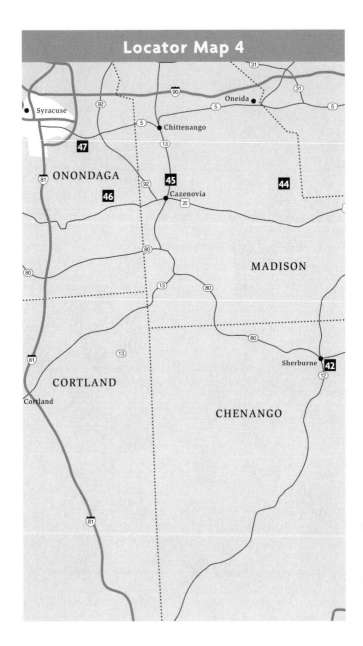

Locator Map 4

Syracuse

ONONDAGA

47

46

Chittenango

45

Cazenovia

44

Oneida

MADISON

CORTLAND

Cortland

CHENANGO

Sherburne **42**

1. Cohoes Falls (35)
2. Falls near Lock 7 (40)
3. Falls between Lock 7 and Rexford (43)
4. Waterfall near Bike Path in Rexford (45)
5. Falls on Indian Kill (47)
6. Krystal Falls (50)
7. Plotter Kill Falls (53)
8. Cascades on Moccasin Kill (68)
9. Falls on Washout Creek (71)
10. Adriutha Falls (Historic) (75)
11. Fall at Cliffside Restaurant (77)
12. Falls at Kirk Douglas Park (78)
13. Little Chuctanunda Falls (81)
14. Cider Mill Falls (83)
15. Falls on Cayadutta Creek (85)
16. Yatesville Falls (87)
17. Flat Creek Falls (Historic) (89)
18. Canajoharie Falls: Upper Gorge (92)
19. Canajoharie Falls: Lower Gorge (95)
20. Cemetery Falls (98)
21. Falls on Tributaries to Nowadaga Creek (101)
22. Scudders Falls (103)
23. Falls at "Inn by the Mill" (106)
24. Fall on Timmerman Creek (109)
25. Beardslee Falls (Historic) (110)
26. Faville Falls (112)
27. Falls by Old Dolgeville Mill (115)
28. High Falls (117)
29. Falls on Spruce Creek (119)
30. Little Falls (121)
31. "Miracle Mile" Cascade (124)
32. Buttermilk Falls (127)
33. French's Falls (132)
34. Bozen Kill Falls (136)
35. Dugway Falls (140)
36. Judd Falls (144)
37. Cascade along Salt Spring-ville Road (146)
38. Fall on Tributary to Cherry Valley Creek (147)
39. Leatherstocking Falls (148)
40. Falls at Van Hornsville (151)
41. Button Falls (155)
42. Rexford Falls (156)
43. Oriskany Falls (159)
44. Stockbridge Falls (161)
45. Chittenango Falls (164)
46. Pratt Falls (167)
47. Clark Reservation (170)
48. Outlet Falls (175)
49. Minelot Falls (177)
50. Falls on Upper Minelot Creek (181)
51. Falls at Hopfield Picnic Area (185)

Locator Maps Key

Waterfalls of the
Mohawk Valley

Introduction

The Mohawk River, at 148 miles in length,[1] is the Hudson River's largest tributary, draining 3,462 square miles of watershed.[2] It rises humbly from the Tug Hill Plateau in upper central New York State, at an elevation of 1,800 feet, and ends its journey between Cohoes and Waterford nearly at sea level as it drops over Cohoes Falls and then down into the Hudson River.

The Mohawk River was created more than 10,000 years ago by the meltwaters of mile-high glaciers in retreat. At that time the topography of New York State was appreciably different from what you see today. The glacial retreat caused an enormous body of water, called Lake Iroquois, to form and occupy much of what would later become the Great Lakes. The Iro-Mohawk River—ancestor to the current Mohawk River—became the outlet drain to this massive lake, evacuating waters east to Lake Albany (covering the present-day Capital Region) and, from there, down the Hudson River into the Atlantic Ocean. This ancient river was even more powerful than the Niagara River that flows over Niagara Falls. The Iro-Mohawk's turbulent, energetic waters carved out an immense valley, which we know today as the Mohawk Valley. Episodes of massive flooding were caused when towering dams of ice suddenly gave way, sending tidal waves of water through the valley and further shaping its development.[3]

Along the Mohawk River, circa 1920.

Several large waterfalls were created by the Iro-Mohawk River. These primordial waterfalls formed where the stream encountered unusually resistant bedrock or barriers of land. None of these early waterfalls have survived into modern times, however. The first ancient waterfall formed at Little Falls. Today, all that remains is a series of drops and rapids totaling over forty vertical feet of relief—hence the name *little* falls. The gigantic glacial potholes on Moss Island, adjacent to the city of Little Falls, however, remain as mute testimony to the once unimaginable power of the ancient Iro-Mohawk River and this early waterfall.

A second waterfall formed over twenty miles further downstream from Little Falls. It, too, has vanished, a victim of its own self-destructive power. Nevertheless, with a little imagination you can visualize how the waterfall once looked. As you're driving along the New York State Thruway (I-90), Rt. 5, or Rt. 5S through Sprakers, keep an eye out for a distinctive formation called The Noses, where rocky hills slope dramatically down nearly to the edge of the river. Picture a high ridge continuing between the two "noses," and then imagine the river coming over the top of this ridge and crashing down into the valley, several hundred feet below. This was the once-mighty waterfall at Sprakers.[4]

A third waterfall, one hundred feet high, formed in the vicinity of Hoffmans (west of Scotia) and vanished long before the arrival of modern civilization.[5] This waterfall was located near the outlet to Lake Amsterdam—a post-glacial body of water that occupied the central Mohawk Valley.[6]

Today, evidence of the Iro-Mohawk's powerful imprint is still all around us. The gently sloping hills along the Mohawk Valley are in fact the side walls of this old river, and the wide valley floor is its ancient riverbed. But the Iro-Mohawk's reign was short-lived. As the glaciers continued their retreat northward, new lands opened up, exposing a more efficient channel through which the water could flow north, this time to the St. Lawrence River. With Lake Iroquois now draining northward, the Iro-Mohawk River shrank to its present size, becoming the Mohawk River. One should not conclude from this fact, however, that the Mohawk River is just a specter of its former self. The river is still prone to flooding during the spring, particularly near Schenectady's downtown Stockade District. In 1914 flooding caused extensive damage to property in the Stockade in what was the worst episode of flooding since regional records were kept. The year before, it had caused massive flooding in Cohoes.

The Iro-Mohawk River created an immense delta at Lake Albany, an enormous post-glacial lake. The height of this delta increased not only from deposits of sediment, but also from the land's slow rise as it rebounded from the gradual easing of glacial weight. As the land rose, it formed a natural barrier, preventing the now weaker Mohawk River from forcing its way east to the Hudson River via the shortest route possible. Thus diverted, the Mohawk River began flowing north towards Ballston Spa and Round Lake, following a pre-glacial valley, and then east via the Anthony Kill to the Hudson River.[7]

Within a short period of time, a secondary channel enlarged near Rexford, allowing the Mohawk to opportunistically usurp this newly created conduit and to now flow into the Hudson River through Waterford in a relatively straightforward manner. If you visit the Rexford Gorge (visible from the Rexford Bridge or, higher up, from Riverview Road), you will discover just how deep the gorge is and how sharply cut its vertical walls are—all indications of the gorge's geological youth. Unlike the rest of the Mohawk Valley, the Rexford Gorge has had little geological time to smooth out its side walls into sloping hills.

Today's Mohawk River may appear deep, but at one time it was very rocky, with shallow rifts and bouncing rapids. In many places the river was actually no higher than a man's thigh. There were ninety-one rifts or rapids along the Mohawk's length, created by gravel and rock that was deposited from the river's many tributaries.[8] The depth of the Mohawk River changed dramatically, however, when a succession of locks and dams were added in 1918 to create the Barge Canal.[9]

The Mohawk Valley is at its widest between Rome and Little Falls, measuring approximately 500 to 8,000 feet across[10] and 400 to 500 feet deep. But these measurements can be deceptive. The valley is actually encased in an even larger valley, which widens out as you proceed further south to the Helderbergs and north to the Adirondack foothills.

The only significant waterfall on the Mohawk River today is the stupendous cascade at Cohoes, located virtually at the confluence of the Mohawk and Hudson rivers. Were it not for the fact that Cohoes Falls has eroded its way upstream several thousand feet during the past few thousand years, it would still be at the union of these two mighty rivers.

There are few other cascades and rapids on the Mohawk River that command attention. As is true with the Hudson River, in order to find significant waterfalls along the Mohawk it is necessary to explore the river's numerous tributaries. Fortunately, the river is blessed with a number of major streams coming into it, and some have produced notable waterfalls in their own right. The Mohawk's main tributaries from the north are West Canada Creek and East Canada Creek. From the south the largest are Oriskany Creek and Schoharie Creek.[11]

History

Long before the arrival of European colonists, the Mohawk Valley was occupied by Native Americans. They established "castles"—villages made out of perishables like wood and brush—and took full advantage of the valley's waterways and exceptionally fertile lands.

These Native Americans called the Mohawk River *Te-non-an-at-che,* meaning "river flowing through the mountains." This is an apt name, for when the ancient Iro-Mohawk River carved out the valley, it fashioned a notch straight through the Appalachian Plateau, forming the only viable passage from the east coast to the western plains between Georgia and the St. Lawrence Valley.[12] It is believed that the name Mohawk originated with the Mohicans, who called the Mohawks *Mohowaug*, meaning "they eat living creatures." The Dutch altered the pronunciation to *Maquaas* (or *Mahakuaas*); New Englanders, in turn, changed the pronunciation to Mohawk.[13]

The Mohawk Valley was very desirable land. Most importantly, the valley was unusually fertile because it had once formed the basin to Lake Albany. The presence of seventy-foot-high Cohoes Falls poised at the eastern terminus of the Mohawk Valley, and the more than forty feet of rapids and small cascades to the west at Little Falls, created a sense of impregnability from invasion, since large ships could not easily bypass such formidable barriers.

Warfare, however, was never far behind as different tribes competed for the lands. The situation hardly improved with the arrival of settlers from Europe. As more colonists spread into the valley, there were inevitable clashes with Native Americans, who felt increasingly marginalized and displaced. Tempers were further inflamed by the growing resentment many settlers felt about having to pay tribute to "mother" England. Eventually the discord erupted into warfare between the colonists and the British and their Tory allies.

In 1777 the British launched a three-pronged campaign to assert their control over the Mohawk and Hudson valleys—the two main river valleys in eastern New York State. The plan was for General John Burgoyne to advance south from Canada, Sir William Howe to advance north from New York City, and Colonel Barry St. Leger to march east from Lake Ontario. The plan rapidly went awry. Howe veered south to engage General Washington in Pennsylvania, instead of proceeding north, and St. Leger was resoundingly defeated at Ft. Stanwix on his march east, leaving Burgoyne without reinforcements at the Battle of Saratoga, which he lost, surrendering his entire army to the colonials.

Throughout the war the Mohawk Valley was thrown into upheaval as fighting erupted between those who were loyal to the British and those who supported the revolution. It is estimated that over one-third of the 7,500 settlers in the area at the start of the war were killed outright, while another one-third, the loyalists, fled for their lives to Canada. It was a period of bitter contention as friends, families, and Native American tribes were split into factions and fought each other desperately. The battle raged back and forth from 1777–1783 in what came to be called "the border wars." Finally, in 1789, with the Treaty of Fort Stanwix, the fighting came to an end, and peace has reigned over the valley ever since.

With the construction of the Erie Canal in 1825, the Mohawk River became a secondary player as a conduit for goods and travelers. When the Barge Canal was created between 1903 and 1918, however, the river was brought back to life and has been serving the recreational needs of New York State ever since.

Through all of this, waterfalls have stood by and watched—mute testimony to the durability of nature over human fragility.

1. Cohoes Falls

Location: Cohoes (Albany County)
NYS Atlas & Gazetteer: p. 66, B4
Accessibility: Roadside; 30-foot walk to overlook

Description: Cohoes Falls, a registered National Historic Landmark, is a 65–70-foot-high, 600-foot-wide waterfall formed on the Mohawk River approximately 2,000 feet upstream from the Mohawk's confluence with the Hudson River.[1-13] There are claims that it is the largest waterfall east of Niagara Falls.[14] In fact, Cohoes Falls once rivaled Niagara Falls as New York State's premier natural wonder and was visited by thousands of tourists each year.

Beached whales were once found at the "sprout" of the Mohawk—the section of the river between the fall and the Hudson River. The whales had come upstream from the Atlantic during a freshet, apparently became disoriented, and ended up grounded.

One of the earliest descriptions of the fall was written by Domine Megapolensis, the first minister to the colony of Rensselaer. In a pamphlet published in Holland in 1644, Megapolensis wrote that the "Mohawk River is 500 to 600 paces wide coming out of the Mahakas County about four leagues north of us … flowing between two high banks and falls from a height equal to that of a church with such noise that we can sometimes hear it with us [at Albany]."[15] Later, in 1780, the fall was described by the Marquis de Chastellux, a French adventurer, as a "vast sheet of water which falls 76 English feet."[16]

In 1804 the waterfall was immortalized by Thomas Moore in a poem entitled "Lines Written at the Cohoes," or "Falls of the Mohawk River."[17] In a footnote to the poem, Moore wrote: "The fine rainbow, which is continually forming and dissolving, as the spray rises into the light of the sun, is perhaps the most interesting beauty which these wonderful cataracts exhibit."

Today, Cohoes Falls generally fails to perform in as spectacular a manner as it once did. Sizable amounts of water are con-
sistently bled off for hydroelectric generation and for servicing the
Barge Canal, leaving the river with little water leftover to show off its
latent splendor.[18] Nevertheless, in early spring or during prolonged
downpours of rain, the waterfall does re-animate and becomes quite
impressive.

The bedrock of Cohoes Falls is composed of Snake Hill shale
and exhibits that rock's characteristically dark complexion. The distinctive block of protruding rock off-center towards the north bank
is called The Noses.

History: According to Native American legend, the founder of the
great Iroquois Confederacy "began his epic quest to unify the war-
ring tribes at the Falls."[19] After inadvertently plunging over Cohoes
Falls, but miraculously surviving, the Peacemaker went on to be
accepted by the Mohawk tribe and continued to promote his concept
of strength in unity. Supposedly, many years later, it was at Cohoes
Falls that Benjamin Franklin first learned about the confederacy from
the Iroquois themselves. Later, he incorporated many of their prin-
ciples of unity into the United States Constitution.[20]

*Cohoes Falls becomes a 70-foot-high avalanche of water during the
spring. Postcard circa 1910.*

During the late-Victorian era, a magnificent hotel called the Cataract House stood on the summit of a 175-foot precipice overlooking the fall. A flight of stairs led 50 feet down from the hotel to an observation deck. No trace of the Cataract House remains today.

Later, for better or worse, the City of Cohoes sealed the waterfall's fate by deciding to exploit the mighty waters for industrial purposes rather than for tourism. In 1811 the Cohoes Manufacturing Company was incorporated and began manufacturing screws near the fall. The factory burned down in 1815. Shortly after, a cotton mill was erected, but that only endured for a short time as well.

It was the construction of the Erie Canal and the Lake Champlain Canal that really put Cohoes on the map and turned it into a bustling center of commerce.[21] Under the leadership of Canvass White, combined with financial backing from a New York City firm and a patroon named Stephen Van Rensselaer, The Cohoes Company was incorporated in 1826. With a vision for the future, the company secured all water rights both above and below the fall, dammed up the Mohawk further upstream from the fall, and constructed a canal system for power generation.

In 1836 the Harmony Manufacturing Company was established to produce woven cotton fabric.[22] The company was named after Peter Harmony, its president.[23] In 1837 the company expanded, creating a series of new buildings, some of which still stand today. During this phase, one out of four residents in Cohoes worked at the mills.[24] By the 1850s and 1860s, Cohoes was the leading cotton manufacturer in the United States. By 1889, 25 mills were in operation, many of them involved in the production of knitted goods such as woolen underwear. When the Great Depression hit, however, the Harmony Mills textile plant closed, in 1932.

By no means is the history of Cohoes Falls all about manufacturing, however. Like Niagara Falls near Buffalo, Cohoes Falls has also had its share of daredevils. In 1899 a stuntman named Bobby Leach jumped into a barrel and rode over the fall on two successive days.[25] Leach used the same barrel for this stunt as he had used earlier while braving the infamous Niagara Whirlpool on the Niagara River, downstream from Niagara Falls.

Anything can happen at a large waterfall, and often does. On July 27, 2004, a 24-year-old man named Michael Jourdanais and an unidentified 15-year-old boy became trapped close to the center of the falls while fishing. Over 50 rescuers from two counties took part in saving the duo as the 60° waters of the river kept rising, threatening not only to subdue the two through hypothermia, but to sweep them over the top of the fall. They were saved just in time. According to Joe Fahd, chief of the Cohoes Fire Department, "They probably had another 10, 15 minutes."[26] The moral to the story: stay far back from the top of a large waterfall.

There are several theories regarding how Cohoes was named. One theory suggests that Cohoes is Native American for "falling canoe" which, if true, speaks volumes for the respect that early natives accorded the fall. Another theory is that Cohoes is a modification of the Algonquian word *Cohoses*, meaning "little holes" (or potholes). To be sure, the fall contains numerous potholes in its bedrock, including the enormous, previously buried pothole wherein the "Cohoes Mastodon" (see next paragraph) was uncovered. Wallace Bruce theorized that Cohoes may translate to "the island at the falls."[27] Still others have speculated that Cohoes was the Native American word for "salmon" or "shad"—fish that at one time were plentiful and easily caught at the fall.[28]

If you carefully study Cohoes Falls through binoculars during low water conditions, you will observe considerable scouring of the bedrock and a plethora of potholes at the base of the fall. In 1866, while workers were busily excavating the north foundation of Harmony Mill, the bones of a prehistoric mastodont were found in a gigantic pothole 60 feet below ground level. The mastodont was displayed in the old New York State Museum until the new museum at the Empire State Plaza was completed in 1977. The mastodont is now on display in the front lobby of the museum. A life-sized replica of the Cohoes Mastodon was constructed at the museum and can be seen at the Cohoes Public Library.

Today, the School Street Hydroelectric Project (a Toronto-based company) is located next to the south side of the fall and produces nearly 40 megawatts of power, enough to provide power to nearly 40,000 homes.[29]

There is currently talk of the City of Cohoes illuminating the falls at night in order to make the cascade more attractive to tourists, and also of constructing a new power plant that would allow more water to tumble over the fall. Concerns have also been expressed by environmentalists that the present turbines are chewing up an unacceptable number of American eel and blueback herring, which migrate upstream from the Atlantic Ocean to spawn. Only time will tell if these measures are enacted. Perhaps the city will eventually install an observation deck much closer to the fall than the current overlook at Cohoes Falls Overlook Park, thus allowing tourists to obtain the pre-industrial view of the fall that the Cataract House observation deck once provided.

Directions: From Albany, take I-787 north to its terminus at Cohoes. Cross over Rt. 32 and continue straight onto New Courtland Street/ North Mohawk Street. Follow the street uphill as you drive north-west, paralleling the Mohawk River, for nearly 0.8 mile from Rt. 32. You will notice several large industrial buildings on your right. After you pass by them, turn right onto School Street (one-way). The fall can be observed from Overlook Park at the end of School Street.

To exit, turn onto Cataract Street (one-way), and then right onto Front Street (also one-way).

2. Falls near Lock 7

Location: Niskayuna (Schenectady County)
NYS Atlas & Gazetteer: p. 66, B3
Accessibility: Canoe or kayak approach from the south bank to base of falls. Roadside views from overlooks along the north bank.
Hours: The Lock 7 park on the south bank is open daily from one-half hour after sunrise to one-half hour after sunset.
Degree of Difficulty: Easy to moderate paddle by canoe or kayak

Description: These broad, ledge-shaped falls are located at Goat Island, a small, irregular-shaped prow of bedrock that is formed near the middle of the Mohawk River below a long dam that extends from Lock 7 across to the Vischer Ferry Hydroelectric Plant. While not high, the falls are fairly broad and expansive, consisting of a mound-shaped rock terrace with numerous ledges, inclined slabs, and pools of collected waters. The falls vary in appearance depending upon the volume of water coursing through the Mohawk Valley at any given moment.

The name "Goat Island" is not unique to the Mohawk River and Cohoes Falls. There is a Goat Island at the confluence of the Mohawk and Hudson rivers. There is even a Goat Island on the Niagara River above Niagara Falls.

History: This section of the Mohawk River is layered with many centuries of history, from Native Americans to post-industrial recreation enthusiasts.

The Niskayuna* lock and dam were completed in 1913 and have remained a vital link in the New York State Barge Canal system ever since.[1, 2] The current hydroelectric plant along the north bank was built in 1925 and is still actively generating power today.

Centuries ago, a Native American village of substantial size flourished along the south bank of the Mohawk River from the "Niska Isle" peninsula to the confluence of the Lisha Kill and Mohawk River. A scenic bike path now parallels this section of the Mohawk River, extending all the way from Albany to Rotterdam Junction. The path is the former railroad bed of the Troy-Schenectady Railroad, built in 1843.[3]

On the opposite side of the river, at the Vischer Ferry Power Plant, is the western terminus of the Vischer Ferry Nature & Historic Preserve's hiking/biking pathway that parallels the old Erie Canal and the Mohawk River.

*The word *Niskayuna* is a Conistigione Indian name for "extensive corn flats," a reference to the high degree of fertility of the land for growing crops of corn.[4]

Directions: *Water Approach*—From I-890 in Schenectady, get off at Exit 7 (for Troy) and drive northeast on Rt. 7 for nearly 2 miles. When you come to the traffic light at Rt. 146 (Balltown Road), continue straight on Rt. 7 for another 0.2 mile. At a traffic light, turn left onto Rosendale Road and proceed east for nearly 1.8 miles until you reach River Road. Continue southeast on River Road for another 0.5 mile. At a sharp curve in the road, turn left onto Lock 7 Road and drive northwest for 0.8 mile to the parking area for Lock 7, on your right.

From the Adirondack Northway (I-87), get off at the Latham Exit and drive northwest on Rt. 7 for roughly 3 miles. At a traffic light, turn right onto River Road and continue west for 2 miles. Then turn right onto Lock 7 Road and continue northwest for 0.8 mile to the parking area.

From the parking area, carry your boat east (downstream) from the lock and dam for a short distance until you reach a point where you can easily and safely put the boat into the river. From there, paddle downstream a short distance to clear the barge canal walls, and then head back upstream, paddling towards the center of the river and Goat Island. Once you reach the island, in 0.8 mile, you are free to explore at your leisure.

Take note that it is also possible to reach Goat Island by putting your boat in at the boat launch site above the dam, and then using the lock system to drop to the lower water level at the base of the dam. If you do so, however, you will have to wait to pair up with a large-sized boat using the lock.

Land Approach—The falls can also be seen from the opposite side of the river along the Mohawk's north bank:

From Lock 7, drive northwest on River Road for 3.7 miles and then turn right onto Rt. 146. Go north for 1.9 miles, crossing over the Mohawk River in the process. At a traffic light turn right onto Riverview Road and proceed southeast for 4.2 miles. Along the way you will notice that the road essentially parallels the Mohawk River. When you come to a sign indicating "Vischer Ferry Plant: New York Power Authority," turn right and drive 0.2 mile south to a parking area above the power plant and falls.

From the Adirondack Northway, get off at Exit 8 for Crescent/Vischer Ferry, and proceed southwest on Crescent Road (Rt. 92) for nearly 4 miles. Along the way Crescent Road turns into Vischer Ferry Road. When you come to the little community of Vischer Ferry, turn right onto Riverview Road and drive northwest for 1.2 miles. Then turn left at the sign for the Vischer Ferry Power Plant (opposite Sugar Hill Road to your right) and drive south for 0.2 mile to a parking area above the power plant.

From this overlook a lateral view of the falls and dam can be obtained, although it is aesthetically compromised by the power plant in the foreground and a fair amount of intervening distance. Fortunately, it is possible to view the falls from a more aesthetic vantage point. Leaving the parking area, walk downhill along a paved road that is restricted to "unauthorized motor vehicles," but open to foot travel. In 0.05 mile, the road abruptly U-turns and heads back west towards the gated power plant. At this point leave the road and follow a pathway/old road that proceeds east, paralleling the Mohawk River. You are now on the western end of the Vischer Ferry Nature & Historic Preserve towpath. The large ditch that you see to your left is a remnant of the old Erie Canal. Within 0.05 mile, you will come to a side path to your right that leads up to a bluff that is crossed by power lines and overlooks the river. From there you will be able to obtain a more pleasing view of the falls, albeit still from a distance.

3. Falls between Lock 7 and Rexford

Location: Niskayuna (Schenectady County)
NYS Atlas & Gazetteer: p. 66, B2–3
Accessibility: 3-mile paddle by canoe or kayak (one way)
Hours: The grounds at Lock 7 are open daily from one-half hour after sunrise to one-half hour after sunset.
Degree of Difficulty: Moderate

Description: There are a number of small but pretty waterfalls formed along the south bank of the Mohawk River between Lock 7 and Rexford. Virtually none of them can be seen or appreciated except from the river. Several of the falls are 10–15 feet high and consist of near-vertical plunges over the top of the south-bank escarpment.[1,2] Two of the falls don't appear to be natural and may have been artificially created or enhanced by the Knolls Atomic Power Laboratory (KAPL) for purposes of drainage.

Even without waterfalls as an enticement, the trip would still be well worth the effort. You will feel as though traveling through primordial times as you paddle through a deeply cut canyon. Near the beginning of the trip, you will encounter large beds of water chestnuts, an invasive species. Soon, as you paddle along the south bank, you will reach the beginning of the escarpment. Here the shale rock walls begin to loom 10 feet above you and then, as you proceed further upstream, rise up to a height of over 30 feet.

During the paddle you will pass by several waterfalls. The last one is reached just before you come to a power line spanning the river (see following chapter for further details). If you pass the last waterfall and continue paddling upstream, you will eventually reach the Rexford Bridge. In the vicinity of the bridge, you will observe that the side walls along the south bank have gradually become lower, whereas the north bank has attained a staggering height of 130 feet or more above the river.[3]

Directions: From I-890 in Schenectady, get off at Exit 7 (for Troy) and drive northeast on Rt. 7 for nearly 2 miles. When you come to the traffic light at Rt. 146 (Balltown Road), continue straight for 0.2 mile to the next traffic light. Turn left onto Rosendale Road and proceed east for nearly 1.8 miles. At this point River Road comes in on the left. Continue southeast (right) on River Road for 0.5 mile. When you come to a sharp curve in the road, turn left onto Lock 7 Road and drive northwest for 0.8 mile. Drive past the first parking area (on your right) and continue uphill to a second parking lot, where a boat launch provides direct access above the dam to the river.

From the boat launch, paddle upstream, hugging the south bank of the river. You will quickly pass a landfill, with views of the bicycle path in the distance. Soon you will reach a point where the escarpment begins and cliffs start to rise up higher and higher as you progress upstream. After roughly 1.5 miles you will reach a point where two artificially created waterfalls can be seen. You will know you are in the right section if you look across to the north bank of the river and see the palatial estate of A. W. Lawrence—former insurance magnate—looming high above the river.

As you continue upstream you will encounter several small but pretty waterfalls (depending upon the season), finally reaching the last waterfall (and also the prettiest), which is contained in a nearly hidden cove on the river.

Waterfalls often form along the side walls of gorges.
Postcard circa 1900.

4. Waterfall near Bike Path in Rexford

Location: Rexford
NYS Atlas & Gazetteer: p. 66, B2-3
Accessibility: Less than 0.6-mile walk
Degree of Difficulty: Easy

Description: This medium-sized cascade is formed on a tiny tributary to the Mohawk River. At one time this stream must have been considerably more dynamic than at present, for it would have taken a much more energetic creek to cut out the deep ravine, extending 60 feet through the bedrock from the Mohawk River, that you see today.

The waterfall is nearly 25 feet high and contained in a pretty grotto-like cove. It can also be accessed from the Mohawk River by canoe or kayak (see previous chapter, "Falls between Lock 7 and Rexford," for river approach).[1] The fall is formed out of shale and is nearly vertical. Because of its limited watershed, the waterfall should be visited in early spring or following significant rainfall when there is sufficient water flow. Several smaller cascades can be found just upstream from the top of the fall.

Directions: From the junction of Rtes. 7 and 146 in Niskayuna, drive north on Rt. 146 for 3.5 miles. Just before you reach the traffic light at the south end of the Rexford Bridge (which spans the Mohawk River), turn right onto East Street. If you reach Williams Street, you have gone too far. Proceed east for 0.1 mile. Park to the right in an area next to the bike path, where several picnic tables and a large garage are visible.

From the parking area, walk (or bike) southeast for 0.5 mile. As soon as you pass under a series of high-tension lines, you will come to a tiny stone bridge that spans a fairly insignificant creek. Cross over the creek and then follow a surprisingly well-worn, unmarked trail that leads off to your left, paralleling the creek. The land is not posted as of this writing. Proceed north for 0.05 mile and you will reach a large clearing at the confluence of the Mohawk River and the small tributary. At this point you are roughly 40 feet above the level of the river, with nearly vertical drops to the streambed and river below. Follow the trail to the left as it leads diagonally down the side of the ravine, heading away from the Mohawk River and back towards the waterfall. After you have made your way halfway down the side of the ravine, you will come to a spot where an excellent view of the waterfall is afforded.

For unparalleled views of the Mohawk River, continue east along the path as it turns right and parallels the 30–40-foot-high bank of the river. The trail continues for over 0.3 mile, but ends when it reaches fenced-in property belonging to General Electric.

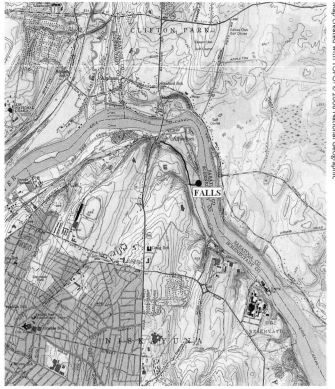

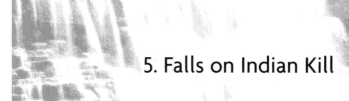

5. Falls on Indian Kill

Location: Indian Kill Nature Preserve, north of Schenectady
(Schenectady County)
NYS Atlas & Gazetteer: p. 66, AB2
Accessibility: 1.0-mile hike one way over uneven terrain
Degree of Difficulty: Moderate

Description: Several small, pretty waterfalls are formed on the
Indian Kill, a modest-sized stream that rises north of Glenville Cen-
ter, flows through a comparatively level tract of land known histori-
cally as Swaagertown (Dutch for "cousin town"), and joins with the
Alplaus Kill just upstream from the Alplaus Kill's confluence with the
Mohawk River.[1-3] Altogether, the Indian Kill runs for 15 miles.

Two of the waterfalls are found within the Indian Kill Nature Preserve, a wilderness-maintained hiking area.[4] The third waterfall lies on
private land outside the park's boundaries and is inaccessible.

The first cascade (which is listed on a map at the preserve as
Waterfall #3) is 3–4 feet high. It is comely, but small as waterfalls go.
The second cascade (listed as Waterfall #2 on the preserve map) is
formed in an attractive glen. It is well over 6 feet in height and flows
into a pool of water at its base. A number of ledges can be seen near
its top. The third fall (listed as waterfall #1 on the preserve map) is
located further upstream, but unfortunately is outside of the preserve's
boundaries and is inaccessible. It is the tallest of the three falls.

History: The falls are part of the 100-acre Indian Kill Nature Preserve,[5]
which is owned by the Schenectady County Nature and Historic Preserve. The park is well-maintained, with groomed paths, wooden
bridges, stairways, and boardwalks placed in strategic locations.

The first mill on the Indian Kill dates back prior to 1800 and
was located on land owned by Lawrence Van Epps.[6] Most historians
believe that it was probably a carding mill.

Directions: From Scotia (junction of Rtes. 5 and 50), take Rt. 50 northeast for 3.5 miles. Turn right onto Glenridge Road and drive east for 1.3 miles. You will initially drive up a steep hill and then down the other side. At the bottom of the hill, turn left onto Maple Avenue and drive north for 0.4 mile. Just past the point where Hetcheltown Road enters from the right, you will see the parking area for the Indian Kill Nature Preserve on your left. If you drive past the Glendale Nursing Home (also on your left), you will have gone too far.

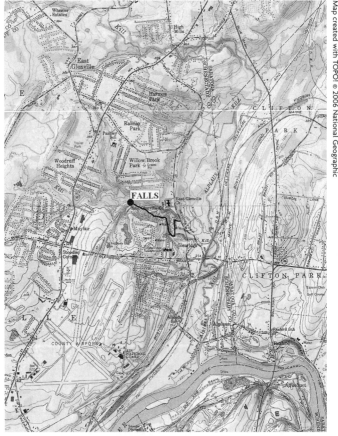

At the parking lot take note of a kiosk with a map of the area. The map is helpful, but once you begin the hike, it is easy to lose your bearings as you cross over and around a maze of gullies and ravines. The trick is to always follow the Indian Kill upstream, staying on the red-blazed Claire Schmitt Trail as you hike westward.

As you walk from the parking lot, you will quickly descend into a gully, where the trail leads you across a metal footbridge spanning the top of a dam. The stream below is the Indian Kill. After crossing the creek, bear to the right and follow the main trail until you eventually reach the Indian Kill again, now further upstream (if you go straight, you will end up on the private grounds of Conifer Park, a rehab center). After a total of over 0.5 mile, you will come to the first waterfall, which is near an open field leading up to the Woodlin Club (a private association for members only). Continue for another 0.2–0.3 mile until you reach a pretty glen where the south bank rises up noticeably above the streambed. The second falls can be seen below. There is even a little bench at the top of the ravine for those who want to linger and enjoy the sound of the cascading waters.

You will notice power lines along an open field in the woods just up from the falls. This marks the end of the Indian Kill Nature Preserve.

6. Krystal Falls

Location: Burnt Hills (Schenectady County)
NYS Atlas & Gazetteer: p. 66, AB2
Accessibility: Roadside

Description: Krystal Falls is formed on the Alplaus Kill, a medium-sized stream that rises near Galway and flows into the Mohawk River at the village of Alplaus. The fall is 15 feet high and surprisingly broad, located where the ravine suddenly opens up to become spacious before narrowing again a short distance downstream where it has carved out walls that rise up to over 60 feet in height.[1]

Near the top of the fall is an enormous depression where a stairway once led visitors down to the bottom of a 10-foot pit. Just upstream from Krystal Falls, west of the Rt. 50 bridge, are several small ledge-shaped falls, the tallest being about 4 feet high.[2] Near roadside, at the top of the south bank, is the old Explorer Post 38 cabin.

History: Centuries ago, the Alplaus Kill was heavily traveled by Native Americans navigating their way north to the Lake Champlain region. Ancient stone tools from the Laurentian tradition have been found in the fields around Alplaus, suggesting that Native Americans may have been present in the area as far back as 3,000 BC.[3]

It was at the nearby hamlet of Alplaus that a party of 96 Native Americans and 114 Frenchmen camped in 1690 before launching a midnight attack on the Stockade section of Schenectady. Sixty residents of Schenectady were killed in what became known historically as the Schenectady Massacre.

The first mill near Krystal Falls was most likely a sawmill. It was soon followed by a gristmill and then, at some point later, by a second sawmill and a woolen factory.[4] It is believed that the woolen factory became specialized as a carding mill, where fleeces were carded into long rolls and then sold to housewives who turned out fabrics on their spinning wheels. Another mill, the High Mills Grist Mill, was operated by the Heckler Brothers and produced rye flour.[5] After time, the area came to be known as High Mills. Little if any evidence remains today of these old industries.

"Alplaus" is derived from the Dutch word *Aalplaats*, meaning "eel place." Although it's hard to imagine it today, the Alplaus Kill was once populated by eels in great number. The eels, which were Caribbean-born, 5 feet long, and weighed an average of 7 pounds, were a favorite staple in the diet of Native Americans and early European settlers. That era came to an abrupt end when a dam was built across the Hudson River at Troy, preventing the eels from returning upstream from the Atlantic Ocean to spawn. If you have visited Cohoes Falls, you might wonder just how the eels were able to get up and over the great height of that falls to reach the Alplaus Kill. The answer is motivation—spurred by the eel's relentless reproductive cycle.

Beginning in 1926 a popular restaurant called Krystal's Inn operated next to the waterfall. In 2005, after considerable renovation, it reopened as the Mill Stone Lodge.

Krystal Falls, circa 1900.

Directions: From Scotia (junction of Rtes. 5 and 50), take Rt. 50 northeast for roughly 6 miles. Just before you cross over a bridge spanning Alplaus Creek, turn right onto Paradowski Road. Drive east for less than 0.2 mile. The falls can be viewed from the side of the road between where Stephen Road and Tryon Street enter Paradowski Road.

The upper falls on Alplaus Creek can be easily viewed from the west side of the Rt. 50 bridge spanning the stream.

Until Krystal's Inn went out of business several years ago, it was possible to walk to the main falls. At that time, visitors could pull into Krystal's Restaurant (now Mill Stone Lodge), park, and walk to the top of the falls via Krystal Falls Park. One can hope that access will be reestablished in the future so that patrons of the restaurant can enjoy not only a good meal, but a great waterfall.

7. Plotter Kill Falls

Location: Near Mariaville (Schenectady County)

NYS Atlas & Gazetteer: p. 66, B1

Accessibility: Moderate hike over uneven terrain to the three main falls. A much lengthier and more demanding hike is required to access the falls in the lower gorge.

Hours: Open dawn to dusk

Degree of Difficulty: Moderate to the three main falls: difficult to the falls in the lower gorge

Description: The Plotter Kill Nature Preserve is a 632-acre tract of land open to hikers and nature lovers. The preserve contains three large waterfalls and more than a dozen smaller falls.[1–8] Two of the large falls are formed on the Plotter Kill,* a small stream that rises near Featherstonhaugh Lake and flows into the Mohawk River below Rotterdam Junction. The third large waterfall is formed on Rynex Creek, a tiny tributary to the Plotter Kill. All three are found within less than 0.3 mile of one another.

There are also numerous smaller cascades formed on the Plotter Kill. One is downstream from the upper fall; several are below the lower fall; and there are at least a dozen smaller falls in the lower section of the Plotter Kill Gorge as the stream rapidly descends towards the Mohawk Valley.

According to Almy and Anne Coggeshall: "The effects of the retreating glacier on the local landscape are seen everywhere in Schenectady County, but in few places are they as dramatic as in the narrow box canyon just west of Schenectady known as the Plotter Kill. Here a retreating waterfall created the steep-sided gorge where its plummeting water undercut the resistant cap rock to maintain a vertical drop. The gorge is now some two miles long and has at its upper end three waterfalls, one seventy feet high."[9]

Indeed, these are high waterfalls. The upper fall on the Plotter Kill is well over 60 feet in height and encased in a horseshoe-shaped amphitheater with lofty side walls.[10] The lower fall is 40 feet in height. Both falls consist of nearly vertical drops. Between the two falls is a small cascade. Just downstream from the lower fall is a 4-foot waterfall, followed by a 7-foot-high, step-like cascade.

The fall on Rynex Creek (the third of the preserve's high waterfalls) is a 40-foot-high vertical drop. Immediately downstream from its base, Rynex Creek flows into the Plotter Kill. It is at this junction where one of the smaller waterfalls on the Plotter Kill can be seen. Much further downstream is a series of smaller, ledge-shaped cascades formed on the lower Plotter Kill and one or two of its tributaries.

The entire area of the Plotter Kill Preserve is chiseled and dynamic in appearance. During the course of three and a half miles, the stream drops over 900 feet from Rynex Corners to the floor of the Mohawk.

Be very careful near the big waterfalls. There have been several accidents and at least one death, in 1993.

Plotter Kill is Dutch for "flat creek"—a reference to the numerous ledges of shale that form giant stairs in the riverbed as you proceed downstream from the main falls.[11]

Directions: From Schenectady, take I-890 west and get off at Exit 2 for Campbell Road. Drive south for 0.8 mile. Opposite the middle entrance to the Rotterdam Square Mall, turn right onto Putnam Road and proceed west for 1.8 miles until you reach Rt. 159 (Mariaville Road). Turn right and drive northwest on Rt. 159 for 1.8 miles.

There are two entrances into the Plotter Kill Preserve, separated by nearly a mile. You may enter the preserve from Rt. 159 or from Coplon Road. Once inside the preserve, the trails are color-coded. Red is for the main trail, which follows the contours of the Plotter Kill and Rynex Creek gorges. The red-blazed path is an enormous trail system that offers many miles and hours of hiking, with significant changes in elevation. Yellow indicates spur trails and small loops that go off of the main (red) trail. Blue is for a short trail along the red trail's southeast end.

From the Rt. 159 entrance: After driving northwest for 1.8 miles from Putnam Road along Rt. 159, you will see Coplon Road on your right. Continue west on Rt. 159 for another 0.4 mile. Look for a Plotter Kill Nature Preserve sign and turn right into a small parking area. Next to the parking lot you will see a large kiosk containing a map of the preserve. It is well worth your time to study the map before undertaking the hike.

The best way to enjoy the falls is to follow the main, red-blazed trail down into the upper section of the gorge, cross over the creek via an impressive footbridge, and hike downstream along the north bank. Within 0.1 mile you will come to the top of the 60-foot-high

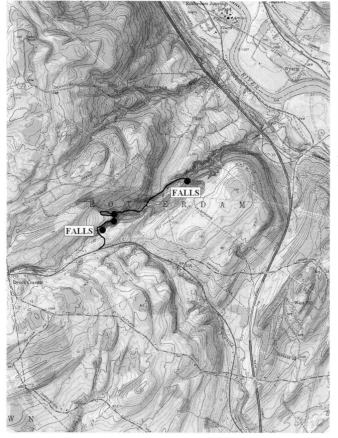

Sixty-foot-high Plotter Kill Falls, circa 1910.

Plotter Kill Falls, Schenectady, N. Y.

upper fall. It is very pretty and is best seen from the side. Use caution. Do not walk out onto the bedrock and approach its brink.

From the upper fall, continue following the red-blazed trail along the north rim of the gorge for 0.2 mile. You will come to an intersection where a yellow-blazed path leads off to the right at an acute angle. The yellow trail will take you quickly down into the gorge. At the bottom you will come upon a pretty, 3-foot-high, ledge cascade.

From here, you now have two choices. One option is to follow the creek upstream, which will lead you to the base of the upper fall in less than 0.2 mile. The hike can be somewhat demanding, however. There is a very well-worn but unmarked trail that proceeds upstream, crosses over the Plotter Kill and then continues on the opposite side, but it quickly peters out and leaves you to negotiate the rest of the trek either by rock-hopping along the streambed or making your way along the edge of the stream. This hike is easy in the summer, but can be tricky if you are visiting in early spring or following significant rainfall, when there is more water flowing through the gorge.

The second option is to follow a well-worn, unmarked path downstream that quickly leads to the top of the 40-foot-high lower fall. Again, use caution and view the fall from the side of the stream, where there is an excellent overlook and far better views than any you could get from the top of the fall itself.

To reach the third large fall in the preserve, return to the top of the gorge and follow the main, red-blazed path west as it parallels the top of what is now Rynex Creek Gorge. Within less than 0.2 mile the path descends to the streambed and then follows Rynex Creek back to the top of the third waterfall, at the intersection of the Rynex Creek and Plotter Kill gorges. There are good views into the gorge, but satisfying lateral views of the third waterfall are somewhat problematic. The waterfall view is particularly disappointing during times of little rainfall. You will notice that there is an informal path on the southwest side of the fall, but this should be avoided. It is steep and heavily eroded, and is not a part of the Plotter Kill trail system.

From the top of Rynex Creek Falls, continue along the red-blazed trail as it climbs steeply back up the north bank. Once you crest the top, the trail descends to a junction in less than 0.4 mile. To the right will take you to the red-blazed trail that follows along the bottom of the middle section of the gorge for a distance before climbing to the top of the opposite side of the gorge. To the left will lead you uphill along the red-blazed trail that follows the rim of the lower section of the gorge.

Let's assume that you take the trail to the right. It will immediately lead you down to the Plotter Kill. From there, instead of crossing over the stream and following the red-blazed trail east along the bottom of the gorge, follow the creek upstream, rock-hopping along the way, until you reach the junction of the Plotter Kill and Rynex Creek. This can be easily done as long as you haven't chosen to visit the gorge after a prolonged, torrential downpour or following spring's snowmelt. From the junction of the Plotter Kill and Rynex Creek, you will have superb views of the lower fall on the Plotter Kill, as well as the fall on Rynex Creek, without having had to engage in any strenuous or dangerous climbing to descend into the gorge.

On the other hand, if you follow the red-blazed Upper Preserve Trail instead of the Lower Preserve Trail, it will lead up to the rim of the gorge where, unfortunately, there are no views of the ravine's interior. By following the trail northeast for another 0.5–0.6 mile, however, you will discover that ultimately there is a payoff. Along the way you will pass under high-tension wires, and then the trail will lead steadily downhill until it levels off. At this point you will soon come to a junction where the Lower Preserve red-blazed trail comes sharply up on your right.

From there, continue straight ahead, following the red-blazed trail. Within a hundred feet you will arrive at another junction. The red-blazed trail veers off to your left, leaving a yellow-blazed trail to continue straight ahead. Go straight ahead on the yellow-blazed trail. (If you stay on the red-blazed trail, it will eventually lead down to the Plotter Kill in over 1.0 mile.) After 0.1 mile you will find yourself walking along a spine of land, with the steeply cut Plotter Kill ravine to your right and another deep ravine off to your left. The trail begins to descend and, within less than 0.3 mile from the start of the yellow-blazed trail, you will come to a very pretty, secluded glen where a 3-foot-high, horseshoe-shaped, ledge cascade falls into

Ledge-shaped cascades abound on the Plotter Kill.
Postcard circa 1900.

a pool of water whose depth has been increased by a little stone dam that hikers have fashioned. It is a pool that invites a quick, refreshing swim. Right next to the fall, descending along the south bank, is a tiny tributary that produces a small cascade of its own. This is one secluded glen that you will not want to miss if you are looking for a peaceful retreat, but bear in mind that it does require some effort to access.

Back at the parking lot, there is a second way to catch a partial view of the large waterfalls on the Plotter Kill from the south side of the gorge. Begin the hike from the kiosk, following the red-blazed trail. In less than 0.1 mile you will reach the south rim of the gorge. Take the blue-blazed trail that leads off to the right, paralleling the top of the gorge's south side. It will lead you to limited views of the Upper Falls and Lower Falls on the Plotter Kill, views that are partially blocked by foliage. For the best views from this vantage, plan your visit for when the foliage is less dense.

From the Coplon Road Entrance: At 0.4 mile east of the Rt. 159 entrance to the Plotter Kill Preserve, turn northeast onto Coplon Road and proceed straight ahead for 0.5 mile. Pull into the clearly designated parking area for the nature preserve on your left.

From the parking lot, follow the trail downhill across a field that immediately leads into the woods. At this point, red-blazed trail markers are visible. Continue following the trail downhill as it rapidly descends into the expansive gorge created by the Plotter Kill. Within 0.3 mile you will come to a junction. If you continue straight, you will follow the red-blazed trail along the south rim of the Plotter Kill Gorge, heading towards the Mohawk River.

Trail to base of Lower Plotter Kill Falls and Rynex Creek Falls: If you turn left, you will follow the red-blazed trail as it heads steadily downhill. Within less than 0.3 mile, you will be level with the Plotter Kill, which is relatively docile and waterfall-free at this point. A low-water crossing will be visible here. Continue following the red-blazed trail, proceeding upstream on the same side of the Plotter Kill. In another 0.3 mile you will reach a point where the trail crosses the Plotter Kill (the high-water crossing). Some rock-hopping is required here, but it is not difficult unless you are hiking after heavy rainfall or snowmelt.

As soon as you cross over the stream, you have two options. **Option #1:** If you follow the red-blazed trail to the right, you will immediately start climbing uphill steadily. Veer left when you come to a junction. In less than 0.4 mile you will reach the top of the Rynex Creek Gorge, where a series of large steps take you down to the brink of a 40-foot waterfall on the Rynex Creek. The problem here, which is a bit confounding, is that it is difficult to get a lateral view of the waterfall.

The red-blazed trail continues along the opposite bank, proceeding upstream for 0.1 mile, and then heads uphill out of the gorge to continue along the rim of the Rynex Kill Gorge. The trail quickly turns to the right at the junction of the Rynex Kill and Plotter Kill gorges. At this point you can take the yellow-blazed spur trail down to the Plotter Kill's streambed, from where, hiking upstream, the Upper Falls can be viewed from below or, walking downstream, the Lower Falls can be seen from its top. Or, if you wish, you can continue along the red-blazed trail, following the gorge upstream for 0.2 mile to the top of the Upper Falls.

Option #2: The other choice (and undoubtedly the one favored by waterfall enthusiasts) is to follow an informal trail that heads

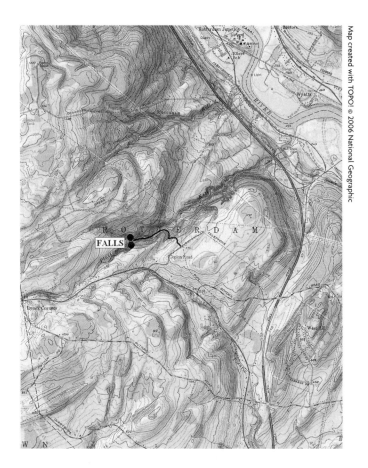

upstream, paralleling the Plotter Kill. Along the way you will have to cross over the Plotter Kill several times. This entails further rock-hopping, but it is not difficult to do unless there is a considerable amount of water flowing through the gorge or the rocks are slippery from rainfall. Blowdown may also be encountered.

This hike will lead you, in less than 0.3 mile, up to the base of the 40-foot-high Lower Falls and also to the base of the 40-foot-high Rynex Creek Falls. These two falls are perpendicular to each other and separated by a distance of only several hundred feet. You will also be able to observe a pretty, 4-foot-high, flume falls on the Plotter Kill, near the base of the Lower Falls, as well as a 7-foot-high, multi-ledge falls on the Plotter Kill (just downstream from the junction of the Plotter Kill and Rynex Kill).

This is a very scenic area, and one that is almost magical. How often do you get to see two large waterfalls so close to one another?

Trail to lower cascades on the Plotter Kill: From the Coplon Street parking lot, follow the path down for over 0.2 mile to the junction of the Lower Preserve Trail and the South Rim Trail. Take the South Rim Trail, which, as the name suggests, follows the south rim of the gorge as the Plotter Kill makes its way down to the Mohawk River. Within 0.3 mile you will arrive at an open field; pass under the power lines that extend far below into the gorge and up the other side. Approximately 0.3 miles beyond this point you will come to a red-colored footbridge spanning a small creek. This tiny tributary to the Plotter Kill has produced a rather chiseled-out ravine of its own. As soon as you cross over the foot-bridge, turn left onto a yellow-blazed trail, called the Scenic Loop Trail. You will see, to your left, a little bench that overlooks a 30–40 foot cascade, although there is really no way to describe the height of this cascade because the stream has cut the shale down to bare bedrock, and the creek continues downhill at a steep angle, making virtually one long continuous waterslide. But bear in mind that little water is carried by this stream except following heavy rain. Within 0.05 mile further downstream, the ravine is filled with earth and loose slabs of rock that have been washed down from the upper regions.

Continue on the yellow path for another 0.05 mile past the cascade. The path parallels the north bank of the gorge produced by this tributary, offering views into the gorge's deep interior when the foliage is sparse. You will reach a point where the yellow trail turns right, paralleling the Plotter Kill Gorge. If you miss this turn, you will immediately start following an informal trail that leads down a very steep slope, coming out at the bottom of the gorge where the Plotter Kill and the small tributary meet and each produce its own cascade and waterfall. You do not need to take this trail downhill (and unnecessarily promote erosion), however, for you can reach the cascades

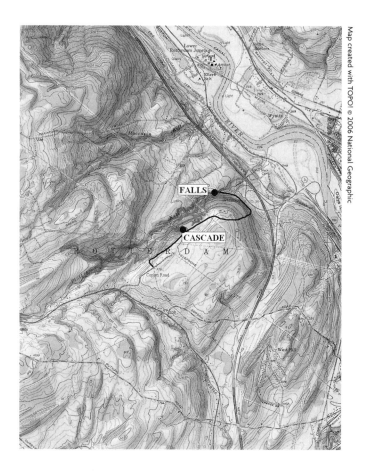

below by following the directions given under the North Rim Trail section (below).

Stay on the yellow-blazed trail as it leads you along the rim of the Plotter Kill and then to the right when it encounters another ravine produced by a second tiny tributary. All the while you will be aware of a huge void to your left, although it is not possible to look down into the Plotter Kill Gorge because of all the trees. The yellow-blazed trail soon leads back over to the red-blazed trail. Continue along this main trail northeast as it follows the south rim. You will soon pass under a second set of power lines that descend into the gorge through an open field. Shortly after this intersection, the red-blazed trail begins to descend steadily, seemingly following an old abandoned road. You can easily hear the roar of traffic on the New York State Thruway (I-90) as you make your way down.

After a while you will reach the bottom of the gorge and the Plotter Kill. If you turn to the right, you will head towards the Thruway. Before you reach the Thruway (which crosses over the Plotter Kill), however, the trail suddenly turns to the left in 0.1 mile and leads down to the bedrock of the stream. If you cross diagonally over the stream at this point, you will pick up the red-blazed trail on the opposite side of the stream and continue your journey, now along the North Rim Trail. If you miss the turn, you will quickly notice that the markers are now blue-blazed and the trail, if you stay on it, will ultimately lead you close to the Thruway embankment in 0.2 mile.

To see waterfalls, look for the sign stating "Jacobs Ladder & Step Falls" and directing you to proceed left when you reach the Plotter Kill (as described above). As you walk upstream along this trail, you will see, immediately to your right, a pretty, 2-foot-high, ledge cascade with a pool of water in the bedrock at the base of the fall.

Continue upstream for several hundred feet further and the trail will lead you right out onto the bedrock at the bottom of a series of cascades. The lowermost fall is a 2-foot-high ledge plunge, followed by a second 2-foot-high ledge falls. Above these is a 12-foot-high cascade.

From there, you can retrace your steps, following the red-blazed trail back downstream until you either return the way you came, up along the South Rim Trail, or cross over the creek and follow the red-blazed trail as it makes its way along the North Rim.

Penetrating the Interior of the Plotter Kill: Some seasoned hikers may want to explore the interior of the Plotter Kill more fully and see its wonderful waterfalls. The following hike, then, is for capable hikers who are bold and adventurous, able to make their way along flat bedrock, including sections covered with stones and boulders, and who can get over and around small cascades:

Plotter Kill Falls, Schenectady, N. Y.

There's always time to relax by a waterfall. Postcard circa 1910.

Plan to undertake this hike when minimal water is flowing through the gorge. From Jacobs Ladder and Step Falls, continue upstream. This will require that you get up and over the 12-foot-high cascade, which necessitates pulling yourself up over the ledge (it is not all that difficult to do) and then bushwhacking upstream. As soon as you clear the top of the falls, you will come to two 2-foot-high falls and then, less than 150 feet upstream from the top of Jacob's Ladder, a pretty, 5-foot-high, ledge fall. It is an area where the bedrock is very flat and scoured.

Follow the creek upstream, as it now turns from bedrock into loose stones and boulders. In over 0.1 mile you will come to a 5-foot-high cascade, and then to a 2-foot-high cascade directly above that. Continue your hike along the streambed for another 0.2 mile or less. You will come to a wide, semi-horseshoe-shaped waterfall that rises approximately 7 feet in height. It is located at a section of the stream where the stream becomes constricted. As you approach the fall, you may at first be fooled by the bend in the stream into thinking that you are seeing a fall on a tributary coming down to the Plotter Kill. What you will notice, however, is a small stream coming down from the south slopes of the gorge and flowing into the base of this fall. During times of high rainfall or snowmelt, this tiny creek becomes animated and produces cascades of its own.

Getting up and over this 7-foot-high waterfall may be difficult, but it can be done. It will require walking over to the left (south) side of the fall, stepping up, and then pulling yourself onto the top of the ledge. Once you have reached the top of the fall, you will notice how the north bank rises vertically to a height of 35–40 feet above you. It is all very dramatic.

Continue your hike upstream. Immediately you will pass by a 1-foot-high cascade and then a 6-foot-high ledge fall, which can easily be bypassed. Within another 100 feet you will come upon a pretty, 2-foot-high, ledge fall. What's unusual about this waterfall is that an 8-foot-long, narrow slab of rock has seemingly been levered out from the edge line of the fall so that it extends perpendicularly. It is just one of several oddities that the gorge has to offer.

At this point you can either retrace your route back to the red-blazed trail (which may be more difficult, since you have to climb *down* the falls now), or you can continue your advance up the Plotter Kill. By forging ahead you will eventually come to a small ledge falls where, exiting from the north side of the stream, you can pick up a yellow-blazed trail that will take you up to the red-blazed North Rim Trail. From there, you can follow the red-blazed trail back to either of the parking areas.

8. Cascades on Moccasin Kill

Location: Near Lower Rotterdam Junction (Schenectady County)
NYS Atlas & Gazetteer: p. 66, AB1
Accessibility: 0.3-mile hike over rolling terrain
Degree of Difficulty: Easy to moderate

Description: There are a number of small, hard-to-see cascades that are located in the 80-acre Moccasin Kill Sanctuary. The cascades are formed on the Moccasin Kill, a little stream that rises in the hills south of Lower Rotterdam Junction and flows into the Mohawk River just north of Rt. 5S.

The cascades consist of 5 to 6 small ledge-shaped falls, ranging in height from 2 feet to 8 feet and formed in a very narrow, steeply walled ravine. There is no way to see the falls from their bases unless you walk right up the ravine, climbing over each fall as you encounter it (something that should not be attempted unless you are adept at scrambling and undertake the venture during times when not much water is flowing through the ravine). For this reason the falls are best seen from the top of the ravine.

As you hike through the sanctuary, you will be surprised at just how deep its several prominent ravines are, and you will undoubtedly wonder how such an insubstantial creek as the present Moccasin could have carved out the immensity before you. Obviously, at a much earlier time, a considerably larger volume of water was coursing through the ravines to cut through rock so deeply and severely.

It should be noted that the Moccasin Kill is just one of several streams that have chiseled out impressive ravines through the south shoulder of the Mohawk Valley. There is the Plotter Kill Gorge to the east. To the west is the Sandsea Kill, located on private land, which Francis Kimball describes as "a turbulent stream, with a sixty-foot cascade" that "races down the town's steep northern slope [actually, it's the southern slope], joining the Mohawk at Pattersonville."[1]

History: The hill on the south side of the Mohawk Valley down which the Moccasin Kill, as well as the Plotter Kill and the Sandsea Kill, descends is called Yantaputchaberg. The hill represents the eastern boundary of what was once the Mohawk tribe's considerable sphere of influence in the valley.[2]

In the 1920s Vincent Schaffer named the stream Moccasin Kill after the pink lady slippers he found there, which reminded him of moccasins. The preserve was acquired from Heinz and Louise Specht in 1966. It is land that has returned to woods after farming was abandoned by the 1920s. The trails were initially mapped and cut by Boy Scout Troop 54.[3, 4]

Directions: From Schenectady, take I-890 west, getting off at the Rotterdam Junction exit for Rt. 5S just before I-890 crosses over the Mohawk River and terminates at Rt. 5. Continue northwest on Rt. 5S for approximately 1.2 miles from the Rotterdam Junction Exit. Turn left onto Lower Greg Road. Go 0.2 mile and then turn left onto Greg Road, heading southwest. Immediately you will cross over railroad tracks. In less than 0.2 mile, turn right onto Crawford Road and drive west, going steadily uphill, for 1.2 miles from the start of Crawford Road. The parking area for the sanctuary is located on the left side of the road. It is just a narrow pull-off and is only able to accommodate a couple of cars at one time.

Before beginning the hike, take a look at the kiosk next to the parking area. It contains a map of the preserve, including a section marked "Cascades."

From the kiosk, follow the red-blazed trail over a small footbridge. Look to your left and you will see giant blocks of rocks below, littering the streambed. Continue on the red-blazed trail for over 0.1 mile. It will lead you down into a deep ravine where you will cross over a usually dry streambed. The stream's dryness is only an illusion, however, for the waters flow underground here, re-emerging immediately downstream from the trail. If you were to follow this creek upstream on foot, it would lead you within several hundred feet to a series of waterfalls.

Continue on the red-blazed trail. Quickly, you will come to a junction where the red trail divides. Bear to the right. Immediately, a blue-blazed trail comes in on the right. Follow it uphill, paralleling the south bank of the stream you just crossed over a moment ago. In less than 0.1 mile the blue-blazed trail and the ravine come closer together. As soon as they begin to pull away from one another, follow an informal path on your right that leads down to the bottom of the ravine. You will end up next to a 6-foot-high cascade formed at a point where the stream abruptly changes direction. Gaze downstream and you will find yourself looking over the tops of several descending cascades as the ravine narrows dramatically.

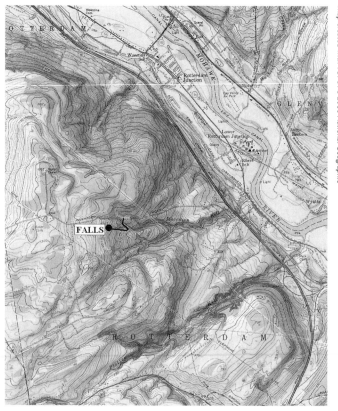

9. Falls on Washout Creek

Location: West Scotia (Schenectady County)
NYS Atlas & Gazetteer: p. 66, AB1-2
Accessibility: Short hike; very short bushwhack
Degree of Difficulty: Easy

Description: There are several small to medium-sized cascades formed on Washout Creek, a little stream that rises in North Glenville and flows into the Mohawk River west of Rector.[1] The falls are contained in the 370-acre Sanders Preserve[2] in a section known as Rabbit Hollow.

The Sanders Preserve is located east of *Tou-ar-e-una*, a name given by Native Americans to the Glenville Hills and its highest point, which rises to nearly 1,100 feet. On the opposite side of the valley, near Rotterdam Junction, is the southern wall's loftiest point, called Yantaputchaberg ("old Yantapoosh"). The word is loosely translated from the Dutch as "Jan Mabee's wood tot"—an historic house that still stands just east of Rotterdam Junction.[3]

The main waterfall contained in the preserve is a pretty, 6-foot-high, ledge cascade. Look closely at the bottom of the cascade and you will see a nearly circular, shallow, nearly 2-foot-diameter pothole that the stream has fashioned. Come back in a couple of centuries and this pothole will most surely have become considerably enlarged.

Two additional waterfalls—a 10-foot-high ledge fall, followed by a 15-footer—are also formed on Washout Creek, but located beyond the boundaries of the preserve.

Washout Creek has been known by several other names during its three centuries of recorded history. During colonial times it was called Arent Mebie's Kill. Later it was known as Walton Creek, after a family who lived along the bank of the stream. In the nineteenth century it acquired its present name after the cloudburst of 1885, which severely damaged the New York Central Railroad bed and tracks.[4, 5]

History: The Sanders Preserve was acquired by the Town of Glenville following the death of John Glen Sanders in 1965. The area containing the preserve is believed to have been the location of the original Sanders farm and summer home, dating back centuries ago. The names "Glen" and "Sanders" have been memorialized in the village of Scotia. There is a Glen Avenue and a Sanders Avenue. But most famous of all is the historic Glen Sanders Mansion at the western end of the "Great Western Gateway" Bridge. The mansion was enlarged in the 1980s and has become one of the region's most respected restaurants.

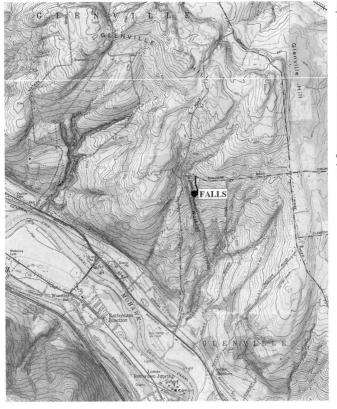

The preserve has been enhanced through a series of Eagle Scout projects undertaken in 1997 by BSA Troop 67. Trails have been firmed up, clear boundary markers were established, and two small bridges have been constructed.[6]

A kiosk next to the parking lot shows a photograph of the waterfall you will be visiting. The kiosk also provides information on how the forest, once harvested, is now in the process of reestablishing itself as it passes through a series of growth stages and species takeovers.

On the opposite side of the road from the preserve is the Johnston Observatory, which is used by amateur astronomers wishing to leave the bright lights of the city for the darker night skies of the country.

Directions: From Schenectady, drive northwest on I-890 for approximately 5 miles. When you come to the terminus of I-890, after crossing over the Mohawk River, turn left onto Rt. 5 and drive northwest for slightly over 1.5 miles. Turn right onto Washout Road and proceed north for 1.6 miles. Then turn right (east) onto Sanders Road. Within 0.2 mile you will come to a parking lot on the right-hand side of the road with a sign that states: "Sanders Preserve, Town of Glenville."

From the parking lot, take the main, blue-blazed path, which is the one closest to the creek, and follow it south for over 0.05 mile. At the point where the ravine and trail begin to come closer together, take a secondary trail that leads off to your right. The trail will quickly take you downhill to the top of a very pretty waterfall, which is the one featured at the kiosk.

The blue-blazed path is well worth following south for another 0.6 mile. The path parallels Washout Creek and passes by several places where views into the interior of the 100-foot-deep gorge are provided. If you stay on the path long enough, you will eventually come to a point where the trail narrows and continues on a spiny, high ridge, with Washout Creek to your right and a tributary coming in from a deeply cut canyon to your left. The path quickly descends and arrives at the confluence of these two streams. A tiny, almost insignificant, cascade on a small tributary can be seen at this point, at roughly 1.0 mile from Sanders Road.

Many of the nearby ravines, like Johnson's Gorge shown in this circa 1910 postcard, have waterfalls of their own.

10. Adriutha Falls (Historic)

Location: Near Cranesville (Montgomery County)
Accessibility: None; fall is located on private land

Description: Adriutha Falls is formed on Lewis Creek, a small stream that rises from two branches in the hills above the Mohawk River. The branch issuing from the north is the one that contains Adriutha Falls. Just downstream from the fall, the two branches join to form the main stream.

Adriutha Falls is approximately 50 feet high, with a smaller, 8-foot-high waterfall upstream from the top of the larger fall.[1-3] Near the base of the waterfall is a mammoth boulder, which stands like a silent stone sentinel.

Approximately 0.1 mile downstream from the waterfall, Lewis Creek is conducted underground by a drain pipe that leads under busy Rt. 5, beneath the railroad tracks, and then out into the Mohawk River.

History: Adriutha Falls has also been known as Buttermilk Falls, a fairly generic name when it comes to waterfalls—the equivalent of a mountain with a rocky summit being called "Bald Mountain."

In 1730 a primitive mill owned by Lewis Groot was established near the south end of the ravine, where a natural spring issued. The spring was approximately 300 feet from present-day Rt. 5. Later, a settler named Swart built a mill on the same site. Undoubtedly, it was from his name that nearby Swart Island and Swart Hill Road arose. Nothing remains of Swart's mill today, however.

The area was also once used as a summer camp by Camp Dorn.[4]

Adriutha Falls, circa 1900.

The Falls of Adrintha, Near Amsterdam, N.Y.

11. Fall at Cliffside Restaurant

Location: Amsterdam (Montgomery County)
NYS Atlas & Gazetteer: p. 65, A7
Accessibility: Wonderful views of the fall can be obtained from the dining room in the restaurant.

Description: This artificially created waterfall is formed at the northwest cliff face of a large rock cut behind the Cliffside Restaurant. The waterfall is 20 feet high and nearly a straight plunge. The only problem is that the fall is formed on a rather insubstantial creek that tends to run dry unless it is recharged by rainfall.

History: In past decades the restaurant was known as the Teepee Restaurant & Motel, and undoubtedly the fall acquired the name Teepee Falls by association. That venture went out of business a number of years ago, and the building fell into disuse until the present management took over and reestablished it as a viable restaurant. The motel has essentially been abandoned. The quarry in which the restaurant is located was developed in the early 1900s by Baid Bros. The stone taken out was used to resurface many of the streets in Amsterdam.[1]

Directions: From the junction of Rtes. 5 and 30 in Amsterdam, proceed southeast on Rt. 5. As you come to the edge of the city of Amsterdam, the two-lane road will suddenly turn into a four-lane highway. Turn left at a green sign pointing the way to East Main Street. Cross over the westbound lane of Rt. 5 and start driving uphill on Chapman Road. Immediately turn left onto a private road that leads up to the Cliffside Restaurant, which is at the northwest end of a quarry, approximately 0.1 mile from Chapman Road.

It is easy to see the fall from the northwest end of the parking lot. Better yet, go inside to enjoy the rare privilege of eating a meal in the presence of a pretty waterfall.

12. Falls at Kirk Douglas Park

Location: Amsterdam (Montgomery County)
NYS Atlas & Gazetteer: p. 65, A7
Accessibility: Views can be readily obtained from east wall of park
Degree of Difficulty: Easy

Description: This series of cascades is formed on the lower section of the North Chuctanunda, a medium-sized stream that rises near Barkersville, is impounded at Galway Lake and, upon being released by the dam, makes its way down to the Mohawk River at Amsterdam. The North Chuctanunda is a fairly dynamic river, descending over 600 feet from Galway Lake before reaching the Mohawk River, with the last 300 feet of descent being concentrated in the final three miles. As a result, by the time the stream reaches Amsterdam, it has taken on the appearance of a wild waterslide.

The falls are located in Kirk Douglas Park, which is more a playground than a nature area. The upper cascade, roughly 10 feet high, can be seen at the north end of the park, nearly opposite a wooden pavilion. Directly downstream is a series of cascades dropping another 20 feet before passing under the High Street Bridge (which, in actual fact, is not a particularly high bridge).

There are a variety of opinions as to what "Chuctanunda" means. One source contends that the word means "twin sisters," a reference to the North Chuctanunda and South Chuctanunda facing each other from opposite sides of the Mohawk River.[1] Another source proposes that the word means "stony houses or stony places."[2, 3]

History: Kirk Douglas Park is named after the famous actor, "the Ragman's Son" (as he titled his autobiography). Kirk Douglas, born in 1916, grew up in Amsterdam. The park was dedicated to him in 1985. Originally, Amsterdam was called Veedersburgh.[4] The city is 36 river miles from the Hudson River and 254 feet in elevation above it.[5]

In 1802 there were 5 mills on the North Chuctanunda. By 1813 the number had increased to 17, including 5 grain mills, 4 carding mills, 4 sawmills, 2 oil mills, and a variety of other factories. During Amsterdam's heyday, over 100 industrial mills and plants at one time or another used the North Chuctanunda for hydropower.[6]

According to Hugh P. Donlon: "some progressive mill owners built dams along the creek [Chuctanunda] prior to 1840 but it was

The Chuctanunda resonates with a history of past industrialization. Postcard circa 1900.

North Chuctanunda Creek Amsterdam, N. Y.

not until 1855 that organized action was taken to control the flow from West Galway towards the Mohawk. The answer to complaints during drought periods came with the formulation of the Amsterdam Water Works Company. The company purchased 174 acres in Galway for the initial impounding"[7]—meaning, the creation of mile-wide Galway Lake. Like the Great Sacandaga Lake (a much larger artificially created body of water), Galway Lake quickly became encircled by summer homes and is now considered a recreational lake.

Directions: From the junction of Rtes. 5 and 30 in Amsterdam, take Rt. 5 northwest. Immediately, you will cross over North Chuctanunda Creek. Quickly turn right onto Market Street, following green signs that point the way to Guy Park Ave. Ext. Turn right onto High Street (which is one-way), and then immediately left into the parking area for Kirk Douglas Park, just before you cross over a bridge spanning the North Chuctanunda.

The best view of the falls is from the bridge over North Chuctanunda Creek.

13. Little Chuctanunda Falls

Location: South Amsterdam (Montgomery County)
NYS Atlas & Gazetteer: p. 65, A7
Accessibility: Roadside

Description: This small but distinguished-looking waterfall is formed on a tiny creek that rises in the hills near Fort Hunter and flows into the South Chuctanunda at the base of the waterfall. What makes the waterfall so distinctive is the narrowly cut ravine at the top of the fall, forming pronounced vertical walls on both sides of the upper half of the waterfall.[1]

Directions: From the intersection of Rtes. 30 and 5S south of Amsterdam, proceed west on Rt. 5S for 0.8 mile. Turn left onto Daniel Street just before you reach a huge bridge. Take an immediate right (Snook's Corner Road). Then turn left onto Florida Avenue (which parallels South Chuctanunda Creek) and drive southwest for no further than 0.2 mile. You will come to a little bridge that crosses over the creek.

The fall, formed on a tiny stream coming into the South Chuctanunda, can be observed from this point. Be sure to stay on roadside, which also provides the best view.

The Little Chuctanunda, circa 1900.

Amsterdam, N.Y.,
The Waterfall
on the Little Chuctanundo.

14. Cider Mill Falls

Location: South Amsterdam (Montgomery County)
NYS Atlas & Gazetteer: p. 65, A7
Accessibility: Roadside

Description: Cider Mill Falls is a small cascade formed on the South Chuctanunda, a medium-sized stream that rises by Mariaville Lake and flows into the Mohawk River at Amsterdam.

The waterfall is 6 feet in height, consists of a series of small ledges and cascades, and is contained in a deep gorge where the western wall rises sharply above the creek.[1, 2] A number of large concrete slabs can be seen along the eastern side of the ravine, remnants of past industrial days.

If you are visiting the area during early spring or following significant rainfall, you will also notice a 30-foot-high cascade formed on each side of the bridge and flowing down the steep wall of the west bank. These cascades will hardly excite waterfall purists, thanks to their proximity to the bridge, but they are worth a look while you are in the area.

History: An old cider mill once stood near the waterfall, which is how the cascade came to be named. Local youths used to frolic in a swimming hole that was not far from an odd-shaped rock projection called the Lion's Head.[3] The rock face, however, is no longer all that recognizable, having badly eroded.

The falls are located in an area of the South Chuctanunda called Mudge Hollow, named after an early resident who, along with Rowland and McDonald, owned and operated a number of mills in the vicinity.[4] The first mills were sawmills and gristmills. Later, a tannery and the cider mill were established.[5]

Directions: From I-90 (the New York State Thruway), get off at the Amsterdam Exit and immediately get on Rt. 5S, proceeding west. After about 0.8 mile, turn left onto Daniel Street and then immediately right. This leads down to South Florida Ave., which parallels the South Chuctanunda Creek. Turn right onto South Florida Ave. As soon as you pass under the towering Rt. 5S bridge, park on the side of the road. The falls are just downstream from where the bridge passes overhead.

Take note that the falls can also be seen from the top of the Rt. 5S bridge, but will appear flattened because of the perspective of looking straight down from a fairly considerable height.

Cider Mill Falls, circa 1900.

15. Falls on Cayadutta Creek

Location: Fonda (Montgomery County)
NYS Atlas & Gazetteer: p. 65, A5
Accessibility: Roadside

Description: This series of small cascades, located directly upstream and downstream from an old stone bridge, are formed on Cayadutta Creek, a medium-sized stream that rises northwest of Gloversville and flows into the Mohawk River at Fonda.

The upper cascades total 3–4 feet in height; the lower falls are concentrated into one or two drops and total 6 feet in height.

There are several larger waterfalls further upstream on the Cayadutta and its tributaries, but none are located in areas that are accessible to the public.

History: Cayadutta Creek once powered the mills and factories that led to the industrial development of Johnstown and Gloversville—the "Twin Cities" as they came to be known. The word *Cayadutta* is Native American for "rippling waters" or "shallow water running over stones."

Directions: From the NYS Thruway (I-87), get off at Exit 28 for Fonda and Fultonville. When you come to Rt. 30A, turn right and cross over the Mohawk River. At 0.4 mile turn left onto Rt. 5, then drive west on Rt. 5 for over 0.5 mile. Turn right onto Cayadutta Street (Rt. 334) and proceed northwest for 2.0 miles. When you come to Commons Road, turn right. You will immediately cross over a bridge spanning Cayadutta Road. Park to the side of the road. The cascades are visible both upstream and downstream from the top of the bridge.

Along the Cayadutta bruk Fonda N.-Y.

Cayadutta Creek, below Johnstown and Gloversville circa 1900.

16. Yatesville Falls

Location: Near Randall (Montgomery County)
NYS Atlas & Gazetteer: p. 65, AB5
Accessibility: Visible from parking area

Description: Yatesville Falls is formed on Yatesville Creek, a small stream that rises in the town of Charlestown and merges with the Mohawk River at Randall.[1, 2] The waterfall has also been known as Buttermilk Falls[3], and possibly Vrooman's Falls as well. Yatesville Falls is approximately 20 feet high and is best seen during the spring, before its limited watershed runs dry. The waterfall is located in Yatesville Falls State Park, a 71-acre preserve managed by the Department of Environmental Conservation.[4]

History: The waterfall must have been frequently visited by the Mohawks, and possibly by the Mohicans as well. In *Wampum, War & Trade Goods West of the Hudson,* Gilbert W. Hagerty writes: "On another high hill commanding a magnificent sweep of the river on the east side of Yatesville Creek about a half mile from the river, pieces of cord-marked pot shards and early prehistoric stone points as well as later prehistoric points appear with 17th Century items."[5]

The now-vanished town of Yatesville, named after John P. Yates, a local merchant, was at one time a main port for shipping hay along the Erie Canal.[6] The hamlet was originally called Unionville. In the mid-1880s the name changed to Leatherville in recognition of the brisk tannery business being conducted on Yatesville Creek.

Nearby Lasher Creek, named after George Lasher, has also produced several pretty falls near Rt. 162 but, unfortunately, the cascades are on private lands and are inaccessible to the public.

Directions: From Fultonville (junction of Rtes. 30A and 5S), take Rt. 5S southwest to Randall. At 4.8 miles turn left onto Currytown

Road and drive southwest for 0.5 mile. Then turn left onto Anderson Road and proceed uphill, going southeast, for 2.7 miles. Turn right onto an unpaved road with a sign stating "Yatesville Falls State Forest." Follow the road southwest to the end, a distance of 1.2 miles. The waterfall is located on the stream next to the parking area.

If you visit the park before May, be prepared to hike in through snow and ice. The road is seasonal and is not plowed during the winter. If you visit during the dry season, there will be little water running over the ledges.

17. Flat Creek Falls (Historic)

Location: Sprakers (Montgomery County)
Accessibility: Inaccessible; located on private land

Description: Flat Creek Falls is a large waterfall formed on Flat Creek, a medium-sized stream that rises south of Root Center and flows into the Mohawk River at Sprakers.[1-4] The waterfall is 60–70 feet high and has also been known as Sprakers Falls,[5] Plattekill Falls, and Onagerea.[6] An old postcard reveals that a wooden bridge once crossed over the creek near the top of the waterfall. A little over 0.1 mile downstream is a second, smaller ledge fall.

At one time a large delta formed at the confluence of Flat Creek and the Mohawk River. It was created by stones and gravel that Flat Creek had flushed downstream to its terminus. This area of fill came to be called Keators Rift and was the worst of 91 shallow areas of fill that obstructed passage along the Mohawk River. Keators Rift no longer exists today, having been dredged when the Barge Canal was created.[7, 8]

History: In the early 1600s, two Mohawk villages flourished in the immediate area of Sprakers—Senatsycrosy (1634) and Tenontogere (1642). Flat Creek Falls must have been visited numerous times by these early Native Americans.

Traces of lead and silver have been found along the bank of the stream.[9] Further upstream from the fall is an old mine shaft that was dug horizontally into the east cliff of the gorge.

The area around Flat Creek Falls was initially called Hamilton's Hollow. Later, the name changed to Sutphen's Hollow.[10] There were several industries in the little hamlet, including a carding mill, sawmill, and flouring mill. Most notable was the Flat Creek Cheese Factory, which produced over 100,000 pounds of cheese annually.[11]

Flat Creek, looking not so flat circa 1910.

Additional Point of Interest: Be sure to look for The Noses as you drive through Sprakers along Rt. 5S or the NYS Thruway. This distinctive geological formation consists of a 500-foot hill on the north side of the Mohawk River, called Big Nose, and a 400-foot hill on the south side of the river, called Little Nose, part of which was blasted away so that two main highways could fit through the notch. Little Nose is also well-known to cavers as the location of Mitchell's Cave, a fairly deep drop into the earth.

The Noses are part of the Appalachian chain of mountains, which once formed an impenetrable rock wall across the valley. Eons ago, however, a mighty cataract perhaps as high as several hundred feet formed as waters from Lake Iroquois rampaged through the valley. Over thousands of years, the waterfall carved out a pass through the valley, eradicating itself in the end, but leaving behind a valley floor that horses, wagons, and later, canals and railroads could follow in order to penetrate the Appalachian Ridge. At an elevation of 300 feet above sea level, the pass is now markedly lower than any other part of the mountain chain.[12] Native Americans called this pass *Tenonaanatche*, meaning "the river that wraps around a mountain."[13]

18. Canajoharie Falls: Upper Gorge

Location: Canajoharie (Montgomery County)
NYS Atlas & Gazetteer: p. 64, A4
Accessibility: 0.5-mile hike
Degree of Difficulty: Easy

Description: Canajoharie Falls is formed on Canajoharie Creek, a medium-sized stream that rises northeast of Cherry Valley and flows into the Mohawk River at Canajoharie. The fall is located north of the main part of Wintergreen Park. Although the fall is 45 feet in height, it actually appears much smaller because it is created in such a stupendous gorge.[1-7]

History: Canajoharie Falls was frequented often by Mohawks, who used it as a favorite spot for courting.[8]

On the darker side, there have been many deaths at the fall, mostly from carelessness and recklessness. But freakish accidents have occurred as well. In 2000, for instance, a Cobleskill woman was swept along by the creek's current and barely escaped with her life by clinging to a tree branch as she drifted to the top of the fall.

The waterfall was recently used by a Canadian film crew as a backdrop to shoot an episode of *Due South*. Three takes were required to get the necessary footage of a Mountie and his prisoner being swept over the top of the fall.

Directions: From the New York State Thruway (I-90), get off at Exit 29 for Canajoharie. Turn right onto Rt. 5S, drive 0.1 mile west, and turn left (south) onto Mitchell Street. You will now be paralleling Canajoharie Creek, to your right. Continue on Mitchell Street as it quickly becomes Moyer Street. Follow Moyer Street uphill for 0.8 mile. At this point it will merge with Carlisle Street. Continue south, driving uphill, for another 0.7 mile. At the point where Carlisle Street veers to the left, going east, continue straight ahead on Old Sharon Road for 0.1 mile. Wintergreen Park is immediately on your right. Drive in the park entrance and pull over at the small parking area on your right before descending into the main section of the park.

Follow a path northward along the rim of the gorge. You will be rewarded with incredible views of the gorge, but don't get too close to the edge. Stay on this path for roughly 0.5 mile and you will eventually come to a large wooden observation deck that overlooks the fall.

The area below and around the fall is restricted. You must stay on the platform to view the fall.

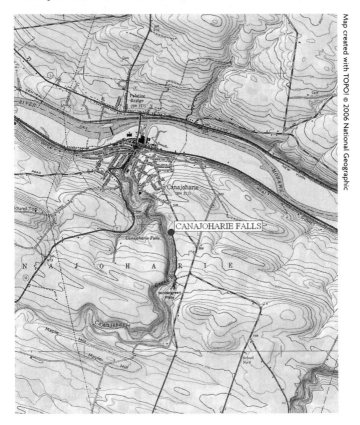

Map created with TOPO! © 2006 National Geographic

Canajoharie Falls, circa 1900.

19. Canajoharie Falls: Lower Gorge

Location: Canajoharie (Montgomery County)
NYS Atlas & Gazetteer: p. 64, A4
Accessibility: 0.1-mile hike along improved trail
Degree of Difficulty: Easy

Description: There are several small falls and cascades formed in the lower section of the Canajoharie Gorge. Most consist of a series of step ledges, and none are of any great height, but several are very pretty. It is the Canajoharie Pothole that is the main attraction. Known locally as the Devil's Ear, it is 24 feet wide and 8 feet deep.[1–3] The pothole is formed midway between several small falls.

History: The name Canajoharie has several possible derivations. Father Bruyas, in 1667, referred to it as *Canna-tsi-chare, laver de chaudiere,* meaning "to wash a large pot." Samuel Kirkland called it *Kanachare,* "the great boiling pot."[4] Both of these early names were references to the enormous pothole contained in the lower gorge.

The famous "Canajoharie Pothole"—Canajoharie's namesake, circa 1910.

The first gristmill erected on Canajoharie Creek was built in 1760 by Goshen (Gose) Van Alstyne. The mill stood on the east bank of the stream. Around 1770 a second gristmill was established by Colonel Hendrick Frey nearly a mile upstream from Canajoharie Creek's confluence with the Mohawk River.[5]

Upstream from the Canajoharie Pothole is a still-functioning dam about 6 feet in height, which was built by Arkell and Smith (a paper bag company) in the 1930s. If you visit the area in the summer when less water is flowing through the gorge, you will notice augured holes in the streambed just below the dam. These holes were drilled so that iron rods could be inserted into the bedrock, providing vertical supports against which wooden planks could be placed to form a primitive dam.

There are many waterfalls in Canajoharie Gorge.
Postcard circa 1920.

Directions: From the New York State Thruway (I-90), get off at Exit 29 for Canajoharie. Turn right onto Rt. 5S, drive west for 0.1 mile, and turn left (south) onto Mitchell Street. Continue uphill as the street turns into Moyer Street. After 0.3 mile, turn right onto Floral Street and park at the end of the lane.

The creek is directly off to your right, with a blacktopped pathway leading down to it. The pathway continues south for a short distance, paralleling the creek. You can walk as far as the Arkell & Smith Dam, but continuing further into the gorge is not permitted. The pathway leading up to the Canajoharie Pothole had become seriously eroded over the years, but was recently restored to good condition. The main cascades are just before you reach the Arkell & Smith Dam and the Canajoharie Pothole.

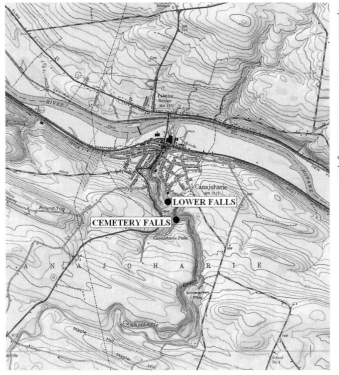

20. Cemetery Falls

Location: Canajoharie (Montgomery County)
NYS Atlas & Gazetteer: p. 64, A4
Accessibility: 30-foot walk to viewing area
Degree of Difficulty: Easy

Description: Cemetery Falls is formed on a tiny tributary to Canajoharie Creek that rises in the hills southwest of Canajoharie and drops into Canajoharie Creek about 0.7 mile south of Wintergreen Park. This very pretty cascade is over 40 feet high and flows down the west wall of the gorge. The fall was named for its location next to the Prospect Hill Cemetery. The top of the waterfall is adjacent to an old, seemingly forgotten part of the cemetery where tall thin tombstones dating back to the early and mid-1800s rise up from a ground covering of green. During the summer the waterfall is moss-covered, suggesting (with a little imagination) decay and death, and thus further living up to its name.

History: Route 10, which leads up from the village of Canajoharie and passes by Prospect Hill Cemetery, is historically significant. It was along this route in 1779 that General James Clinton led an army of 2,000 men with 300 wagons, 200 bateaux (a double-ended, flat-bottomed rowboat), and supplies to Otsego Lake to begin the Sullivan-Clinton Campaign against the Iroquois.

Approximately 0.2 mile before you reach Prospect Hill Cemetery, you will pass by a pull-off on your left. Although there are no noteworthy views into the Canajoharie Gorge from here, you will find a historical marker that tells how Canajoharie came to be named.

Directions: The waterfall is roughly 0.3 mile upstream from the Canajoharie Pothole and is located in a part of the gorge that is inaccessible and posted with warnings because of the number of fatalities that have occurred at Canajoharie Falls, which is about 0.2 mile beyond Cemetery Falls. If walking in, do not go any further up the gorge than the Arkell & Smith Dam.

There is a safe, easy way to access the fall, however. From the center of Canajoharie (junction of Rtes. 10 and 5S), turn south onto Rt. 10 and drive uphill for approximately 1.0 mile. When you come

Cemetery Falls, circa 1900.

to Prospect Hill Cemetery on your left, drive in through the main gate and proceed east to the back of the cemetery, which parallels the rim of the Canajoharie Gorge. Turn left and then immediately left again. Park at this point.

You will be next to a portion of the cemetery that houses the Spraker family plot. Walk to the far northeast corner of this plot, which is also the northeast end of the cemetery's boundary. From there, look upstream (south) into the gorge. Cemetery Falls is clearly visible as it flows down the side wall of the gorge.

21. Falls on Tributaries to Nowadaga Creek

Location: Newville (Herkimer County)
NYS Atlas & Gazetteer: p. 64, A2
Accessibility: Roadside

Description: There are several medium-sized waterfalls that can be seen along Nowadaga Creek. All are formed on tributaries that rush over the top of the west bank escarpment and down into the gorge. The water from each tributary, in turn, then continues down Nowadaga Creek and out into the Mohawk River west of Five Miles Dam.

The first cascade, visible at some distance from roadside, is over 30 feet high, but only its bottom portion can be clearly discerned; a large evergreen obscures its upper section. The second cascade is over 40 feet high and quite spectacular in the early spring when its small creek is sufficiently animated by snowmelt. The third cascade consists of a 15–20-foot drop. The fourth cascade is 10 feet high and, like the first cascade, is viewed from a distance.

History: Nowadaga Creek was at one time home to a Native American castle (village), which endured until the nineteenth century.[1] Just east of the creek along Rt. 5S can be seen the Indian Castle Church, built in 1769 by Sir William Johnson, arguably the most prominent colonial figure in the Mohawk Valley. Johnson saw unlimited potential in the New World and acquired vast tracts of land in the Mohawk Valley. He established deep and abiding trade relations with the Native Americans he encountered and became a respected mediator and diplomat.

Directions: From I-90 (the NYS Thruway), get off at Exit 29 for Canajoharie. Turn right onto Rt. 5S, drive through Canajoharie, and continue northwest until you reach the village of Fort Plain in 3.5 miles. From the junction of Rtes. 5S and 80 in Fort Plain, continue northwest on Rt. 5S for 10 miles. As soon as you cross over Nowadaga Creek, turn left onto Creek Road. Drive southwest now, setting your odometer at 0.0. At 0.8 mile you will cross over a bridge spanning Nowadaga Creek. Look upstream to your right and you will see a small cascade. Look a little further beyond that cascade and you will see a tiny tributary coming down the west bank that produces a tall cascade of its own.

Continue driving southwest. At approximately 1.1 miles you will cross over Nowadaga Creek again. The stream will now be on your left. At 1.7 miles you will come to a small bridge where Nowadaga Creek switches back over to your right. In another 0.3 mile (or slightly over 2.0 miles from the beginning of Creek Road) look for a pull-off to your right where a pretty, towering cascade can be seen across the stream along the west bank.

Drive southwest for a couple of hundred feet further and you will see a third cascade on your right, formed along the north bank.

Finally, the last cascade is reached at 2.8 miles (0.3 mile before Bellinger Road), just before you pass by several houses. You will have to be satisfied with a distant view of this fall from roadside.

22. Scudders Falls

Location: St. Johnsville (Montgomery County)
NYS Atlas & Gazetteer: p. 78, D3
Accessibility: Roadside

Description: This pagoda-shaped, 50-foot-high waterfall is formed on Zimmerman Creek, a medium-sized stream that rises northeast from the St. Johnsville Reservoir and flows into the Mohawk River at St. Johnsville.[1] The waterfall consists of a series of ledges that form an enormous staircase of water.

The large, circular, cement cistern located next to the waterfall is the village water treatment plant, built in 1948. Old stone ruins from an early mill can be seen between Lassellville Street and the private gated road that leads down to the treatment plant.

Just a short distance upstream from the main fall can be seen a small but pretty cascade.

History: St. Johnsville was founded in 1775 by Jacob Zimmerman, a Swiss immigrant who built a gristmill on Zimmerman Creek. The mill ground corn and wheat. Zimmerman established good trading relations with Native Americans throughout the Mohawk Valley and in 1719 married an Indian princess from the Lower Mohawk Castle (at present-day Fort Hunter) whose christened name became Anna Margaret.[2]

In 1801 a second gristmill was built by George Klock. In 1804 a third was established by David Quackenbush.

The village of St. Johnsville is named after Alex St. John, surveyor and commissioner.

This section of the Mohawk Valley is sometimes referred to as Crystal Valley because of the abundance of clear, doubly-terminated quartz crystals.[3]

Scudders Falls rises like a Chinese pagoda. Postcard circa 1930.

Directions: From I-90 (the NYS Thruway), get off at Exit 29 for Cana-joharie. Turn right onto Rt. 5S, drive west for 0.2 mile, and turn right onto Church Street (Rt. 10). Proceed north for 0.3 mile, crossing over the Mohawk River to Palatine Bridge. Then turn left onto Rt. 5 and head northwest on Rt. 5 for 9.0 miles, paralleling the north bank of the Mohawk River. When you reach the center of St. Johnsville, turn right at the traffic light onto North Division Street and drive uphill for 0.8 mile. When you come to Lassellville Street, bear right. Within 0.3 mile you will see a little road leading downhill to the right. The waterfall is located at the bottom of this short road, next to the water treatment plant. Take note that the land is posted.

Continue uphill for less than 0.1 mile to where the stream crosses under Lassellville Road. Park in a pull-off to your left. A small upper cascade can be seen upstream from the bridge, and the top of the main fall is visible looking downstream from the bridge.

23. Falls at "Inn by the Mill"

Location: St. Johnsville (Montgomery County)
NYS Atlas & Gazetteer: p. 78, D3
Accessibility: Near roadside
Degree of Difficulty: Easy

Description: This series of cascading waterfalls is formed on Timmerman Creek, a medium-sized stream that rises near Dempster Corner and flows into the Mohawk River at Upper St. Johnsville. From the Stone Grist Mill (known in the mid-1800s as the Beekman Mill), three cascades totaling 40 feet in height can be seen—a small fall, followed by a spectacular, long cascade, ending in a short drop.

From the Cliff Side Cottage (just up the road from the Stone Grist Mill), several additional, smaller cascades are visible.

The Inn by the Mill, a bed & breakfast, provides the rare opportunity of staying at an elegant retreat with its own natural gorge and waterfalls.

History: The Inn by the Mill not only has an abundance of waterfalls, but an interesting history to go with it. The inn consists of four principal buildings: the Stone Grist Mill, the Hog'n Haus Cottage, the Mill House, and the Cliff Side Cottage.

The historic 1835 Stone Grist Mill next to the cascades contains some mill machinery, including an old turbine. In the nineteenth century the mill, using an overshot waterwheel 30 feet in diameter and 8 feet wide, produced flour and animal feed, and was operated by the Beekman brothers.[1] In its time, the mill was considered the best-equipped flour mill in the state. It is now listed on the Federal and New York State Registers of Historic Places.

The Hog'n Haus Cottage overlooks the cascades and is awash with the sound of tumbling falls, which are only a few yards feet away. The cottage was built in 1888 as a hog house.

The Mill House, constructed in 1894, is located directly across the street from the Stone Grist Mill. It now provides lodging to guests who enjoy a more muffled sound of cascades at night. The Cliff Side Cottage is of more recent vintage and overlooks several of the upper, smaller, cascades.

The Stone Grist Mill has a unique history. Prior to the Civil War it was part of the Underground Railroad, which helped African-American slaves make their way northwest up the Mohawk River to Canada and freedom. A tunnel still leads underground from the Grist Mill to the site of a lower mill.[2]

Additional Point of Interest: Further upstream is Hills Falls, near Klock Park. Although the falls are located on private property, it may be possible to obtain permission to access them, particularly if you are staying at the inn.

Directions: From I-90 (the NYS Thruway), get off at Exit 29 and turn right onto Rt. 5S. After 0.2 mile turn right onto Church Street (Rt. 10) and drive north, crossing over the Mohawk River into the village of Palatine Bridge. When you come to Rt. 5, turn left and drive north-

Hills Falls near Klock Park, circa 1940.

west on Rt. 5 for 9.0 miles until you reach the traffic light at the center of St. Johnsville. From there, continue west on Rt. 5 for another 1.0 mile, then turn right onto Mill Road and drive north, uphill, for less than 0.5 mile. The mill and access to the falls are on your right, opposite the decorative Mill House.

From the Stone Grist Mill, a short path paralleling the stream leads up to an overlook of the middle (and largest) cascade, where a dam once spanned the creek. Remnants of the old dam are still visible. The path follows a buried pipe that leads from the dam to power a turbine at the gristmill. At night the pathways and falls are illuminated.

24. Fall on Timmerman Creek

Location: St. Johnsville (Montgomery County)
NYS Atlas & Gazetteer: p. 78, D3
Accessibility: Roadside

Description: This small, 10-foot-high waterfall is formed on Timmerman Creek, a medium-sized stream that rises near Dempster Corner and flows into the Mohawk River. You will see the fall looming directly in front of you as you come to the intersection of Mill Road and Crum Creek Road.

History: Timmerman Creek has also been known as Klock Creek and Old Mill Creek.[1] Hills Falls, a considerably larger and more spectacular cascade, is also formed on Timmerman Creek, but is located further downstream on private, posted land and cannot be accessed without permission.

Directions: From I-90 (the NYS Thruway), get off at Exit 29 and turn right onto Rt. 5S. After 0.2 mile turn right onto Church Street (Rt. 10) and drive north, crossing over the Mohawk River into the village of Palatine Bridge. When you come to Rt. 5, turn left and drive northwest on Rt. 5 for 9.0 miles until you reach the traffic light at the center of St. Johnsville. From there, continue west on Rt. 5 for another 1.0 mile, then turn right onto Mill Road and drive north, going uphill, for 1.6 miles until you come to the intersection of Mill Road and Crum Road where the waterfall can be clearly seen straight ahead. Proceed for another 0.1 mile to the fall.

The waterfall is located next to a private residence. Stay at roadside to view the fall.

If you continue further north on Mill Road, you will see several minor cascades that have formed on Timmerman Creek, but none are substantial in size.

25. Beardslee Falls (Historic)

Location: East Canada Creek (Herkimer County)
Accessibility: Inaccessible, located on privately owned and posted land

Description: Beardslee Falls is formed on East Canada Creek, a large stream that rises at Christian Lake and flows into the Mohawk River shortly below the falls. The waterfall is just one of several significant falls that have developed on East Canada Creek between the Mohawk River and Dolgeville.

Beardslee Falls is located just upstream from an old Niagara-Mohawk plant and is 25 feet in height. It consists of a rather steep cascade that hugs the western side of the stream.[1] At the top of the fall, the streambed flattens out noticeably. Here, several large potholes have formed—one almost 30 feet in diameter. The river has also cut a miniature ravine into the streambed, creating a deep narrow channel.

A second fall, 15 feet in height, is located further upstream and consists of a series of wide, descending ledges, giving the stream the appearance of an outdoor arena.

History: Beardslee Falls is named after Guy R. Beardslee, an army engineer who purchased the land around the waterfall after leaving the military.[2] In 1898, Beardslee erected a powerhouse at the falls and began providing electrical power to St. Johnsville. By 1901 he was also supplying electricity to Fort Plain and Canajoharie. In 1924 a new dam and power plant were built to replace the old Beardslee station. It still stands.

The Beardslee estate is reminiscent of an English Tudor castle and was built along Rt. 5 not far from the fall. Many years later it was converted into a popular restaurant called Beardslee Manor. A fire two decades ago caused considerable damage and reduced the dimensions of the building to its present size.

The Mohawks called East Canada Creek *Ci-o-ha-na*, meaning "large creek."

Beardslee Falls, circa 1910.

26. Faville Falls

Location: Near Dolgeville (Herkimer County)
NYS Atlas & Gazetteer: p. 78, CD2
Accessibility: Short hike over uneven terrain
Degree of Difficulty: Easy to moderate

Description: Faville Falls are formed on Ransom Creek (also called Gillette Creek), a small stream that rises in the hills northwest of Dolgeville and flows into Kyser Lake slightly south of Dolgeville. The stream contains two main cascades, as well as a number of smaller drops and plunges in between. The upper cascade is 10 feet high and formed just downstream from the bridge that crosses Ransom Creek. The lower waterfall is 20 feet in height and formed in a tiny gorge littered with huge blocks of talus.[1, 2]

History: John Faville, a Revolutionary War soldier born in Bound Brooks, New Jersey,[3] settled near the creek in 1795, establishing first a gristmill and later a sawmill. From this early beginning, a small settlement formed. Old foundations from the 1800s can still be glimpsed near the west bank of the creek by the parking lot. According to H. P. Cushing, the gorge was created by the Little Falls fault.[4]

Directions: From St. Johnsville (junction of Rt. 5 and North Division Street), proceed northwest on Rt. 5 for roughly 9.0 miles (or 5.8 miles from East Canada Creek). Before you reach Little Falls, turn right onto Rt. 167 and drive northeast towards Dolgeville for 6.7 miles. Turn left onto Spencer Street and drive west for approximately 1.7 miles. Take note that the name of the road will change from Spencer Street to Peckville as you pass through the intersection of Lyons Road. At 1.7 miles you will cross over a little bridge spanning Ransom Creek. Immediately turn left into a parking area for the falls.

Proceeding on foot, follow a trail that quickly leads to a metal footbridge spanning Ransom Creek. From the top of the bridge you will get a commanding view of the upper falls, and of several smaller cascades directly below. Cross over the stream and continue along the north bank for less than 0.2 mile, following the trail as it slowly descends to the bottom of the gorge and up to the base of the second falls.

Considerable time and effort has obviously gone into opening up this scenic gorge to the public.

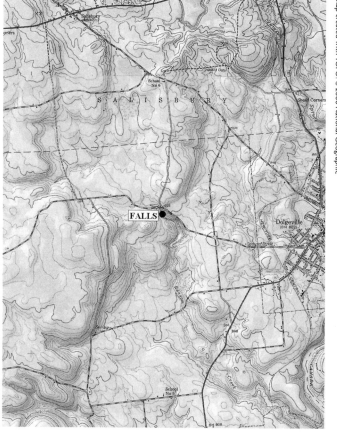

Faville Falls, circa 1900.

27. Falls by Old Dolgeville Mill

Location: Dolgeville (Herkimer County)
NYS Atlas & Gazetteer: p. 78, CD2-3
Accessibility: Roadside

Description: Two small cascades, each 3–4 feet in height, can be seen downstream from a wide dam spanning East Canada Creek. These tiny cascades offer little hint of the big falls located further downstream. (See next chapter, "High Falls.")

History: The cascades are located just upstream from the historic Dolgeville Mill, which now serves as an antique center. The factory and complex was built by Alfred Dolge between 1882 and 1895.[1]

According to a brochure distributed by Dolgeville Mill Inc., Dolgeville is the birthplace of modern Social Security (1879), the first public kindergarten (1889), and the first hydroelectric plant using Edison's second dynamo (1881).

Small cascades can be seen upstream from the bridge. Postcard circa 1920.

Directions: From St. Johnsville (junction of Rt. 5 and North Division Street), proceed northwest on Rt. 5 for roughly 9.0 miles (or 5.8 miles from East Canada Creek). Before you reach the city of Little Falls, turn right onto Rt. 167 and drive northeast for 7.0 miles. Near the center of Dolgeville, look to your right for the Dolgeville Mill—an enormous three-story-high stone structure opposite Elm Street.

Park and walk over to the north end of the former mill, and then follow a road that goes between two buildings and leads to a bridge that has recently been converted into a pedestrian footbridge. Stand on top of the bridge and you will have first-rate views upstream of the falls and dam.

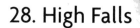

28. High Falls

Location: Dolgeville (Herkimer County)
NYS Atlas & Gazetteer: p. 78, CD2-3
Accessibility: Roadside

Description: High Falls is formed on East Canada Creek, a large stream that rises at Christian Lake, four miles southwest of Irond-equoit Bay in Piseco Lake, and flows into the Mohawk River west of St. Johnsville.[1, 2]

Be prepared for a view that is less than pristine. A large hydro-electric power plant and water treatment site have been built next to the falls. Furthermore, you will be looking down at the falls from a considerable height and distance, which serves to flatten the falls and make them appear smaller than they actually are.

History: East Canada Creek got its name from early settlers who believed that the stream coursed all the way down to the Mohawk River from Canada. Walter F. Burmeister describes the stream as "a wild tumultuous torrent cutting a tortuous channel into the southern edge of the Adirondack plateau."[3]

At one time there was a park, called High Falls Park, south of Dolgeville near East Canada Creek. The park had a hotel, dance hall, outdoor playground and a ball field, and a path led over to the base of High Falls. Before that, the land containing High Falls was part of the Reuben Faville farm. In 1887 Alfred Dolge purchased 500 acres of land overlooking High Falls and donated it to the people of Dol-geville.[4] Today, the land once encompassing the park is again privately owned and not open to the public.

This area was originally known as Bracketts Bridge. It was renamed Dolgeville after Alfred Dolge, who came to the area in 1874.[5] Dolge worked ardently to bring the town into the future, and in many ways was as progressive as Zadock Pratt, founder of Prattsville

High Falls is wider than it is high. Postcard circa 1900.

High Falls, Dolgeville, N. Y.

in the Catskills. In 1879, Dolge bought Thomas Edison's second dynamo—the first to be run by waterpower—and had it installed in his factory. Unfortunately, Dolge ultimately overextended himself financially and ended up having to leave town penniless.

Directions: From St. Johnsville (junction of Rt. 5 and North Division Street), proceed northwest on Rt. 5 for roughly 9.0 miles (or 5.8 miles from East Canada Creek). Before you reach the city of Little Falls, turn right onto Rt. 167 and drive northeast for 7.2 miles. When Rt. 167 ends, turn right onto Rt. 29 east and cross over Brocketts Bridge, which spans East Canada Creek. As soon as you cross over the bridge, turn right onto Dolge Avenue and follow the road south, paralleling the river, for nearly 1.2 miles. Just before you reach the top of a hill, you will see a small clearing to your right, by the guardrails. Pull over into a small area on the left and be very careful as you cross the road to the guardrails, from where a limited view of the falls can be had. Downstream, the massive walls of the west bank create quite an imposing sight.

29. Falls on Spruce Creek

Location: Salisbury Center (Herkimer County)
NYS Atlas & Gazetteer: p. 78, CD2
Accessibility: Roadside

Description: This 10-foot-high cascade is formed on Spruce Creek, a medium-sized stream that rises from Spruce Lake and flows into East Canada Creek above Dolgeville. The cascade tumbles through a wide rocky area of streambed,[1, 2] where a pretty park, complete with picnic tables, has been established along the east bank. The waterfall has also been known as Ellwell's Falls in the past.

At the west end of the covered bridge, an attractive footbridge takes you over to a tiny rocky island where views of a small upstream cascade, as well as of the covered bridge, can be obtained looking back. The island is formed at a point where the stream is split into two before rejoining below the covered bridge. Girl Scout Cadette Troop 93 should be congratulated for their 2005 Silver Award Project and beautification of this very scenic area.

A lower cascade has developed as well, roughly 0.05 mile further downstream. It consists of a long slide that ends in a short drop. Unfortunately, the fall is difficult to see in its entirety from roadside. There are also small falls several miles further upstream on Spruce Creek in the area of Ives Hollow and visible from Curtiss Road.

History: The 42-foot-long Burr Arch truss-span covered bridge that crosses Spruce Creek near the top of the cascades was constructed in 1857 by Alvah Hopson and was later moved to its present site.[3] It is now a nationally registered historic site. Although once closed to vehicular traffic, the bridge has now reopened (seasonally) to cars, but with a two-ton weight limit. In the winter the bridge is closed, for the obvious reason that the weight of a snowplow would damage the structure.

A historic marker next to the bridge states that Spruce Creek at one time furnished hydropower for nine nearby mills. Old foundation ruins can be seen along the east bank just upstream from the covered bridge.

Directions: From St. Johnsville (junction of Rt. 5 and North Division Street), proceed northwest on Rt. 5 for roughly 9.0 miles. Before you reach Little Falls, turn right onto Rt. 167 and drive northeast towards Dolgeville for 7.2 miles until you reach Rt. 29. Turn left onto Rt. 29 west and drive north for 2.9 miles. Just before reaching the intersection of Rtes. 29 and 29A, turn left onto Fairview Road. In less than 0.05 mile you will come to an old covered bridge. Park to your left. The falls are visible downstream from the bridge and can be seen close-up from all along the east bank of the park.

To view the top of the lower falls, as well as sections of the upper falls, return to Rt. 29, turn right, drive south for less than 0.1 mile, and turn right onto Kingsley Road. Within 0.1 mile you will come to a small bridge crossing the stream. From there, excellent views can be obtained of the upper falls by looking upstream towards the covered bridge. Look downstream and you will see the top of the lower falls, just west of the bridge.

30. Little Falls

Location: Little Falls (Herkimer County)
NYS Atlas & Gazetteer: p. 78, D2
Accessibility: Roadside

Description: Although the name Little Falls suggests a waterfall of diminutive size, you will be hard-pressed to find a waterfall of *any* size—just rapids and white water.[1-6] At one time, however, Little Falls had an enormous waterfall. This cascade formed when the Iro-Mohawk River—a precursor to the Mohawk River—raged through the valley as it drained a prodigious body of water known as Lake Iroquois (only parts of which still exist today as the Great Lakes). Evidence of the power of this earlier river is evident everywhere at Moss Island (next to Lock 17 near Little Falls), where enormous potholes have been left behind. The largest pothole, however, is hidden from view underneath the waters of the Mohawk River next to Moss Island. The pothole is the "fossil imprint" of an earlier and very powerful waterfall.[7, 8]

The Mohawk River drops 42 feet in less than 0.5 mile as it flows past the village of Little Falls.[9] The fact that the river looks deep at both ends of the village is because nineteenth-century locks were established so that boats could be afforded clear passage. There are now 20 locks on the Mohawk River, starting at its confluence with the Hudson and continuing all the way up to Rome, raising and lowering boats a total of 420 feet.

History: As to what the falls and gorge looked like in the 1700s, prior to the locks' creation and the industrialization of Little Falls, we must hearken back to what early travelers saw. According to one account: "At that date the rapids and their adjoining shores were in all their primitive grandeur, unadorned or marred by the works of man. Undoubtedly the water-power early attracted to their border the saw and grist mills, whose dams probably were an unwelcome barrier to the daring warriors who trusted their lives to the birchen canoe in shooting the rapids. In every direction would have been seen rocks and running water, and rocky hills crowned with the primeval forest. For nearly a mile extended the cascades between perpendicular cliffs from two to four hundred feet high."[10]

The Mohawks' name for Little Falls was *As-te-ron-ga*, meaning "rocky place." Native Americans derived a sense of security from living between Cohoes Falls to the east and Little Falls to the west, believing that they were reasonably safe from attack by large vessels. It was this strategic position that undoubtedly contributed to giving the Mohawks primacy in the Iroquois Council.

By 1725, Little Falls was taken over by Palatine Germans who began charging river-users a toll in order to portage their bateaux and canoes around the rapids. Later, Nicholas Herkimer, an eighteenth-century farmer and enterprising trader, made a considerable profit by organizing slaves to carry small boats overland around the falls.[11]

le falls, N.Y. The Ragged Rocks on the Mohawk River.

There are very little falls to see in Little Falls. Postcard circa 1910.

Directions: From I-90 (the NYS Thruway), get off at the exit for Little Falls and take Rt. 169 northwest to Little Falls. Or, if you are driving northwest on Rt. 5, continue on Rt. 5 until you reach Little Falls. As you drive west on Rt. 5 through the south end of Little Falls, turn right where signs indicate the way to Rt. 167. This route takes you up to Albany Street (a one-way street). Proceed east on the one-way street for one block and then turn right onto Rt. 167 (Overhead Street). Drive south on a high bridge spanning Rt. 5 and the railroad tracks. Before crossing over the Mohawk River, turn left onto "East Ramp" for Canal Place (Elizabeth Street). The ramp immediately leads down to South Ann Street. Turn right onto South Ann Street and drive to its end, where you can park along the street or in one of several parking areas.

Look upstream from the bridge at the end of the street and you will see a series of rapids and tiny cascades interspersed amongst a rubble of rocks and boulders. You are looking at the main cascades at Little Falls, which admittedly *are* little.

Cross over the bridge on foot and follow a pedestrian road east that parallels the Mohawk River (to your left) and the Barge Canal (to the right). Within 0.3 mile you will walk past a brick building on your left. Immediately after, follow a tiny path left that leads to overlooks of the Mohawk River. From this vantage point, you will see a small dam spanning the top of a small cascade—another of Little Falls' little falls.

31. "Miracle Mile" Cascade

Location: Little Falls (Herkimer County)
NYS Atlas & Gazetteer: p. 78, D2
Accessibility: 0.2-mile walk along paved former railroad bed, with no change in elevation
Degree of Difficulty: Easy

Description: This 30-foot-high cascade is formed on a tiny unnamed tributary to the Mohawk River. The cascade is pretty and moss-covered, but only distinguishes itself in the early spring or following heavy rainfall because of its limited watershed.

The "Miracle Mile" Trail is a fitness walk established by Herkimer County. The trail not only leads you past the south side of Little Falls and Moss Island (an island of fascinating geological potholes), but ultimately, within three miles, to General Herkimer's House. Herkimer was a gentleman farmer and second only to Sir William Johnson as a prominent colonial figure in the Mohawk

Once a rail, it's now a trail. Postcard circa 1900.

Valley. During the American Revolution, Herkimer sided with the Americans, while Johnson (a "Loyalist" or "Tory") sided with the British. Herkimer was killed at the Battle of Oriskany while leading colonial forces against the British.

Directions: Driving west through Little Falls on Rt. 5, turn right where a sign directs you to Rt. 167. You will immediately come up to a one-way street called Albany Street. Drive east for one block and then turn right onto Rt. 167 (Overhead Street). Proceed south over a

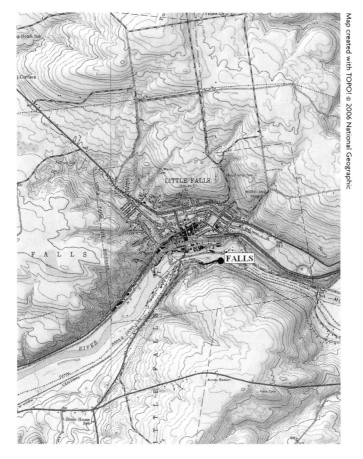

high bridge spanning Rt. 5, railroad tracks, and the Mohawk River. As soon as you come to the south end of the bridge, turn left onto Casler Street. You will then come directly to Flint Street. Turn left, and then immediately right onto West Shore Street. Drive to the end of the street, where there is a large parking area.

Proceeding on foot, follow the designated "Miracle Mile Trail" (a paved-over railroad bed) as it heads east. The walk in itself is fascinating, for you will be strolling through a deep, narrow rock cut that was blasted out of solid rock to create a pass for the rail line. In just over 0.1 mile you will come to a short tunnel. After passing through, in less than 0.05 mile, you will arrive at a tiny stream that is conducted under the path and to the edge of the escarpment, where it falls into the canal below. Turn right and follow a very discernable path south for less than 50 feet. You will see the cascade coming down the steep incline of the hill, less than 30 feet from the trail.

32. Buttermilk Falls

Location: Little Falls (Herkimer County)
NYS Atlas & Gazetteer: p. 78, D1-2
Accessibility: 0.1-mile hike
Degree of Difficulty: Easy

Description: Buttermilk Falls is formed on a small stream that rises in the hills north of Little Falls and flows into the Mohawk River, completing the last half mile of its journey via an aqueduct under the village of Little Falls. The cascade is roughly 50 feet high and consists of a wall of rock that is slightly inclined, which gives the fall a washboard look.

A short distance upstream from Buttermilk Falls is a 6-foot ledge waterfall, but this fall cannot be seen from below.

Directions: Approaching Little Falls from the east along Rt. 5, turn right at a traffic light at the edge of town onto East Main Street (which is Rt. 169N). Follow East Main Street for 0.5 mile, then turn right onto North Ann Street (still following Rt. 169N) and continue for less than 0.2 mile. Turn left onto Monroe Street (continuing on Rt. 169N) and drive uphill, west, for 0.4 mile. As soon as you pass by an old school on your right, turn right onto Sherman Street, go 0.1 mile, and turn left onto Burch Street. You will see a green sign indicating the way to the "field."

When you come to an athletic field, park your car. There is a large cement building at the north end of the field. This is a bath-house that is located next to a large outdoor pool. As you walk up to the bathhouse, take note of a stream passing by the right side of the building and then flowing into an underground duct. This is the stream that contains Buttermilk Falls. Take note that you cannot approach the stream from this side of the building. Walk around to the left side of the building and continue to the back where a little playground is located next to the pool. From there, you will discover a tiny path, paralleling the stream, which leads to the fall in 0.1 mile.

Buttermilk Falls—an oasis of natural beauty. Postcard circa 1900.

Waterfalls Along
Route 20

Introduction

Before 1825 and the creation of the Erie Canal, roads served as the main system of transportation westward across New York State. Many of these roads began as Native American trails. Route 20, known then as the Great Western Turnpike (and, at other times, as The Cherry Valley Turnpike), offered an improved toll road that allowed travelers to journey from Albany to Pompey (south of Syracuse) in as much comfort as that era permitted, given the fact that all land travel then consisted of riding on horseback, carriage, or stagecoach. The Great Western Turnpike followed an old Seneca Trail, which gave it an historic character. The turnpike became incorporated in 1799, and by 1804 a total of fifty-two miles of road had been constructed between Albany and Cherry Valley. By 1809 the route was extended to Cazenovia.[1]

In its heyday, the turnpike had many way stations and rest stops. All told, there were over sixty-two taverns just between Albany and Cherry Valley alone. This averages out to more than one tavern per mile along this fifty-mile stretch of highway. There were also the inevitable toll stations, which were generally encountered every ten miles. Toll collectors would charge 12 cents for each wagon and 25 cents for each coach. Church-goers, physicians, midwives, jury duty designees, and citizens on their way to vote in an election were exempt from tolls.

Several of the towns along Route 20, including Sharon Springs, may seem like minor stopovers today, but they were once major destinations for tourists and travelers.

With the creation of the Erie Canal and then the advent of the locomotive—both of which provided an efficient means for transporting large quantities of goods over vast distances at comparatively low costs—Route 20 fell into relative obscurity. Then came the age of the automobile and new life was infused into the communities, albeit only for a short period of time. After the 1940s, major sections of the road were increased from two lanes to four. But the establishment of the New York State Thruway (I-90), in 1954, diverted a huge volume of traffic and potential customers away from Route 20. The historic thoroughfare was once again bypassed.

Cherry Valley Turnpike, circa 1930.

33. French's Falls

Location: Near Guilderland Center (Albany County)
NYS Atlas & Gazetteer: p. 66, C2
Accessibility: Roadside

Description: French's Falls are formed on the Normans Kill, a medium-sized stream that rises near Duanesburg, is temporarily intercepted by the Watervliet Reservoir, and then released to continue its relentless descent to the Hudson River near Glenmont. Native Americans called the stream *Towasentha*.

French's Falls consist of two broad, ledge-shaped waterfalls.[1, 2] The upper fall is 8 feet high and is located slightly upstream from an old bridge that spans the gorge. Directly beneath the bridge are several tiny cascades, and just downstream is the second fall, which is 6 feet high and also ledge-shaped. The falls are spectacular during the spring, but can become sluggish during the summer.

French's Falls, circa 1920.

French's Falls, circa 1900.

Several hundred yards upstream from the falls is the Watervliet Reservoir, a modest-sized impoundment created in 1917. The reservoir is currently owned and operated by the town of Watervliet, which is about 17 miles distant. There is talk today of increasing the height of the reservoir to compensate for the loss of volume created by sediment settling on the floor of the reservoir. At one time the impoundment was known as French's Mills Reservoir.

History: An historic sign at the junction of French's Mill Road and Rt. 20 states that French's Hollow was the site of an early sawmill as well as a cloth works established by Peter K. Broeck in 1795. In 1800 the factory was acquired by Abel French, for whom the hollow and the falls were ultimately named.[3]

In the same general area was an industry known as Spawn's Grist Mill, which endured until 1825. In 1869 Henry Witherwax built a 162-foot-long covered bridge across the Normans Kill at the falls. By then the area downstream from the bridge, called French's Hollow, had grown into one of the oldest settlements in the Town of Guilderland.[4-6]

French's Woolen Mill lasted until 1860.[7] From then on the abandoned building was used for church suppers, town gatherings, Methodist church meetings, and miscellaneous functions until 1917, when it was demolished around the time that the reservoir was created. The site is presently occupied by the reservoir's pump station.

By 1910 the tiny hamlet of French's Hollow had turned into a ghost town. This was principally a result of the creation of the Saratoga & Hudson Railroad in 1865, which enabled products to be exchanged by rail and obviated the need for local factories. By 1933 even the physical structures, such as the old mills and covered bridge, were gone.

An automobile bridge was constructed in 1933, crossing the gorge at exactly the same spot as the covered bridge once did. The bridge conveniently passed between the two ledge falls. After having been closed off to traffic for a number of years, the bridge has recently been repaved and turned into a pedestrian crossing.[8]

Upstream from the falls, next to the enormous dam containing the Watervliet Reservoir, can be seen two elevated, parallel train trestles built in 1865. They are still in use today.

If you look downstream from the falls, you will see the City of Watervliet's Water Supply & Hydroelectric Facility. What's not so obvious is that the entire hydroelectric plant is underground and hidden from view![9]

Additional Point of Interest: The Normans Kill possesses a number of small tributaries. One of these, Vly Creek, has given rise to a 40-foot waterfall called LaGrange Falls (also known as Horton Falls) in Voorheesville.[10, 11] This fall has been effectively isolated from public view by a number of surrounding private homes, but it was once a favorite haunt of tourists staying in various boarding homes in Voorheesville. It was even given honorable mention in the *History of the County of Albany, NY. From 1609–1886.*[12]

Directions: Take Rt. 20 northwest from Albany. After you pass by Rt. 146N (to your right), drive northwest on Rt. 20 for another 0.8 mile and then turn left onto French's Mill Road. Follow French's Mill Road southwest for 0.9 mile until you reach its junction with Fullers Station Road. The falls can be seen from the pedestrian bridge, directly to your left.

From Schenectady, take Rt. 158 south until you reach Rt. 20. Turn left and go southeast on Rt. 20 for 1.7 miles, then turn right onto Fullers Station Road and proceed south for 0.9 mile to the falls.

LaGrange Falls, circa 1920.

34. Bozen Kill Falls

Location: Duanesburg (Schenectady County)
NYS Atlas & Gazetteer: p. 66, BC1
Accessibility: Fairly short, 0.4-mile hike over uneven terrain
Degree of Difficulty: Easy to moderate

Description: Bozen Kill Falls is formed on the Bozen Kill, a medium-sized stream that rises south of Delanson and flows into the Watervliet Reservoir near Guilderland.[1] In times past the Bozen Kill was known by the less dignified name of Drunkard's Creek.[2]

The fall is broad, 15 to 20 feet in height, and formed out of shale and sandstone.[3] Since shale erodes more quickly than sandstone, the less permanent, underlying shale wears away more quickly than the sandstone cap rock forming the ledges.[4]

Some sources list the height of the fall as 30 feet[5-7]; one source goes so far as to suggest 70 feet.[8] The latter figure is either a more accurate estimate of the height of all of the waterfalls in the sanctuary combined, or of the waterfalls further downstream on the Bozen Kill (which are presently inaccessible).

Directly across from Bozen Kill Falls is an attractive lean-to where hikers can enjoy a snack or just relax while enjoying the hypnotic sound of water falling in the background.

There are several small falls above the main one, but those are located on posted land. Fortunately, as you proceed downstream from the main fall, you will encounter a series of smaller, but pretty, ledge-shaped falls along a 0.2-mile tract of stream. All of these are worth seeing.

History: Bozen Kill Falls is located near Duanesburg in the Christman Sanctuary, a small nature preserve owned and operated by the Nature Conservancy and now a designated National Historic Landmark. The sanctuary is part of what was once the Christman homestead, initially purchased by Spencer Christman in 1854 and later farmed by his son and daughter-in-law, William and Catherine Christman. If you walk along a trail near the eastern perimeter of the sanctuary, you will encounter two plaques affixed to large rocks honoring W. W. Christman (1869–1937) and Catherine Bradt Christman (1867–1946), the second-generation owners of the land.

William Christman reforested 60 acres of his farm, creating a plantation of white pine, locust, red pine, scotch pine, and larch. He retired from the farm at age 59 and then went on to write four

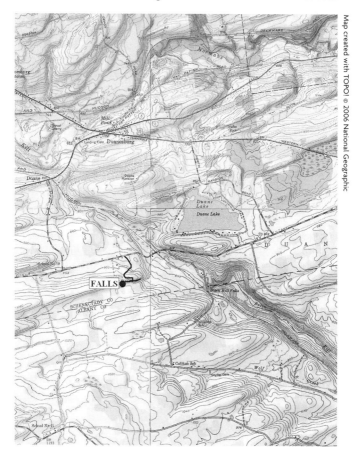

Bozen Kill Falls, circa 1900.

volumes of poetry.[9, 10] One volume, entitled *Wild Pasture Pine*, won a John Burroughs Memorial Association award. Some critics likened Christman's writings to that of Walt Whitman.[11]

The Bozen Kill was home to a number of mills in the vicinity of Duanesburg. The Van Patten family ran a gristmill and a sawmill on the Bozen Kill.[12] Another sawmill was operated by Robert Liddle on farmland adjacent to the Bozen Kill.[13]

There are a number of fairly prominent waterfalls on tributaries of the Bozen Kill, several of which are even taller than Bozen Kill Falls. The tributaries containing these falls enter the Bozen Kill further upstream, virtually next to Rt. 7, but unfortunately they are located on posted land and are not accessible to the public.

Directions: From I-90 (the NYS Thruway), get off at Exit 25A for Schenectady and Binghamton and drive southwest on I-88 to the village of Duanesburg. Get off at Exit 24 for Duanesburg. Turn left at the end of the ramp and drive south for less than 0.2 mile. When you come to Rt. 20, turn left and go east for 2.2 miles. Then turn right onto the Schoharie Turnpike and drive southwest for 3.1 miles. The parking area for the Christman Sanctuary is on your left.[14]

Follow a well-worn trail from the parking lot that leads into the woods within less than 0.1 mile. Stay to the right when the path divides next to the trail registry, and you will immediately descend into a little gully and cross over a small creek via a pretty footbridge that was erected in September 2004. Continue uphill through the woods. When you finally reach a large ravine containing the Bozen Kill, turn left and walk along the top of the bank downstream for over 0.1 mile until you come to a secondary trail on your right that immediately takes you between a narrow cleft in the rock and then down to the stream. Follow the Bozen Kill upstream for 0.05 mile to the fall. The fall is located at the western boundary of the park's perimeter.

Return to the main path and follow it downstream. Within a span of 0.2 mile, you will encounter a series of small cascades and ledge falls—all worth seeing during your visit to the sanctuary.

Lower Bozen Kill, circa 1920.

35. Dugway Falls

Location: Sharon Springs (Schoharie County)
NYS Atlas & Gazetteer: p. 64, B4
Accessibility: Roadside

Description: This 40-foot-high waterfall, also known as Sulphur Springs Falls, Brimstone Falls, and Ravine Falls, is formed on a small stream that rises near Sharon Springs and merges with Canajoharie Creek midway between Staleyville and Marshville.[1, 2, 3] The *NYS Atlas & Gazetteer* lists the stream as Brimstone Creek, as do historic plaques that proliferate throughout the village of Sharon Springs. An antique twentieth-century postcard, however, identifies the stream as Sulphur Springs Creek. Whether it's Brimstone or Sulfur, the alternate names of the stream testify to the olfactory-stimulating properties of the waters of Sharon Springs.

The waterfall is located in a fairly conspicuous spot, directly under a bridge. According to an historic plaque near the intersection of Alder Road and Rt. 10, the waterfall acquired its name during a period of time when the hollow was called The Dugway.

There is a second fall in the ravine. If you walk downhill from the bridge along Rt. 10 for less than 0.05 mile, you will notice, to your left and close to roadside, a fairly high and narrow waterfall coming down the wall of the ravine when sufficient water is flowing. It is very pretty, and distinguished by the abundance of green moss growing along its base.

History: Sharon Springs is known for its numerous mineralsprings containing sulfur, magnesia, and chalybeate.[4] Native Americans were the first to regard the sulfur springs as havingcurative powers, and made pilgrimages to the springs when healing was needed. By 1825 David Elbredge, recognizing that there was money to be made from the effervescent, sulfurous waters, turned the springs into a commercial enterprise. This was during the era when the principal modes of travel were by horse, carriage, or boat, and Sharon Springs, prominently situated between the crossroads of the Great Western Turnpike and the Loonenburg Turnpike (which came up north from Durham and Middleburgh), was a natural destination for land travelers. Travelers also came from the Mohawk Valley via the Erie Canal, followed by a 10-mile stagecoach ride. From all directions, over 10,000 tourists a year made their way to the 60 hotels that flourished at Sharon Springs. Sharon Springs was blessed with an excellent supply of mineral waters: "White sulphur springs, a natural sulphur-and-magnesia-stained spring (located in the center of the village) poured forth at an average of four barrels a minute."[5] During the village's heyday, there was no shortage of healing waters for anyone willing to believe the ballyhoo. The "healing" waters were taken both externally and internally: externally, in the form of slate tub baths for skin and arthritic conditions; internally, by either drinking the waters for "malarial difficulties" and "biliary derangements," or by inhaling the fumes for pulmonary disorders. Even today, the smell of sulfur is pervasive as you stroll through parts of the village.

All of this is worth thinking about as you watch the flowing waters of Brimstone Creek as it drops over the falls.

Next to the top of the waterfall can be seen an old stone powerhouse of fairly modest size. If you look closely enough along the bank of the east side of the cascade, you will notice fragments of a retaining wall that once supported a small structure. Just upstream, on the opposite side of the road, is a breached stone dam. The first industry established near the waterfall was a sawmill. That was followed by a gristmill, which was built in 1798 by Omed (or possibly Omeo or Oma) LaGrange.[6]

A fairly substantial structure, called Schaefer Baths, along with a duck house and plane factory, were located just upstream from the bridge. All have vanished, and no signs remain except some bits of pipes.

Just uphill from the top of the waterfall, on Adler Road, is the still-intact structure of the Adler Hotel, which was built in 1927 and contained 150 rooms. Dugway Falls was a natural destination for those who wanted to take a short stroll down from the hotel.

Dugway Falls, circa 1900.

Additional Points of Interest: While in town, you would be remiss not to visit the famous White Sulphur Spring, which can still be readily accessed. It is almost directly across the road from Pavilion Avenue (which is just up the street from Adler Road). The spring is surrounded by a circular stone wall and is part of a complex of several structures that the town has preserved.

The town sits on top of a sloping bed of limestone, whose porosity ensures that underground rivulets appear in numerous places as bubbling springs. Some of the springs carry a high concentration of sulfur and give forth a very strong odor of rotten eggs. One spring has the taste of magnesium. Another spring—the Eye Water Spring—has virtually no taste at all.

A quick look at a topographical map or the *NYS Atlas & Gazetteer* shows that Sulphur Spring Creek, after leaving Bowmaker Pond, travels underground for a considerable distance before reappearing in the historic section of Sharon Springs. The insurgence (where the stream disappears) is called Old Maid's Hole and is about 50 feet south of Rt. 20. There, the stream drops into a large, deep sinkhole, producing a 6-foot-high cascade in the process. In 1998 the hole clogged up and water flooded across Route 20 to a depth of 18 inches.

Directions: From Duanesburg (junction of Rtes. 20 and 7), drive west on Rt. 20 for 26 miles to Sharon Springs. Turn right at the intersection of Rtes. 20 and 10, and follow Rt. 10 northeast, going downhill for roughly 0.8 mile. Just before you reach Alder Road on your right, park next to a historic marker erected in 1999 by the Sharon Historical Society.

From there, proceed on foot, walking carefully down Rt. 10 for less than 0.1 mile—all the while staying well to the side of the road—until you reach a little bridge where Rt. 10 spans a small stream. The waterfall is directly below the bridge, on your right.

From the Mohawk Valley, starting at Canajoharie (junction of Rtes. 5S and 10), drive southwest on Rt. 10 for nearly 10 miles. The waterfall will be on your left as you cross over a small bridge before arriving in the historic part of Sharon Springs.

36. Judd Falls

Location: North of Cherry Valley (Otsego County)
NYS Atlas & Gazetteer: p. 64, B2-3
Accessibility: Roadside. A partial view into the great gulf at the head of the canyon can be seen from Vanderwerker Road.

Description: Judd Falls is a hulking, 135-foot-high cascade formed on a small stream that rises north of Cherry Valley and flows into Bowman's Creek downstream from the waterfall.[1-4] The waterfall, although one continuous drop, consists of three main sections: a long, steeply angled slide that leads to a high plunge and ends in a final pitched cascade. The waterfall is poised at the mouth of a canyon that seems impossibly large, given the size of the stream falling into it.

Despite the gorge's location, virtually next to Rt. 20, it remains hidden from sight as busy motorists travel by. This is because the stream is carried under Rt. 20 by a large pipe and only reappears at the top of the gorge.

History: Centuries ago, Native Americans called Judd Falls *Tekaharawa* (also spelled *Tekaharaw*), meaning "place of high waters,"[5] which is an apt description of this towering waterfall. That name never caught on with European settlers, however, and, like most falls of northeastern New York, ended up acquiring a more prosaic name that Europeans could pronounce easily. The modern name came from the Judd Iron Works, which once used the waterfall for power generation.[6]

Because of its great depth and rocky terrain, the canyon has been used in the past by paramedics, EMTs, and emergency mountain rescue squads for vertical rope work.

Directions: From Duanesburg (junction of Rtes. 7 and 20), take Rt. 20 west for approximately 32 miles. (Or, from the junction of Rtes. 20

and 10 at Sharon Springs, continue west for another 6.4 miles.) You will reach a right-hand turn for Rt. 166, which ultimately leads to Cherry Valley. Turn right here. As soon as you arrive at the end of the exit ramp, you will notice that Rt. 166 veers to your left, Rt. 32 to your right, and Vanderwerker Road goes straight ahead. Continue straight onto Vanderwerker Road for less than 100 feet and you will see a colossal canyon to your right. The falls are at the head of the gorge, almost next to the road, and the stream would certainly be visible were it not for the fact that it has been channeled under Rt. 20, issuing from a pipe at the top of the cascade.

Judd Falls, circa 1920.

37. Cascade along Salt Springville Road

Location: North of Cherry Valley (Otsego County)
NYS Atlas & Gazetteer: p. 64, B2-3
Accessibility: Roadside

Description: This lofty, steeply inclined, 60-foot high cascade is formed on a small stream that rises from a swampy area east of Shankley Mountain. A portion of the waterfall continues under the bridge and then makes its way downhill through a gorge.

An old abandoned bridge can be seen directly next to the current bridge.

Directions: Follow the same directions given for Judd Falls (see previous chapter). From Judd Falls, proceed north on Vanderwerker Road for 0.3 mile. At a fork in the road, bear left onto Salt Springville Road and drive northwest for 1.3 miles. The cascade is directly to your left where the road passes over a stream.

Take note that the land is posted. Fortunately, however, the best views are from roadside.

38. Fall on Tributary to Cherry Valley Creek

Location: Cherry Valley (Otsego County)
NYS Atlas & Gazetteer: p. 64, BC2-3
Accessibility: Roadside

Description: This large waterfall is formed on a small tributary to Cherry Valley Creek. The stream drops precipitously over a discrete rock edge into a deep and foreboding gulf whose side walls rise up nearly vertically. The waterfall is easily 50–60 feet high and only outmatched in size by the containing walls of the gorge. There are excellent views of Cherry Valley from the top of the fall, looking west.

Directions: From the junction of Rtes. 20 and 166 north of Cherry Valley, drive southwest on Rt. 166 for over 2 miles. Just before you reach the main intersection in the village of Cherry Valley (where Rt. 166 turns abruptly left at a traffic light), turn sharply left onto Lancaster Street (which becomes Rt. 50), and drive southeast for over 1.7 miles. Then turn right onto O'Neil Road and travel south for 0.1 mile. You will pass by a formidable gulf to your right where a little stream goes under the road. Park to the right of the road just beyond this point.

From roadside you can look right over the top of the fall into the enormous gulf, whose steep walls seem so improbable given the light flow of the current stream. A lower section of the waterfall, more cascade-like, can be glimpsed from roadside by walking a few feet south from the top of the fall.

Take note of the posted signs and remain at roadside. Even if posted signs were not present, however, the chasm's immensity and steep sides would preclude any thought of descent.

39. Leatherstocking Falls

Location: Cooperstown (Otsego County)
NYS Atlas & Gazetteer: p. 64, BC1
Accessibility: Roadside

Description: Leatherstocking Falls is formed on Leatherstocking Creek,[1] a small stream that rises east of Metcalf Hill and flows into Otsego Lake less than 0.5 mile downstream from the waterfall.[2-4] The fall is 20 feet high and is named for James Fenimore Cooper, who lived in Cooperstown for part of his life. Cooper's Leatherstocking Tales—a series of novels set in the 1700s and based upon a fictitious frontier character named Hawkeye (also known as the Pathfinder, La long Carabine, and Natty Bumppo)—made references to the waterfall.

Antique postcards show the waterfall in a more natural setting, without the trappings of civilization. Later postcards show the waterfall with a sturdy-looking wooden bridge spanning its top. At some point the wooden bridge was replaced by an old stone bridge, which today leads to an establishment called Leatherstocking Farms.

There used to be a nature trail that led from Rt. 80 up through the ravine to the base of the waterfall, but this historic access is now posted.

History: Otsego Lake was called *O-te-sa-ga* by Native Americans.[5] James Fenimore Cooper called it Glimmerglass, but it remains Otsego today (although Glimmerglass is now the name of an opera company on the lake).

In the early nineteenth century a gristmill operated near the fall. According to one account it burned down and was abandoned before the Civil War.[6] Another account states that the old gristmill was dismantled by Dr. William E. Guy when he purchased Leatherstocking Farms, and the stones were used in the construction of a

Leatherstocking Falls, circa 1900.

new summer residence on the property.[7] This raises the possibility that there might have been two different gristmills on the site at different times.

Additional Point of Interest: Leatherstocking Falls is not the only natural wonder near Otsego Lake to have been incorporated into one of Cooper's novels. On the escarpment near the east shore is Natty Bumppo's Cave (though it is more of a shelter than a cave).[8] In *The Pioneers* the cave provided Elizabeth Temple, one of Cooper's protagonists, with a refuge from a raging forest fire.

Directions: From Duanesburg (junction of Rtes. 20 and 7), drive west on Rt. 20 for roughly 40 miles. (Or, from the junction of Rtes. 10 and 20 at Sharon Springs, continue west on Rt. 20 for around 14 miles.) Turn left onto Rt. 80 and drive south for approximately 8.5 miles. During most of the ride, Otsego Lake will be directly to your left. Along the way you will pass Five Mile Point and Three Mile Point. Ignore the first right-hand turn for Rt. 28, at 2.7 miles. Then at 8.5 miles, turn sharply right onto Rt. 28 and drive uphill for 0.1 mile.

You will come to a pull-off on the right from where the waterfall can be glimpsed through trees.[9] You can also catch fleeting glimpses of the waterfall as you walk uphill along Rt. 28 for a hundred feet. The land here is posted and cannot be entered. It used to be possible to visit Leatherstocking Falls by following the creek upstream from Rt. 80 for 0.1 mile. That land has been posted for many years, however, and this approach, too, is now off limits.

It is imperative that you visit when there is no foliage whatsoever; otherwise you will be able to see almost nothing of the fall.

40. Falls at Van Hornsville

Location: Van Hornsville (Herkimer County)
NYS Atlas & Gazetteer: p. 64, AB2
Accessibility: Short hike over uneven terrain
Hours: Sunrise to sunset
Restrictions: Rules are posted at entrance and include no fishing, hunting or swimming.
Degree of Difficulty: Easy to moderate

Description: There are a number of pretty waterfalls and cascades that have formed on and along Otsquago Creek, a medium-sized stream that rises near Summit Lake and flows into the Mohawk River at Fort Plain. This is an area that is especially waterfall-rich.

The main fall on Otsquago Creek is block-shaped and 10 feet high, and is formed directly next to the renowned Tufa Caves. Towering above the main fall is a 50-foot, staircase-shaped cascade, called Creamery Falls, that is formed on Creamery Creek, a small tributary. The two falls are so close together as to seemingly form one large, L-shaped waterfall.[1] Just below the main waterfall is a long, 8-foot-high cascade.

Near the beginning of the hike is a pretty, moss-covered, 8-foot-high, block-shaped fall, where an old sawmill foundation and machinery can be seen.[2] Between this waterfall and Creamery Falls, further downstream, are at least three more cascades and falls. A short distance downstream from the 8-foot-high cascade below Creamery Falls is a 10-foot-high, block-shaped waterfall, formed on a tiny tributary to Otsquago Creek that comes in on the right. A small footbridge spans its top. Less than 0.1 mile further downstream is another cascade coming in on the east side (to the right), formed on another tiny tributary to Otsquago Creek. This cascade is roughly 40 feet in height, but it is fairly insignificant because of the small amount of water it carries.

Lower Otsquago Creek, circa 1920.

Otsquago Creek, Fort Plain, N. Y.

History: This series of waterfalls is located at the Robert D. Woodruff Outdoor Learning Center, which includes more than 30 acres of nature trails. The main trail is a deserted nineteenth-century road that once connected Fort Plain with Cooperstown. After the road was abandoned, the bridge fell into ruin and the waterfalls and caves became inaccessible to all except fishermen and curiosity-seekers who were willing to ford the stream. In 1984, however, work began on reopening the area. The main footbridge crossing Otsquago Creek was rebuilt by members of the 464th Engineering Battalion of the U.S. Army Reserve, and access to the preserve was reestablished.

The first waterfall one encounters is located at the site of an old sawmill. Downstream is the foundation of what was once a cheese box factory. As you continue along the bank of the stream for less than 0.2 mile, you will be amply rewarded with the sights and sounds of falling water. But the best is still to come. Within 0.2 mile from the start of the hike, you will arrive at the famous Tufa Caves.[3] The caves are formed in porous, calcareous rock that looks remarkably like a sponge. The Tufa Caves were considered so unique and unusual that a mural of the caves was put on display at the 1939 World's Fair. Right next to the Tufa Caves can be seen Creamery

Falls and the main fall on Otsquago Creek. The base of the main fall is accessible via a wooden stairway. Van Hornsville is named after Abraham Van Horne, the town's founder.

Directions: The village of Van Hornsville can be reached by two routes: from Rt. 5S in Fort Plain, take Rt. 80 southwest for over 12.5 miles until you reach Van Hornsville; or, from Rt. 20 near Otsego Lake, turn north onto Rt. 80 and drive northeast for 5.0 miles until you reach Van Hornsville. Either way, once you are in the village of Van Hornsville, look for the Owen D. Young Central School on the southeast side of Rt. 80. Turn in at the school and drive down to a lower parking area, right next to Otsquago Creek. The area, according to a sign, is "intended for the residents and students of the Owen D. Young Central School District," but the sign also states, "All others are welcome" as well.

Cross over a footbridge that leads to the Outdoor Learning Center, where a small pavilion and several other structures can be found. Follow the main trail, which parallels Otsquago Creek, and proceed downstream, going northeast. There are several small trails off to the left that lead to the secondary falls. At one point you will pass by the site of an old mill. Continue until you reach the area of the Tufa Caves. Creamery Falls and a prominent waterfall on Otsquago Creek's tiny tributary can be found there. There are several additional waterfalls further downstream, both on Otsquago Creek and its tributaries, and they are all within 0.1 mile.

There is more to see along Rt. 20 if you don't mind continuing west for another 55 miles. Route 20 is a surprisingly fast, pleasant excursion on what is mostly a four-lane road, and you will pass through a number of towns and villages that are historically significant. What makes the trip particularly worthwhile is that you will get to see a number of cool cascades including one of New York State's most majestic waterfalls, at Chittenango Falls State Park. At the conclusion of the tour you will end up at Clark Reservation State Park, where you will be able to visit a colossal plunge basin that was formed by a now-extinct cataract.

Scenic beauty of Route 20, circa 1950.

41. Button Falls

Location: Near Leonardsville (Madison County)
NYS Atlas & Gazetteer: p. 63, B5-6
Accessibility: Roadside

Description: Button Falls is formed on Button Creek, a small stream that rises in the hills northwest of Leonardsville and flows into the West Branch of Unadilla River south of Leonardsville. The waterfall consists of two cascades: The one closest to the bridge is eight feet in height. It is quickly followed by a second cascade that drops over 40 feet into an enormous canyon whose walls rise up vertically to nearly 60 feet in height.[1,2]

History: The first sawmill was erected in 1792. Later that year John Button built a gristmill on the same stream, south of the sawmill. Over time the creek came to be known as Buttons Mill Creek, which in later years was shortened to Button Creek.[3]

Leonardsville is named after Reuben Leonard, who established a store in the town in 1801.

Directions: From Richfield Springs (junction of Rtes. 20 and 167), drive west on Rt. 20 for 14.5 miles. Turn left onto Rt. 8 and drive south for 6.6 miles. Turn right onto Button Falls Road and proceed west for nearly 0.5 mile. Pull over to your right just before crossing the bridge.

The top of the falls can be glimpsed by standing on the south side of the bridge and looking downstream.

42. Rexford Falls

Location: Sherburne (Chenango County)
NYS Atlas & Gazetteer: p. 62, C4
Accessibility: Great views from a footbridge spanning the gorge above the fall, and also from the rim of the north bank
Degree of Difficulty: Easy

Description: Rexford Falls is formed on Mad Brook,[1] which rises from several tributaries east of Sherburne and flows into Chenango River south of Sherburne. The cascade is 30–40 feet high and encased in a stupendous canyon whose towering walls rise up to nearly 100 feet.[2-5]

History: The waterfall and park were donated to the Town of Sherburne by friends and relatives of Nelson C. Rexford.[6]

The first mill erected in the canyon was a sawmill located approximately 0.5 mile downstream from Rexford Falls. At that time the waterfall, or the area next to it, was known as Sulphur Spring.[7] Later, John Gilmore erected a gristmill closer to the fall.[8]

Mad Brook has also been known in the past as Sulphur Spring and as Harris Falls.[9] The bridge spanning Mad Brook Gorge was constructed by the Thompson Iron Works out of Norwich in 1877.[10, 11]

Directions: From Sangerfield (junction of Rtes. 20 and 12), drive southwest on Rt. 12 for over 19 miles. When you get to the center of Sherburne, at a stoplight (junction of Rtes. 12 and 80), continue south on Rt. 12 for less than 0.2 mile. Turn left onto Chapel Street and drive east for 0.7 mile. You will cross over Mad Brook and join with a road coming in from the right. You are now on Rexford Falls Road. Continue east for another 0.7 mile. Pull into a parking area on your left for Rexford Falls.

This is a very scenic place, with tall pine trees and pine needles covering the ground. Walk 50 feet over to a green-colored footbridge that spans an enormous gorge. Turnstiles have been set into place at both ends of the bridge, presumably to ward off vehicles from attempting to cross. Walk out onto the center of the bridge and look down. About 50 feet below you is Rexford Falls.

For lateral views of the cascade, continue across the footbridge to the north side, then follow the rim of the gorge downstream for 50 feet. You will get an impressive view of the waterfall by looking across and down from the rim.

Rexford Falls and its high bridge, circa 1900.

To access a second cascade that has formed on a tiny, unnamed tributary to Mad Brook, follow the north rim downstream for another 50 feet until you can go no further. If sufficient water is flowing, you will notice a cascade, straight ahead and slightly to the right, that drops sharply down from the top of the north rim. This cascade may be seasonal, so be sure to visit after considerable rainfall or snowmelt.

For those who have just visited nearby Button Falls, there is a shorter way to get to Rexford Falls. From Button Falls Road, drive south on Rt. 8 for nearly 8.5 miles. Then turn right onto Rt. 25 and head west. After roughly 2.5 miles, Rt. 25 becomes Rt. 80. After traveling over 7.5 miles from Rt. 8, you will arrive at a bridge crossing Mad Brook. Turn left just before the bridge onto Rexford Falls Road, and drive west for 0.2 mile. The parking area for the fall will be on your right.

43. Oriskany Falls

Location: Oriskany (Oneida County)
NYS Atlas & Gazetteer: p. 62, A4
Accessibility: Roadside

Description: Oriskany Falls is formed on Oriskany Creek, a moderate-sized stream that rises southwest of Oriskany Falls. The falls consist of a series of short drops totaling approximately 15 feet in height. Of particular interest is the curiously designed, V-shaped dam that sits on top of the falls.

A dam and a platform overlook, which are part of the NYS-DEC's Hinman Memorial Fishing Access Site, can be seen down by Cassety Bridge.

History: "Oriskany" is derived from the Mohawk (and perhaps Oneida, too) *Oriska*, meaning "the place of the nettles."[1]

According to an historical marker on the south side of the Rt. 26/12B bridge, Oriskany Falls was formerly known as Cassety Hollow and was named after Col. Thomas Cassety, who settled in the community in 1794 and erected a gristmill near the falls. Over the succeeding years the stream has been heavily industrialized by a variety of factories including a tannery, sawmill, distillery, and woolen mill.[2, 3] If you look over the railing at the north side of the Rt. 26/12B bridge, you will notice that the stream has been funneled into a man-made channel, just before it plunges over the top of the dam and falls.

Additional Point of Interest: As you drive east on Rt. 20 from the junction of Rtes. 20 and 26/12B, look up at the hills to your south and you will see a series of giant windmills, tirelessly extracting energy from the currents of moving air. These high-tech windmills may be to this century what waterwheels once were to the Industrial Revolution.

Directions: From Sangerfield (junction of Rtes. 20 and 12), drive west on Rt. 20 for 5.6 miles. Turn right onto Rtes. 26 and 12B, and drive northeast for 2.6 miles. As soon as you cross over a small bridge spanning Oriskany Creek in the village of Oriskany, turn right onto Broad Street and immediately park to the side of the road where space is available. Cassety Street, which crosses over Oriskany Creek, is directly ahead, less than 0.05 mile from where you just turned.

Proceeding on foot, go right on Cassety Street and walk onto the bridge that spans Oriskany Creek. By looking upstream from the bridge, you can readily see the small falls and dam below the Rt. 26/12B bridge. It is also possible to look down at the top of the falls from the Rt. 26/12B bridge if you walk upstream from where you parked.

At the end of the Cassety Street bridge, you will notice a wheelchair-accessible platform that overlooks a 6-foot-high, dam-created falls.

44. Stockbridge Falls

Location: Near Stockbridge (Madison County)
NYS Atlas & Gazetteer: p. 62, A2-3
Accessibility: Roadside

Description: Stockbridge Falls is formed on Oneida Creek, a medium-sized stream that rises in the hills to the west. The falls are quite impressive and consist of a series of ledges totaling over 50 feet in height.[1-3] Most of the falls have formed upstream from the bridge. An 8-foot-high fall, however, can be seen directly downstream from the top of the bridge. The bedrock almost gives the appearance of wet cement.

Just upstream from the bridge, along the north bank, is an old foundation from an early industry. Unfortunately, however, the ruins cannot be seen easily from roadside until the foliage is gone.

Stockbridge Falls, circa 1900.

Stockbridge Falls, circa 1930.

History: The town and falls are named after the Stockbridge Native Americans who succeeded the Oneidas and Tuscaroras.[4]

Hydraulic limestone, a material that sets and hardens after combining with water, was once taken out from a quarry near the falls.[5]

Directions: From Sangerfield (junction of Rtes. 20 and 12), drive west on Rt. 20 for 11 miles. (Or, from the junction of Rtes. 20 and 12B, drive 2.5 miles west on Rt. 20.) Turn right onto Rt. 46. Drive west for less than 0.2 mile, then turn left (northwest) onto Pratt Road (Rt. 49). After several miles you will pass through Pratt Hollow. At 3.5 miles, turn left onto Streeter Road, which takes you up a steep hill, going northwest. After 0.4 mile Streeter Street bears left. Continue straight ahead onto Falls Road and drive north for another 1.2 miles. As soon as you cross over a small bridge, pull over into a parking space on either side of the road.

The falls can be observed from either side of the bridge. Take note of the posted signs and stay at roadside.

45. Chittenango Falls

Location: Cazenovia (Madison County)
NYS Atlas & Gazetteer: p. 62, A1
Accessibility: The top of the falls can be easily reached without effort. The bottom is accessed by a moderate, 170-foot descent along a graded walkway and steps. For those desiring a more vigorous hike, the entire "gorge trail" loop can be done in 1.1 miles.
Fee: A modest fee is charged to enter Chittenango Falls State Park from Memorial Day through Labor Day.
Hours: Open year round. The trail to the viewing bridge near the base of the falls is closed during winter.
Degree of Difficulty: Easy to top; moderate to bottom

Description: Chittenango Falls is a large, 167-foot-high, multi-tiered waterfall formed on Chittenango Creek, a medium-sized stream that rises southeast of Cazenovia and flows into Oneida Lake.[1, 2] At one time the stream served as a feeder for the old Erie Canal.[3]

The waterfall is located at the 192-acre Chittenango Falls State Park, which has been named by Reserve America as one of the nation's most popular outdoor sites.[4] The fall is formed out of a series of limestone terraces that developed following the last ice age. The best view of the fall is from a footbridge downstream from the base of the cataract.

History: Cazenovia Lake, the creek's lake source, was called *Owah-gena* by Native Americans, meaning "the lake where the yellow fish swim" or "yellow perch lake."[5] The falls have been employed by a number of mills and factories in the past, including William's Stone Quarry, H. L. Jones' Paper Mill, and Foster's Sawmill.[6] In addition, according to *Route 20 Pulse: The Heartbeat of the Highway of Dreams,* "a papermill, cheese factory, and limestone quarry were once located here, the settlement being called Bingley."[7]

In 1887 the land seemed destined for continued privatization. Derrick Boardman, who then owned the falls, had an opportunity to sell the property to a gunpowder manufacturer, but Boardman reconsidered and instead sold the property at reduced cost to Helen Fairchild with the stipulation that it would be in the public domain

Chittenango Falls, circa 1900.

from that point on. With that, the Chittenango Falls Park Association was formed. Later, in 1922, the land became a New York State park. The park is host to an endangered species of snail called the Chittenango ovate amber snail.[8]

Nearby Chittenango is best known as being the birth place of L. Frank Baum, the author of *The Wizard of Oz.*

Geology: Chittenango Falls is made out of Onondaga limestone, a sedimentary rock that formed around 400 million years ago at the bottom of a shallow sea. Around that time, North America was just beginning to form and was located directly over the equator, thousands of miles from its present location[9] and with a much more tropical climate.

Directions: From Duanesburg (junction of Rtes. 7 and 20) drive west on Rt. 20 for nearly 95 miles until you reach Cazenovia, which is located at the southeast corner of Cazenovia Lake. Turn right onto Rt. 13N (Gorge Road) and drive northeast for 4 miles. The entrance to Chittenango Falls State Park will be directly on your left.

Park in the main parking area. The top of Chittenango Falls is virtually at the same level as the parking lot and can be easily reached with minimal effort.

Accessing the base of the waterfall requires more effort and involves a descent of over 170 feet via a series of paths and steps. The trip is well worth the effort, however, for it allows you to gaze at the full enormity of Chittenango Falls from a footbridge crossing the creek just downstream from the base.

If you continue across the bridge and up the opposite side of the fall, the round trip will end up being a 1.1-mile hike.

46. Pratt Falls

Location: Near Pompey (Onondaga County)
NYS Atlas & Gazetteer: p. 61, A6-7
Accessibility: Short walk to top of falls; 120-foot descent along a graded carriage road and some stairs to the base of the falls
Fee: A nominal fee is charged.
Hours: Open year round
Degree of Difficulty: Easy to the top; moderate to the bottom

Description: Pratt Falls is formed on a tiny stream that rises east of Pompey and flows into the West Branch of Limestone Creek. The waterfall is 137 feet high and cascades into a surprisingly (considering the present size of the stream) deeply cut gorge.[1-3] The fall is located in Pratt Falls County Park.

Limestone Creek is no stranger to waterfalls. On its east branch, near Delphi Falls, can be found two cascades reputed to be 90 feet and 60–70 feet in height, respectively.[4, 5]

History: Centuries ago the area around the fall was a Native American campground.[6] A number of Indian skeletons and artifacts were dug up by the Civilian Conservation Corps while the park was being constructed in the 1930s.

According to an historical marker at the top of the waterfall, Pratt Falls was the first waterfall in Onondaga County to be industrialized when a mill was built by Manoah Pratt, Sr. and Abraham Smith in 1796. Initially it served as a sawmill, and then became a flour mill in 1798. A vertical saw from the mill is exhibited near the historic marker, and a tiny mill pond can be seen upstream from the top of the fall.

Directions: Follow the directions already given to Cazenovia (see previous chapter, "Chittenango Falls"). From the junction of Rtes. 20 and 13S

Pratt Falls, circa 1950.

(on the outskirts of Cazenovia), drive west on Rt. 20 for 6.7 miles. Turn right onto Watervale Road, just after passing a green sign that points the way to Pratt Falls County Park. Drive north on Watervale Road for roughly 0.5 mile, then turn left onto Pratt Falls Road and drive west for about 1.0 mile. The entrance to the park will be on your right.

After paying a modest entrance fee, continue to the main parking area. From there, follow a path (more like a carriage road) with occasional stairs that leads down to an observation point near the base of the fall. To prevent further erosion to the area, do not follow the steep, informal path by the gorge that heads downhill near the metal fence.

Although the views are limited from the fenced-in overlook at the top of the waterfall, if you follow the fence northeast, you will ultimately be rewarded with a wonderful view looking back at the waterfall from a high overlook along the east rim of the gorge.

47. Clark Reservation

Location: Near Jamesville (Onondaga County)
NYS Atlas & Gazetteer: p. 61, A6
Accessibility: 0.3-mile walk
Fee: Modest admission fee
Hours: Open year round
Degree of Difficulty: Easy, except for uneven footing

Description: This is not an actual waterfall, but rather, the fossil imprint of one. Still, what a magnificent, enormous fossil it is! This extinct waterfall is located at the 365-acre Clark Reservation State Park, named after Myron Clark, governor of New York from 1855–1857. The Clark Reservation provides the rare opportunity to walk along the dry bed of a former mighty river and to stand at the brink of what was once a stupendous waterfall.

The mighty cataract left behind in its wake an enormous plunge basin, 175 feet deep,[1] which now contains a small, ten-acre lake. The plunge basin was created at the end of the last glaciation, when an enormous torrent of water flowed through Butternut Valley for about 2,000 years.

History: In early times Native American called the lake at the bottom of the plunge basin *kai-yah-koo*, meaning "satisfied with tobacco." According to legend, the name arose after a child drowned in the lake. Every year thereafter his mother would visit the lake and throw tobacco onto the waters so that the spirits would be appeased and continue to look after her child. In 1878 an entrepreneur from Pennsylvania named James McFarlane built a small hotel at the top of the basin and a series of walks, including a stairway that led down to the lake. The hotel failed, however, and the structures were subsequently razed.

In 1915, 108 acres by the lake were purchased by Mary Clark Thompson and donated to New York State to memorialize her father, former Governor Myron Clark. The land became a state park in 1926.

Geology: The limestone beds forming the reservation were laid down 250–400 million years ago when the region was at the bottom of a shallow, salty sea.

Ten millenniums ago, as the last ice age ended, meltwaters from mile-high glaciers in retreat carved out the feature that you see today. It began further along Butternut Creek, and then receded southwest as the rock eroded. The west side of the basin and parts of the north and south banks were once part of an enormous horseshoe-shaped waterfall whose volume was greater than that of today's American Falls at Niagara Falls.

As a point of further interest, the lake at the bottom of the basin is meromictic, meaning that its surface and bottom waters remain unmixed—the result of the lake having a limited surface area relative to its depth of 62 feet. In this respect the lake is one of only a few of its kind in the United States.

Directions: Follow the directions given to Pratt Falls County Park (see previous chapter, "Pratt Falls"). From Pratt Falls County Park, go back east on Pratt Falls Road to Watervale Road. Turn left onto Watervale Road and drive north for 4.6 miles (or a total of 5.6 miles if you are beginning at the junction of Rtes. 20 and Watervale Road). When you reach Rt. 173, turn left and drive west for 5.3 miles (in the process passing through Jamesville). Turn right into the entrance for the Clark Reservation State Park and drive for 0.2 mile to the main parking area.

You will have no trouble locating the glacial basin and lake; a brochure containing a map is given to you as you enter the reservation. If you meander over to the west side of the basin to an area called Table Rock, you will be standing at virtually the midpoint of what once was a horseshoe-shaped waterfall that extended around part of the rim of the basin.

Ilion Falls, postcard circa 1906.

Fox's Falls, Ilion, N.Y.

Waterfalls of
the Helderbergs

Introduction

The Helderbergs represent the northeastern extension of the Appalachian Plateau, formed principally out of limestone that was deposited in the middle Paleozoic Era. During the early Tertiary Period (the Eocene Epoch), the area was uplifted to form what is today's Helderberg plateau. It is the Helderbergs' limestone, easily dissolved by water, which has allowed areas of karst (sinkholes, fissures, and caves) and an occasional spectacular waterfall to form—such as Minelot Falls at John Boyd Thacher Park.

"Helderberg" is a Dutch corruption of the Old German word *Helle-berg*, meaning "clear mountain." The Helderbergs were named by early Schoharie County settlers who spotted the *bergs* (mountains) off in the distance as they traveled west from Albany.

Indian Ladder, circa 1910.

48. Outlet Falls

Location: Indian Ladder at John Boyd Thacher Park
(Albany County)
NYS Atlas & Gazetteer: p. 66, CD1-2
Accessibility: 0.3-mile hike along base of escarpment following a 100-foot descent via stone and metal stairs
Fee: There is a seasonal fee for parking at the picnic areas; no fee is charged at the "Cliff Edge" parking area.
Hours: The Indian Ladder Trail is open 8 AM to dusk from May 1 through November 15, weather permitting.
Degree of Difficulty: Moderate

Description: Outlet Falls is formed on Outlet Creek, a small stream that rises in the hills south of Thacher Park and flows into Minelot Creek a short distance downstream from the fall. The waterfall plunges for 100 feet from the top of the Indian Ladder escarpment.[1, 2]

Indian Ladder is a towering, 100-foot-high escarpment at the northern edge of what once was an ancient, shallow, inland sea whose bedrock later became raised up to its present height by massive geological forces. The trail at the base of the escarpment, called the Lower Bear Path, is well maintained and extends for slightly under 0.5 mile.

Outlet Falls is not an especially energetic waterfall. This is due in part because its stream carries a considerably smaller volume of water than its companion stream, Minelot Creek, which is located further east along the escarpment wall and produces Minelot Falls. Furthermore, a significant portion of Outlet Creek's waters are pirated underground through a 1,000-foot, low-lying passageway to emerge near the waterfall's base.[3] For this reason the waterfall has also come to be known as Dry Falls—a name whose origin becomes readily apparent as the middle of summer approaches.[4]

What is most noteworthy about Outlet Falls and what differentiates it from virtually any other waterfall in eastern New York State, is that a separate, 4–5 foot cascade has formed at its base. The end result is something highly unusual—double waterfalls, with the plunge fall from Outlet Falls dropping in front of the lower cascade.

History: Outlet Falls is located in John Boyd Thacher Park—a multi-purpose, more than 2,000-acre recreational area located 14 miles outside of Albany and named after John Boyd Thacher, historian and past mayor of Albany.

Directions: From Albany (junction of 1-90 and Rt. 85), drive southwest on Rt. 85 for slightly over 4 miles. When you reach New Scotland Avenue at Slingerlands, turn right and drive west on Rt. 85 for nearly 8 miles, passing through New Scotland and then New Salem in the process. As you leave New Salem behind and near the top of a long, winding hill, turn right onto Rt. 157. Drive northwest for 4.0 miles and you will reach the main recreational area for John Boyd Thacher Park, where the swimming facilities are located. Turn right here onto Hailes Cave Road, which leads immediately to a tollbooth. As soon as you pass through the tollbooth, turn right again and drive to the end of the parking lot.

Proceeding on foot, follow signs that direct you to the Indian Ladder Trail. Within several hundred feet you will walk down a stone stairway that leads to a flight of metal stairs descending to the base of the Indian Ladder Escarpment, some 100 feet below the top of the escarpment. Once you have descended to the base of the escarpment, follow the lower escarpment trail until you come to Outlet Falls, approximately 0.3 mile from where you started.

49. Minelot Falls

Location: Indian Ladder at John Boyd Thacher Park
(Albany County)
NYS Atlas & Gazetteer: p. 66, CD1-2
Accessibility: 0.4-mile hike along base of escarpment following a
descent of 100 feet via a flight of stone and metal stairs. Expect some
uneven terrain.
Fee: A seasonal fee is charged for parking at the picnic areas.
Hours: The Indian Ladder Trail is open 8 AM to dusk from May 1
through November 15, weather permitting.
Degree of Difficulty: Easy to moderate

Description: Minelot Falls is a stupendous cataract formed on
Minelot Creek, a small stream that rises in the hills west of John Boyd
Thacher Park and flows into Black Creek. The waterfall is 116 feet in
height, plunging off the top of the escarpment.[1-6] Minelot Falls has
also been known as Big Falls and Indian Ladder Falls in years past.

One of the earliest descriptions of the waterfall dates back
nearly 150 years: "From the edge of the overhanging precipice, more
than a hundred feet above your head, streams down a silvery rope
of spray, with a whispering rush, sweeping before it damp, chilly
eddies of fugitive air that sway the watery cable to and fro."[7]

During spring's snowmelt, Minelot Falls turns into a dynamic
tornado of falling water, hitting the rocks below like a pile driver.
During the summer, it narrows and becomes more snake-like, writh-
ing in the breeze. Hikers will frequently stand at its base during
hot, humid days and shower under the falling spray. Minelot Falls
is no less magnificent in the winter, often appearing as an inverted
cone of ice. Take note, however, that Indian Ladder is closed from
late fall to mid-spring—and for good reason. The trail is typically
glazed over with ice, making it dangerous and virtually impassable.
Fortunately, the frozen cataract can be viewed from an escarpment

overlook south of the fall. What you will typically see is not a water-fall, but a mound of ice rising up to more than half the height of the escarpment.

Like many of the streams along the Helderberg escarpment, Minelot Creek loses some of its water to underground drainage.[8] If you stand under the huge amphitheater behind Minelot Falls, you

Minelot Falls, circa 1910.

Minelot Falls in the winter, circa 1920.

will observe a number of tiny rivulets issuing from the base of the escarpment.[9]

History: The long stone stairway to the base of Indian Ladder follows a rift in the escarpment that was created in 1828 to make a carriage road that ascended from the floor of the valley to the plateau. It was along this carriage road that visitors had their first glimpse of Indian Ladder, and a magnificent view it was, for, unlike today, when you must reach the base by descending down the escarpment, early travelers on the carriage road could get the full measure of the escarpment buttress as they approached from below.

Directions: Follow the directions given in the previous chapter ("Outlet Falls") to reach the base of Indian Ladder.[10] From there, walk east, following the Lower Bear Path. You will first come to Outlet Falls, at 0.3 mile, and then to Minelot Falls, at nearly 0.5 mile.

If you wish, you can continue further east along the Lower Bear Path for another 0.1 mile, and then ascend via a flight of metal stairs back up to the top of the escarpment near the Grange Bush Picnic Area. From there, you can walk back to your car along the top of the escarpment.

Minelot Falls can also be viewd from the top of the Indian Ladder escarpment. Starting from the east end of the Indian Ladder Trail, walk west along the top of the escarpment for 100 feet to a fabulous overlook of the waterfall. Outlet Falls can also be seen in the far distance.

50. Falls on Upper Minelot Creek

Location: John Boyd Thacher Park (Albany County)
NYS Atlas & Gazetteer: p. 66, CD1-2
Accessibility: Short hike, less than 0.3 mile
Fee: A seasonal fee is charged for parking at the picnic areas.
Hours: Open year round, 8 AM to dusk
Degree of Difficulty: Easy to moderate

Description: In addition to Minelot Creek's principal waterfall, Minelot Falls, there are several smaller cascades formed further upstream. The first waterfall is six feet high and is visible from the Paint Mine Parking area. It consists of a series of small ledges at the entrance to a small ravine.

The second waterfall is 12 feet high—a 6-foot-high plunge dropping onto a 6-foot-high cascade, creating the appearance of one, 12-foot-high fall. The waterfall is located at the mouth of a medium-sized ravine. Just above the top of the fall is a 4-foot cascade.

Approximately 0.2 mile further upstream is another pretty waterfall formed by Minelot Creek and one of its tributaries. The unnamed tributary issues from a spring that can be found a short distance upstream from the fall. The tributary produces an 8-foot-high cascade that drops directly onto Minelot Creek, where another 12-foot-high cascade has formed. From a distance the two appear to be one L-shaped cascade about 20 feet high.

There is still more to see. Several hundred feet further upstream, Minelot Creek passes through a large drainpipe as it flows under a dirt road (marked with red blazes) and immediately drops 12 feet, forming a small cascade.

Directions: From Albany (junction of I-90 and Rt. 85), drive southwest on Rt. 85 for roughly 12 miles. When you come to Rt. 157 above North Salem, turn right and proceed northwest on Rt. 157 for

3.7 miles. Just before you reach the park's main entrance (0.3 mile further), turn left into the Paint Mine Picnic Area and park at the southern end, where several pavilions and numerous picnic tables can be seen.

The first cascade is clearly visible from the parking lot. Proceeding on foot, follow a wide dirt path for less than 100 feet that leads over to the stream and up to the base of the fall. From the base of the fall, follow the dirt path up a small but steep hill, and then continue straight ahead for several hundred feet further until

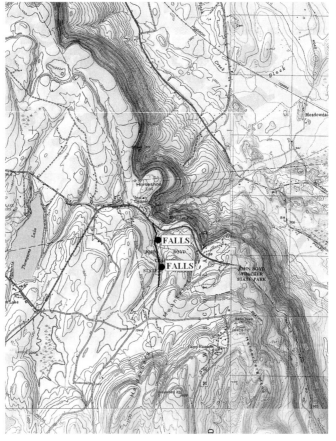

Map created with TOPO! © 2006 National Geographic

you come to a view of the second cascade from the top of the ravine. From there, the dirt path immediately comes out onto an asphalt road. Go left and walk up the road for 100 feet. At this point the road becomes gravel, and you will see a sign indicating that you have reached the beginning of the "Nature Trail." If you wish to see more of the second waterfall, cross over the little foot-bridge and then follow a path immediately to your left, which leads quickly over to the top of the cascade. An informal path descends to the base of the fall.

Return to the "Nature Trail" sign and start walking up the gravel road blazed with red and aqua markers. The stream will again be to your left. Within 0.1 mile the ravine suddenly begins to narrow and becomes much deeper as you continue uphill. Within 0.2 mile you will reach a point where you can see the falling waters of a tiny tributary up ahead as it drops onto Minelot Creek. Fifty feet beyond a wooden fence that park officials have erected to safeguard hikers from an exposed section of the road is an informal overlook of the waterfall, no more than 10 feet from the road. From there, you will observe an 8-foot-high cascade formed on a tiny tributary that drops directly onto the top of a 12-foot cascade on Minelot Creek. During times of limited water flow, this tributary carries significantly more water than Minelot Creek does. The likelihood is that the tributary has siphoned off through an underground system much of the water that was originally carried by Minelot Creek. If there is sufficient water flowing down Minelot Creek, you will also observe a 12-foot-high cascade further upstream in the deep gorge that Minelot Creek has carved out.

Leaving the overlook, continue up the road for another 50 feet, paralleling the narrow, youthful ravine that the tributary has cut. You will notice that the tributary issues from a spring on the right-hand side of the road, virtually at the junction of the red-blazed and aqua-blazed roads. If you wish to see the upper 12-foot cascade on Minelot Creek more closely, turn left onto the red-blazed road at this junction. Walk several hundred feet, crossing over an embankment that was created to bridge Minelot Creek. As soon as you are on the other side, follow an informal path to your left that leads down an embankment and around to an overlook where you can see Minelot Creek issuing from a drainpipe and then plummeting down a 12-foot-high cascade.

Additional Point of Interest: If you would like to see how a stream can vanish into the earth, only to resurface later, then you will find the upper section of Minelot Creek absolutely fascinating. This is an area riddled with limestone, containing such nearby caves as Witches Hole, Forgotten Cave, and William van Zandt Cave. The only caveat is that you must visit upper Minelot Creek when little water is flowing; otherwise, the creek's underground drainage system is overwhelmed and the streambed fills with water, leaving virtually nothing for you to see of Thacher Park's underground world.

From the junction of the red-blazed and aqua-blazed roads, continue uphill on the aqua-blazed road. After a couple of hundred feet, the road divides. Stay to the left, following the aqua blazes. The road quickly crosses over Minelot Creek. A couple of hundred feet further, you will come to a point where the road starts to climb uphill steeply. Bear to your right where the road divides. Before going any distance up the hill, bushwhack over to Minelot Creek (it is clearly in sight), which is flowing out of a swampy area to the right of the hill. Just a short distance downstream from a tiny cement dam at the end of the swamp can be seen a natural, underground drain where the entire stream disappears into the earth. Quite possibly it is a portion of these waters, pirated away, that reappear downhill at the spring from which Minelot Creek's tributary rises.

There is one more sight worth taking in. Return to the aqua-blazed road. Continue uphill for another 50 feet and follow an informal path to your right. It will lead you immediately to an impressive view of the swamp and the limestone cliffs enclosing it.

51. Falls at Hopfield Picnic Area

Location: John Boyd Thacher Park (Albany County)
NYS Atlas & Gazetteer: p. 66, CD1-2
Accessibility: Short walk, less than 0.1 mile to first fall; 0.3 mile to second ravine and cascades
Fee: A seasonal fee is charged for parking at the picnic areas.
Hours: Open year round, 8 AM to dusk
Degree of Difficulty: Easy to first fall; Easy to moderate to second falls

Description: The first waterfall that you will encounter is formed on a tiny stream that rises from a swampy area in John Boyd Thacher Park and flows through the Hopfield Picnic Area on its way down to the Helderberg escarpment. The waterfall consists of a 15-foot-high cascade with multiple ledges and is located in a short ravine that opens up into a large open area just downstream from the cascade. After leaving the ravine, the creek meanders for another 0.3 mile before plunging over the edge of the Helderberg escarpment, east of the Glen Doone Picnic Area.

The second falls are formed on a small, unnamed stream that also rises from the southern hills in the park, and which ultimately plunges over the Helderberg escarpment further downstream, east of the Green House Picnic Area. The falls are contained in a fairly narrow, deep ravine. The main cascade is easily 10 feet high and can be glimpsed from either the side of the ravine or from its top.

Directions: From Albany (junction of I-90 and Rt. 85), take Rt. 85 southwest for about 12 miles. At the top of a hill southwest above New Salem, turn right onto Rt. 157 and drive northwest for over 2.7 miles until you see the parking area for the Hopfield Picnic Area on your left. Park close to the entrance.

To First Fall: Follow a grassy path south through a wide open area where a steep escarpment wall rises to your left and a thick grove of pine trees is on your right. Continue walking for less than 0.1 mile. You will come to a ravine on the left, where a pretty waterfall can be easily seen. For those who require a more intimate connection with the fall, an informal path leads 20 feet into the ravine.

To Second Falls: From the first fall, continue following the dirt road uphill through a road cut. After several hundred feet, bear left, and then cross over a tiny footbridge that spans the creek. As soon as you cross over the stream, bear left where the road divides and follow a yellow-blazed hiking road that parallels the east bank of the stream. Within several hundred feet, the road veers away from the ravine and begins to parallel Rt. 157. After you have walked close to 0.2 mile from the footbridge crossing, you will reach a point where the road begins to veer sharply right. Continue uphill for another 0.05 mile. The ravine will quickly come into view on your left. When you reach an open area to your left containing a picnic table, you are near the top of the uppermost fall. Follow a short path down to the streambed, from where you can look over the top of the main cascade. Just be sure to stay near the side of the ravine when you do your looking.

There are several smaller cascades downstream in the ravine. There is an easy way to see them without having to climb down into the ravine. From the Hopfield Picnic Area, drive east on Rt. 157 for 0.2 mile. Pull into a parking area on your right, opposite the Greenhouse & Yellow Rocks Picnic Area. From there, you can look up into the mouth of the ravine and see a 10-foot-high cascade.

Additional Point of Interest: A trip to Thacher Park would not be complete without enjoying views of the Mohawk Valley from the Cliff Edge Overlook—a long parking area with scenic vistas.

From the Hopfield Picnic Area, drive west for 0.4 mile and turn right into the area designated "Cliff Edge Overlook." From the overlook, you can see the eastern Adirondacks, the Taconics, the Green Mountains of Vermont, and the Berkshires (including Mt. Greylock, Massachusetts' highest point). If the weather is exceptionally clear, you may even be able to see Mt. Mansfield, Vermont's highest mountain, approximately 140 miles away. In the foreground can be seen the South Mall buildings in Albany.

52. Falls by Long Road

Location: East of East Berne (Albany County)
NYS Atlas & Gazetteer: p. 66, CD1-2
Accessibility: Roadside

Description: These small falls are formed on a tiny stream that rises in the hills northwest of Helderberg Lake and flows into a swampy area just south of Thompson Lake. The upper waterfall consists of a 12-foot-high double cascade. The lower fall, immediately downstream, is 6 feet in height. The falls are contained in a ravine that is surprisingly deeply cut, considering that it seems to arise suddenly out of nowhere.

Directions: From I-90, get off at the Slingerlands Exit and drive west on Rt. 85 for nearly 12 miles. When you reach the top of a winding hill above New Salem, turn right onto Rt. 157 and drive northwest. At 0.8 mile, turn left onto Beaver Dam Road (Rt. 311) and drive uphill, going northwest, for 2.6 miles. Then turn left onto Bush Road and drive southwest for 0.9 mile. Turn right (west) onto Long Road, and in less than 0.1 mile you will see the ravine directly to your right.

The falls are formed at the head of the ravine, virtually next to the road. Stay at roadside.

53. Onesquethaw Falls (Historic)

Location: Clarksville (Albany County)
NYS Atlas & Gazetteer: p. 66, D2
Accessibility: Not open to the public. The waterfall is surrounded by private lands.

Description: Onesquethaw Falls is formed on Onesquethaw Creek, a medium-sized stream that rises in the Helderberg Mountains northwest of Clarksville and flows into the Hudson River at Coeymans. The waterfall is approximately 25 feet high[1, 2] and surprisingly broad, considering that the creek quickly narrows into a deeply cut canyon downstream from the fall, where several chute-like cascades have formed.

Onesquethaw Creek meanders through much of Clarksville. During the summer, segments of the creek bed will appear dry. This is because the waters are channeled into an underground drainage system, only to resurface farther downhill. It is thanks to the porosity of the limestone bedrock, which underlies much of Clarksville and the Helderbergs in general, that Albany and Schoharie counties are so rich in caves.

Farther upstream is an area known as "Indian Head," where the erosive power of Onesquethaw Creek has created a series of falls and caves. Unfortunately, this site is also not accessible to the public.

History: The village of Clarksville was named after Adam A. Clark, who settled in the area in 1822. Before that, possibly as early as 1755, a mill was erected along the stream.

Onsquethaw Falls, Clarksville, N. Y.

Onesquethaw Falls, circa 1900.

54. Cascade at Hannacroix Ravine Preserve

Location: Clarksville (Albany County)
NYS Atlas & Gazetteer: p. 66, D1-2
Accessibility: 0.05-mile hike to view of fall from top of ravine
Degree of Difficulty: Easy

Description: The 30-foot cascade at Hannacroix Ravine is formed on Hannacroix Creek, a medium-sized stream that rises in the hills west of Clarksville and flows into the Hudson River south of Coeymans. The bedrock is formed out of Hamilton shale and sandstone that was laid down 370 million years ago.

The waterfall is located in the Hannacroix Ravine Preserve, a 440-acre wilderness area owned by the Nature Conservancy.[1] Sections of the preserve were acquired between 1968 and 1981 through the generosity of George Cooley and Christopher Stahler. The land containing the preserve has been untouched during the last 70 years, except for limited logging.[2]

The Hannacroix Ravine extends far beyond the preserve's boundaries for a total distance of roughly two miles, with a depth of up to 60 feet.[3]

Five other falls produced by Hannacroix Creek can be found several miles downstream from the preserve. Three are inaccessible—Dickinson Falls next to the Alcove Reservoir, Deans Mill Falls by Aquetuck, and a series of falls off Tan Hollow Road near Westerlo. Although it is not open to the public, Dickinson Falls can be glimpsed from roadside in late fall or early spring. The other two waterfalls are accessible—the Fall at Alcove (see chapter on that fall in this book) and Ravena Falls near Ravena (see *Hudson Valley Waterfall Guide* for more information).

History: "Hannacroix" (also spelled Hannacrois) is derived from the old Dutch word, *hanagecraeys*, meaning "cock crow." According to popular legend, the name arose when onlookers observed a barn being swept downriver in a raging flood, with a defiant rooster crowing loudly on its roof.[4, 5]

Cass Hill Road, which crosses Hannacroix Creek, was at one time a colonial stagecoach route along the old Albany-Schoharie Turnpike.

Directions: From Albany, go southwest on Rt. 443 for roughly 12 miles until you reach the village of Clarksville. From Clarksville (junction of Rtes. 443 and 301), continue west on Rt. 443 for 0.5 mile. Then turn left onto Cass Hill Road and drive uphill, going west and gaining elevation quickly. Eventually you will descend into a deep ravine. At 1.8 miles turn left into the parking area for the Hannacroix Ravine Preserve. Should you continue downhill on Cass Hill Road for another 0.1 mile, you will reach the bottom of the ravine, where Hannacroix Creek crosses under the road.

From the parking area, follow the orange-blazed trail south for 0.05 mile. You will find yourself close to the top of Hannacroix Ravine, from where the fall can be heard. It can also be partially glimpsed from here if you are visiting in spring when there is little foliage and much water flowing through the ravine. By continuing downstream along the top of the ravine for several hundred feet, you will gradually follow the contour of the rim to the right and down to a lower point, from where the fall can be seen head-on, albeit from a distance. The foliage is typically dense and the stream often insubstantial, so visit in mid-spring when visibility is optimal, the fall is most animated, and there is no snow or ice to create slippery footing.

55. Fall on Tributary to Helderberg Lake

Location: Near Helderberg Lake (Albany County)
NYS Atlas & Gazetteer: p. 66, CD1-2
Accessibility: Roadside

Description: This pretty, 8-foot-high cascade is formed on a tiny creek that rises in the hills south of Helderberg Lake and flows into the lake just a short distance downstream from the fall. The waterfall is difficult to see while driving along Rt. 443/85, because of the contour of the ravine. If you are coming up West Shore Drive from Helderberg Lake, however, the waterfall is strikingly visible and obviously must be well known to users of the lake.

Directions: From the junction of Rtes. 157 and 85 above New Salem, continue south on Rt. 85 for just over 2 miles. Then turn right onto Rt. 443/85, and drive west for 1.9 miles. Pull off to the side of the road just as you reach the right-hand turn for West Shore Drive/ Glenwood Drive (which, if taken, leads down to the south end of Helderberg Lake).

On the opposite side of Rt. 85 from West Shore Drive can be seen a small cascade contained in a serpentine ravine roughly 50 feet from the road.

56. Fall at Alcove

Location: Alcove (Albany County)
NYS Atlas & Gazetteer: p. 52, A2
Accessibility: Next to roadside

Description: This small, 15-foot-high waterfall is formed on Hannacroix Creek, a medium-sized stream that rises in the hills west of Clarksville and flows into the Hudson River south of Coeymans. Just below the base of the waterfall, Hannacroix Creek runs into a towering vertical wall of solid rock and turns abruptly east at a right angle. It is an apt reminder that water always follows the path of least resistance.

Two small cascades can be seen directly upstream from the bridge. They were once buried under the waters of a dam-created pond just upstream from the bridge. The pond allowed water to be channeled through a cement conduit to a gristmill. The dam has long since been breached and, with that, the cascades have returned to public view again.

History: The Alcove Reservoir was created in 1930 to provide a dependable source of water for Albany residents. (The Hudson River had long ago become polluted and a carrier of disease.) Prior to the reservoir's creation, the valley was occupied by a little farming hamlet of 75 people called Indian Fields, which consisted of two foundries, a harness shop, three stores, a hotel, a Baptist church, and 18 houses. The entire area now lies under 13.5 billion gallons of water spread out across 1,440 acres.[1]

The ruins of an old gristmill can be seen next to the fall, directly along the west bank. Across the stream, on the east bank, is a stone house that once served as a store and is now a private home. If you look upstream from the bridge, you will see part of an old, 10-foot-high, stone dam. It extends westward, paralleling the bank of the stream for some distance. Judging from its size, it held back a fairly sizable impoundment of water. A flax mill once stood next to the bridge, between the road and the dam.

Directions: *From Ravena* (junction of Rtes. 9W and 143), drive west on Rt. 143 for 6.1 miles. When you come to Coeyman's Hollow, just east of the reservoir, turn left onto Rt. 111, cross over the stream, and drive uphill for 0.4 mile. Take note of the amazingly tall, derelict chimney to your left as soon as you cross over the creek. As soon as you pass by Alcove Road on your left, Rt. 111 crosses over a small stream. Park to your right immediately after you cross over the bridge. There will be a sign near the pull-off on your right stating that you are in the village of Alcove. The main fall is directly downstream and quite visible from the top of the bridge.

The two cascades can be viewed by looking upstream from the bridge.

Fall at Alcove, circa 1910.

From Albany (junction of I-787 and Rt. 9W), drive south on Rt. 9W for 1.5 miles. When Rtes. 9W and 32 divide at a fork in the road, continue straight onto Rt. 32 and drive southwest for nearly 14 miles. When you reach the junction of Rtes. 143 and 32, turn left onto Rt. 143 and drive south for 2.8 miles. At Coeyman's Hollow, turn right onto Rt. 111 and then drive uphill for 0.4 mile to Alcove.

57. Fall near Alcove Reservoir

Location: Near Alcove (Albany County)
NYS Atlas & Gazetteer: p. 66, D2
Accessibility: Roadside

Description: This waterfall is formed on a tiny creek that issues from a small pond east of the Alcove Reservoir. The stream drops over a 6-foot-high, broad ledge at the terminus of a short ravine, and then quickly dissipates as its waters flow into the Alcove Reservoir a short distance downstream from the fall.

Directions: *From Ravena* (junction of Rtes. 9W and 143), drive west on Rt. 143 for 6.1 miles to Coeymans Hollow (junction of Rtes. 143 and 111). From there, continue northwest on Rt. 143 for another 2.3 miles. Look for a pull-off on your right. The fall can be readily seen from roadside.

From Albany (junction of I-787 and Rt. 9W), drive south on Rt. 9W for 1.5 miles. At a fork in the road, where Rt. 9W and Rt. 32 split, continue straight onto Rt. 32 and drive southwest for nearly 14 miles. When you reach the junction of Rtes. 143 and 32, turn left on Rt. 143 and drive south for 0.5 mile. The pull-off and fall will be on your left.

Keep your expectations low; this stream has minimal flow in the summer.

58. Dickinson Falls

Location: Alcove (Albany County)
NYS Atlas & Gazetteer: p. 52, A2
Accessibility: Roadside

Description: Dickinson Falls is a fairly robust waterfall formed on Hannacroix Creek, a medium-sized stream that rises in the hills to the west of Clarksville and flows into the Hudson River south of Coeymans. The waterfall is 30 feet high, but looks even taller from a distance.[1] It is located only a short distance upstream from the Alcove Reservoir.

History: Dickinson Falls is named after a famous eighteenth-century Presbyterian preacher named Jonathan Dickinson. Dickinson was a leader in the "Great Awakening" and a co-founder and first president of what would become Princeton University.

Like many other waterfalls in the area, Dickinson Falls was once heavily industrialized. Old foundations abound near the top and base of the fall, but can no longer be accessed because the land is posted and closely monitored.

The Alcove Reservoir was created in the first third of the twentieth century when reservoir building was at its peak in upstate New York. The Sacandaga Reservoir (now called the Great Sacandaga Lake), Ashokan Reservoir, Neversink Reservoir, Pepacton Reservoir, Schoharie Reservoir, Cannonsville Reservoir, and Rondout Reservoir were all constructed during roughly the same period of time as the Alcove Reservoir.

Directions: *From Ravena* (junction of Rtes. 9W and 143), drive west on Rt. 143 for nearly 9 miles. At the junction of Rtes. 143 and 32, next to the Alcove Reservoir, turn left and follow Rtes. 143/32 for 1.5 miles. Look for the fall to your left as you drive up a long hill 0.3 mile from where Carr Road comes in on the right.

From Albany (junction of I-787 and Rt. 9W), drive south on Rt. 9W for 1.5 miles. At a fork in the road, where Rt. 9W and Rt. 32 split, continue straight onto Rt. 32 and drive southwest for nearly 14 miles. When you reach the junction of Rtes. 143 and 32, bear right onto Rt. 143/32 and drive southwest for 1.5 mile.

Although Dickinson Falls is not directly accessible, it is partially visible through the trees from roadside. The waterfall is on land posted by the City of Albany. Do not attempt to directly access the fall under any circumstances. The reservoir has been heavily patrolled since September 11, 2001, and trespassers are prosecuted. Obey the posted signs and stay on the road. For the best views, visit in the early spring or late fall when the trees are fairly barren.

59. Lobdell Mill Falls

Location: South of Westerlo (Albany County)
NYS Atlas & Gazetteer: p. 66, D1
Accessibility: Roadside

Description: Lobdell Mill Falls is a 12-foot-high waterfall formed on Basic Creek, a medium-sized stream that rises in the hills northwest of Westerlo and flows into Catskill Creek near Freehold. The waterfall is fairly broad and horseshoe-shaped.

Near roadside is a short sluiceway at the top of the fall, where water was formerly diverted to power a small mill. The foundation walls of this mill are still partially visible near the base of the waterfall. One can surmise that the top of the waterfall must have been dammed at one time, for the sluiceway would not have been able to work unless the water was at an elevation several feet higher than its present level. The reinforced bank along the stream's side wall suggests that this indeed was the case.

History: An historic marker across the road from the fall states that a mill was first established on this site by Lobdell and Baker in 1795. The marker also mentions that the area was named Westerlo after the Reverend Eilardus Westerlo, minister of the First Dutch Reformed Church in Albany.

There is conjecture that the name "Basic Creek" may have arisen from the Dutch word *bezig,* meaning "busy." Since the Dutch pronounce their "e" like an "a," and their "g" like a harder-sounding "k," it seems reasonable to assume that *bezig* would have sounded like "basic" to non-Dutch speakers.[1] Certainly the stream would have fit the description of "busy" with its numerous mills in continuous operation.

Directions: From Ravena (junction of Rtes. 9W and 143), take Rt. 143 west for nearly 9 miles until you reach the junction of Rtes. 143 and 32 next to the Alcove Reservoir. Turn left onto Rtes. 143/32 and drive west for 2.3 miles, At the point where Rtes. 143 and 32 divide, go right on Rt. 143 and drive west for 3.4 miles until you reach Westerlo (junction of Rtes. 143 and 401). Turn left onto Rt. 401 and drive south for 1.2 miles. Then turn left onto Lobdell Mill Road and drive east for 0.4 mile. You will see the fall to your right as you cross over a small bridge spanning Basic Creek.

Take note that the land by the waterfall is posted; stay at roadside.

As you drive back up Lobdell Mill Road and turn right onto Rt. 401, you will see a small cascade down in the stream below. (Take note, however, that this cascade is also on posted land.)

60. Falls #1 at Partridge Run: Partridge Run Road

Location: Partridge Run Wildlife Management Area (Albany County)

NYS Atlas & Gazetteer: p. 65, D7

Accessibility: 0.2-mile walk along old road; quick scramble into ravine

Degree of Difficulty: Easy to moderate

Description: There are two pretty waterfalls formed on a small stream that rises from White Birch Pond. The stream eventually flows into the Switz Kill at some distance downstream from the falls. The first waterfall is an 8-foot drop into a pretty glen. The second, just downstream from the first, is a 12-foot cascade that gushes into a lovely, deep pool of water.

The falls are contained in the Partridge Run Wildlife Management Area, a 6,000-acre nature preserve containing woods, fields, ponds, streams, and over 40 miles of trails and roads.[1] From Partridge Run, the stream forming the two falls descends over 1,000 feet before reaching the village of Berne.[2] The lands contained at Partridge Run are found at a fairly high elevation, with Henry Hill being not only the highest point in the preserve (at an elevation of 2,160 feet), but also the highest point in the entire Helderbergs.[3]

History: The land encompassing the falls was originally part of Rensselaerswyck, a huge tract of land owned by Kiliaen Van Rensselaer, a wealthy Dutch patroon of the 1600s. In the nineteenth century, settlers vainly tried to farm the land. Later, some farmers did manage to eke out a living by raising sheep and producing woolen goods. By the 1930s, however, even the most determined settlers had abandoned their farms.

The Civilian Conservation Corp was brought in to plant hundreds of acres of red pine and spruce in order to bring back the land. They also created two small lakes—White Birch Pond and Fawn Lake. In 1962 the property was turned over to the New York State Department of Environmental Conservation (ENCON) so that it might be preserved.

Directions: From Albany (junction of I-90 and Rt. 85), drive southwest on Rt. 85 for roughly 4 miles to New Scotland Road. Turn right onto New Scotland Road and follow Rt. 85 for approximately 10 miles as it passes through New Scotland and New Salem, finally reaching

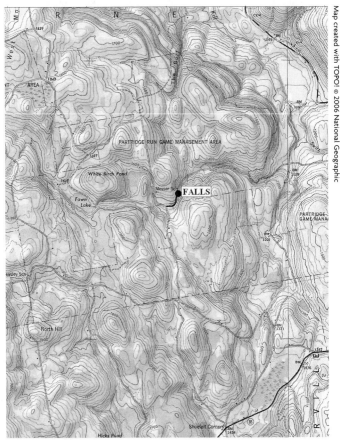

Rt. 443 outside of Clarksville. Turn right onto Rtes. 85 and 443, and proceed west. When you get to a fork in the road at 2.0 miles from the junction of Rtes. 85 and 443, bear to the left on Rt. 85 as Rt. 443 veers to the right. Continue southwest on Rt. 85 for roughly 9 miles further. When you come to Rt. 6, which is 0.9 mile north of the village of Rensselaerville, turn right onto Rt. 6 and drive north for 2.6 miles. Look for a gravel road going off to the right at the point where blue-colored DEC markers and signs for Partridge Run can be seen.

Park there, then follow Partridge Run Road for 0.1 mile to the first waterfall, which will be on your right as you crest the top of a hill. The second waterfall is 0.05 mile further downstream, just behind a tiny hillock on your right, which prevents you from seeing the waterfall immediately from the road.

61. Falls #2 at Partridge Run: Redbelly Trail

Location: Partridge Run Wildlife Area Management
(Albany County)
NYS Atlas & Gazetteer: p. 65, D7
Accessibility: Less than 0.1-mile hike, half of which is an easy bushwhack
Degree of Difficulty: Moderate

Description: There are a number of falls formed on a small stream that rises in the hills north of White Birch Pond and flows into the stream paralleling Partridge Run Road. In descending order, they are: a 6-foot-high cascade, immediately followed by a 4-foot-high cascade; an old stone dam; several small falls and cascades; then, at the brink of an abyss, a 12-foot fall, immediately followed by two, 6-foot-high cascades. It is a very dynamic and scenic area.

Look carefully for a scattering of foundation ruins between the dam and top of the falls.

Directions: Follow the same directions given in previous chapter (Falls #1 at Partridge Run) to reach the junction of Rtes. 85 and 6. Turn right onto Rt. 6, exactly 0.9 mile before you reach Rensselaerville. Drive north for 3.4 miles. At the intersection of Rtes. 6 and 13, turn right into a parking area opposite Rt. 13.

Follow the Redbelly Snowmobile Trail (an old road). It immediately parallels a stream, which will be on your left. Within a hundred feet you will see a 6-foot-high cascade in the stream below, which is immediately followed by a smaller, 4-foot-high cascade. After another hundred feet, the old road begins to pull away from the stream as the creek veers off to the left. A very short bushwhack is now required. Follow the creek as it proceeds downstream. Within a couple of hundred feet, you will encounter a massive, three-foot-wide breached stone dam. Just downstream can be seen several

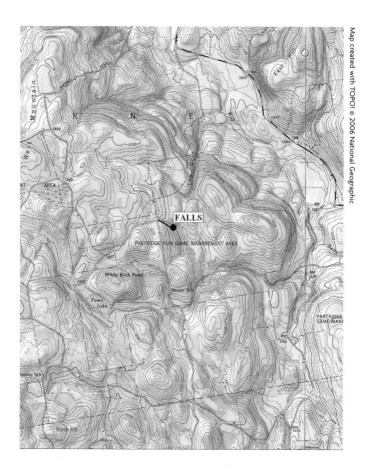

small cascades that lead up to a precipitous drop where the stream plunges into the valley below. This drop consists of a 12-foot-high cascade, followed by two, 6-foot-high drops, with the stream ending up far below on the valley floor.

If you desire to see the falls from the bottom of the valley, it is best to cross the stream at some distance above the falls and then make your way down a moderate slope along the north bank to the bottom. The slope along the south bank is too steep and difficult to easily negotiate.

62. Rensselaerville Falls

Location: Rensselaerville (Albany County)
NYS Atlas & Gazetteer: p. 65, D7
Accessibility: 0.1-mile walk to base of fall, with little elevation change; 0.3–0.4-mile hike to top of fall, with moderate change in elevation
Degree of Difficulty: Easy to base of falls; moderate to top of falls

Description: Rensselaerville Falls is formed on Ten Mile Creek, a medium-sized stream that rises from Lake Myosotis and merges with Catskill Creek near Oak Hill. The waterfall consists of a series of stair-case drops and cascades totaling over 100 feet in height.[1-3] The falls are composed of Devonian sandstone, siltstone, and shale.[4] Small footbridges provide an attractive crossing just downstream from the base of the fall, and across its top.

Lake Myosotis, which was artificially created around 1800 to ensure that a consistent supply of water would be available to power the numerous mills and factories that once populated Rensselaerville, is 0.3 mile upstream from Rensselaerville Falls. Myosotis is the botanical term for the flowers we know as forget-me-nots.

Downstream from the Rt. 353 bridge can be seen a 6-foot-high dam, followed by a series of cascades and ledge drops as Ten Mile Creek continues its rapid descent downhill. A long wooden conduit along the north bank leads directly to the old gristmill that now serves as the site of the Rensselaerville Historical Society.

History: The falls are located in the Edmund Niles Huyck Preserve, a 2,000-acre private sanctuary established in 1931 for biological research and nature appreciation. The initial grant of land was given by Huyck's widow after his death in 1930.

Rensselaerville has a rather remarkable history. At one time it was the mercantile capital of this area and was the only town beside Albany to be listed as a principal city in Albany county.

Upper section of Rensselaerville Falls, circa 1920.

At the top of Rensselaerville Falls, circa 1910.

At the base of Rensselaerville Falls can be seen the stone foundation of one of the first felt mills in North America, built in 1870 and owned by Frances Conkling Huyck and Henry Waterbury.

Directions: From Albany (junction of 1-90 and Rt. 85), take Rt. 85 southwest to its terminus at Rensselaerville, a drive of approximately 27 miles. At the end of Rt. 85, turn right onto Rt. 353 and proceed west for 0.1 mile. You will come to a bridge spanning Ten Mile Creek. Instead of crossing over the bridge, continue straight ahead into a tiny parking area for the Edmund Niles Huyck Preserve.

To Main Falls: From the rear of the parking area, follow Ten Mile Creek upstream for 0.1 mile. Excellent views of the lower and midsection of Rensselaerville Falls can be obtained from the footbridge spanning the creek. After you have crossed over the footbridge, you can follow a short, well-defined trail along the south bank, which leads quickly up to a closer view of the waterfall.

If you stay on the main, red-on-yellow blazed trail, ascending uphill, you will eventually come back down to Ten Mile Creek directly at the top of Rensselaerville Falls, where a second attractive footbridge spans the creek. From the footbridge you can look down into the gorge, but only partially, because of the ravine's shape. If you continue across to the other side of the bridge, the 10-foot-high, block-shaped waterfall that lies directly below the footbridge is more easily seen and appreciated.

On your return trip there is a spur trail worth taking. After you pass by the junction for the Lake Trail and Pond Hill Road, take your first left, an unmarked trail. This trail quickly leads over to the earthen remains of an old sluiceway that once carried water down from the Waterbury Dam at the top of Rensselaerville Falls to the felt mill at the base of the fall.

To Lower Falls: There are also a number of falls downstream from the parking lot. Walk across the road and look down from the top of the bridge. You will see a 6-foot-high dam above a couple of cascades. You will also observe an old wooden conduit on the left bank. This brought water down to the old Grist Mill, which now houses the Rensselaerville Historical Society. There are good views of the dam-created fall and cascades from the side of the Grist Mill, and from inside the building during the hours when it is open to the public.

It is also possible to look at several more falls directly below the gristmill. From the parking lot, walk or drive downhill on Rt. 353/351 for nearly 0.3 mile and turn right onto Bennet Lane. The road quickly ends at a dirt road that parallels Ten Mile Creek. If you are driving, turn left and park at what appears to be a parking area for public fishing. Walk back on the dirt road, following the creek upstream. In less than 0.1 mile you will see three cascades ahead, the highest one being next to the gristmill.

Take note that you cannot walk much farther up the road before it turns into a private driveway.

63. Cascades on Inlet Stream to Lake Myosotis

Location: Rensselaerville (Albany County)
NYS Atlas & Gazetteer: p. 65, D7
Accessibility: 0.5-mile walk along old roads, with 0.2-mile bush-whack as you follow a small creek upstream; some change in elevation
Degree of Difficulty: Moderate

Description: This cascade is formed on a small stream that rises from a swampy area west of Rensselaerville and flows into Lake Myosotis within 0.6 mile from the swamp. The waterfall consists of two tiers totaling 20 feet in height.

Directions: From Albany, take Rt. 85 to Rensselaerville, a distance of approximately 27 miles. As indicated in the previous chapter ("Rens-selaerville Falls"), park in the tiny lot next to the biological research station at the Edmund Niles Huyck Preserve.

Proceeding on foot, walk upstream on the trail paralleling Ten Mile Creek for 0.1 mile. You will cross over a pretty footbridge that spans the creek directly in front of Rensselaerville Falls. Continue following the red-on-yellow blazed trail as it climbs uphill and then curves around towards the top of Rensselaerville Falls.

Within 0.3 mile you will come to a junction where the Lake Trail continues straight ahead and Pond Hill Road goes to the right. Follow the Lake Trail west for over 0.1 mile. When you come to a second junction, take the trail to the left again, which heads towards Lincoln Pond. After 0.1 mile you will come to a stream that flows into Lake Myosotis (visible in the distance off to your right). It is this stream that bears the cascade.

Follow the creek upstream for 0.2 mile, bushwhacking—but only in the sense that you are following the contour of the top of the ravine, and not a marked trail. The dirt road on your left, which initially parallels the stream, quickly pulls away as it heads south up to Rt. 353. Persevere and you will soon reach the waterfall. Although this is a bushwhack, there is no way you can get lost if you stay next to the stream.

It is also possible to access the falls fairly expeditiously from Rt. 353. From the parking lot for the Edmund Niles Huyck Preserve, drive west on Rt. 353 for 0.7 mile. Look for an old grass-covered road that goes off into the woods on your right. Park the car off the road here. Take note of the preserve's posted signs, which state that no motor vehicles, guns, bows, or traps are allowed, and that the public assumes all risks upon entering the preserve.

Walk down the road for several hundred feet. Then enter the woods to your left and bushwhack over to the top of the ravine, which is several hundred feet away. You should come out close to the falls, which can then be accessed with a modicum of effort if you scamper down the sloping ravine to the streambed below.

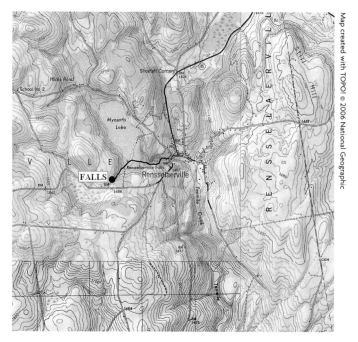

64. Falls at Berne

Location: Berne (Albany County)
NYS Atlas & Gazetteer: p. 65, CD7
Accessibility: Less than 0.05-mile walk, following short, tiny paths from the park that lead to different sections of the stream
Hours: The Fox Creek Park is open until dusk
Degree of Difficulty: Easy

Description: There is a series of small falls that have formed on Fox Creek, a medium-sized stream that rises near Helderberg Lake and flows into Schoharie Creek near Vroman Corners.[1] The waterfalls are located in Fox Creek Park, which is run by the Town of Berne.

The first two falls are located just downstream from the Rt. 443 bridge and are 10 feet and 5 feet in height, respectively. The falls are contained in a small gorge where potholes and much erosion of the limestone bedrock are evident. Within several hundred feet can be seen three other falls, roughly 3 feet, 5 feet, and 8 feet in height, respectively. Old foundation stones are visible at several sites along the stream.

If you look upstream from the east side of the Rt. 443 bridge, you will observe a succession of tiny falls below a small dam. This part of the stream has been massively altered, its walls encased in concrete and stone to form a sluiceway.

History: According to Robert M. Toole, "The Foxkill which thunders past East Berne provided the power used to grind local wheat into flour."[2] The first mill, located near today's Rt. 443 bridge, was constructed in 1750 by Jacob Wiedman. Downstream from the intersection of Rtes. 443 and 156, a carding and fulling mill were erected by Malachi Whipple, William H. Bell, and Lyman Dwight.

According to a roadside historic marker along Rt. 156, an ax factory was established by Daniel Simmons in 1825 and was reputed to be the first factory in the United States to make axes from cast steel. Simmons was a blacksmith who had moved from Albany in order to use the greater waterpower furnished by Fox Creek. His mill, which included a variety of triphammers and grindstones, churned out 600 axes a day as well as a number of other edged tools. Nevertheless, by 1849, Simmons had relocated again, this time to Cohoes because of its closer proximity to the Hudson and Mohawk waterways.

Berne was originally settled in 1750 by Palatines of German stock. The town was at first spelled "Bern," like the capital of Switzerland. A century later the "e" was added at the end.

Directions: From Albany, take Rt. 443 west until you reach the hamlet of Berne (junction of Rtes. 156 and 443); this will be roughly 7 miles west from the intersection of Rtes. 85S and 443W. Turn left onto Rt. 443, cross over Fox Creek, and immediately turn right onto a little road that takes you right down to the Fox Creek Park. Park in the lowermost area. Excellent views of the falls can be obtained from along the south bank.

Falls at Berne, circa 1900.

Poem Number One

Where the sun on water glinted
I saw coins of foamy white.

From the falls these coins were minted—
In the pool they caught the light.

Ceaselessly these coins revolved
Round where water roiled there,

So remaining uninvolved
Till they reached the boulders where

Lines of liquid ribbon fell
Making cataracts descend

Drowning all in swollen swell
All the way to the river bend.

From *forty falls* © 2003 by Chuck Gibson

Waterfalls of the
Schoharie Valley

Introduction

The name "Schoharie" is from the Native American *Skoharje*, for "driftwood" or "flood wood," and goes back far into time.[1] Long before European settlers set foot on the continent, the Native Americans of the Schoharie Valley were living near the confluence of the Little Schoharie, Line Kill, and Schoharie creeks, near present-day Middleburgh. Receding floodwaters from these streams left behind huge piles of driftwood every spring, and it was from this mass of driftwood that the name "Schoharie" arose.

The Schoharie Valley is dominated by Schoharie Creek, an 89-mile-long stream that rises over one-half mile northwest of a little pond at Platte Clove,[2] high in the Catskill Mountains, and descends over 2,500 feet to its confluence with the Mohawk River by Fort Hunter. It is the only major stream in the eastern Allegheny Plateau that drains across the Helderberg scarp in a northward direction. Schoharie Creek initially carved out a valley 700 feet wide in the plain. Over many thousands of years, the valley widened to a breadth of between 1–1.5 miles. When geological forces raised the plain up higher, Schoharie Creek began carving out a second valley within the one already created, cutting down as deeply as 200 feet. This valley gorge within Schoharie Valley is not visible today because the glaciers filled it in with debris as they retreated northward at the end of the last ice age. The Schoharie Creek today is still in the process of cutting through the fill and re-excavating this ancient streambed.

In this respect the Schoharie Creek is by no means unique. Virtually all of the major streams in this region at one time or another possessed valleys that were 50 to 200 feet deeper than their present levels, and are busily in the process of trying to remove all of the fill that the glaciers deposited.

The Schoharie Creek's principal tributaries entering from the west are Cobleskill Creek, Line Kill, Panther Creek, West Creek, and Mine Kill. Entering from the east are Fox Creek, Little Schoharie Creek, Stony Brook, Keyser Kill, Platten Kill, and Manor Kill.

In prehistoric times Schoharie Valley contained a massive body of water called Lake Schoharie. The lake was fed by melting glaciers as sheets of ice over one mile high began retreating northward at the end of the last ice age. It is because of the past existence of this glacial lake and the sedimentation left behind from the Wisconsin deglaciation that the land in the Schoharie Valley is so unusually fertile.

The first white settlers that arrived in the valley in the early 1700s were of German and Dutch descent. Taking advantage of the rich soil, they set up large tracts of farmlands and began producing crops, which grew in abundance.

By the mid-1700s, as the struggle between the colonists and the British erupted into outright war, the valley became known as the "Breadbasket of the American Revolution," producing over 80,000 bushels of wheat a year for General George Washington's Continental Army. By the 1880s there were over 70 mills in the valley grinding grains, sawing lumber, and turning out a wide variety of other products.[3]

It was inevitable that roads would follow the natural architecture of the valley. The main highway paralleling Schoharie Creek is Route 30, which passes by a number of small but historically significant towns that grew up along the river. In 1970, Rt. 30 became more colorfully known as the "Timothy Murphy Trail," in honor of the famous sharpshooter and soldier who lived in the area in the 1700s. Murphy is credited with mortally wounding British General Fraser at

Schoharie Valley, circa 1930.

the Battle of Saratoga in 1777, an incident that contributed immeasurably to the final outcome of the battle.[4]

Schoharie County contains a variety of fascinating natural wonders, including Howe Caverns—the largest commercialized cave in the northeastern United States (McFail's Cave in Carlisle, at 6.7 miles in length, is the largest undeveloped cave in this region)—and Secret Caverns, which contains a stupendous, 100-foot-high underground waterfall.

Vromans Nose (called by Native Americans *Onistagrawa*, or "corn mountain"), located just southwest of Middleburgh, is a small mountain with high ledges that provide superb views of the fertile flatlands of the valley.

65. Falls on Wilsey Creek

Location: Burtonsville (Montgomery County)
NYS Atlas & Gazetteer: p. 65, B6
Accessibility: Roadside; 0.05-mile walk to side view of falls

Description: This medium-sized waterfall is formed on Wilsey Creek, a small stream that rises southwest of Lost Valley and flows into Schoharie Creek north of Burtonsville.[1-2] Wilsey Creek has also been known as Wilsey Mill Creek.[3]

The waterfall is approximately 25–30 feet high and located just below a small bridge spanning Wilsey Creek. The fall consists of several drops, the main one being 15 feet high.

Directly upstream from the bridge is a 5-foot-high ledge cascade, and slightly above that is an even smaller, 2-foot-high fall.

The falls are contained in the 198-acre Schoharie Creek Preserve located on the south side of the bridge. The preserve is managed by the Mohawk-Hudson Land Conservancy.[4] The land was donated by doctors Lester Citrin and Clifford Tepper.[5]

History: Burtonsville is named after Judah Burton who operated a gristmill on nearby Colyer Road. The area was settled after the Revolutionary War and, in addition to Burton's mill, had a woolen mill, nail factory, tannery, and lumber mill.[6] As you cross over Schoharie Creek and enter Burtonsville, look to your left and you will see an upright millstone that was taken from Burton's mill.

Directions: From Amsterdam (junction of Rtes. 30 and 5S), drive south on Rt. 30 for about 10 miles. When you come to Braman Corners, where Rt. 30 bears sharply to the left, go straight onto Braman Corners Road and proceed west (downhill). At 1.9 miles you will cross over Schoharie Creek. When you reach the hamlet of Burtonsville at the end of the bridge (at roughly 2.1 miles), turn right onto

Colyer Road and drive north for 0.8 mile. Then turn right onto Butler Road and follow it downhill for 0.5 mile until you reach a tiny bridge. Park immediately to the right of the bridge after crossing it.

If you are approaching from the south, drive northeast from Esperance (junction of Rtes. 30 and 20 just east of town) for 3.6 miles, and then turn left (west) onto Braman Corners Road. Continue from there as above.

The top of the fall is clearly visible from the bridge, as are the smaller falls upstream.

The waterfall can also be easily seen from along the top of the bank. For this view, walk south across the bridge and down the road for 30 feet to where the guardrail ends, and then follow a path uphill, paralleling the stream, traversing land that is managed by the Mohawk-Hudson Land Conservancy. Fairly decent views of the fall can be obtained through the tree line along the top of the ravine.

It is not recommended that you continue farther on this path. A short distance later the trail continues along a knife edge, with Wilsey Creek dropping off sharply to your left and Schoharie Creek precipitously to your right. The Schoharie Creek is not only very wide at this point, but also very shallow. Parts of this path are only several feet wide. This is definitely not an area to hike with children.

Additional Point of Interest: As you cross over Schoharie Creek into Burtonsville, turn left immediately at the end of the bridge. A short road will lead you down to a parking area next to the bridge, where you'll find the massive stonework of an old, abandoned bridge. If you look upstream, you can see a number of tiny cascades, each probably no greater than 1–2 feet in height. Burmeister mentions that if you go a distance upstream from the Burtonsville Bridge, "swift water cascades over a series of four ledges arranged layer-like in a spiral staircase formation."[7]

66. Waterfall at Secret Caverns

Location: Howes Cave (Schoharie County)
NYS Atlas & Gazetteer: p. 65, C5
Accessibility: Less than 0.2-mile walk through a descending underground passageway
Hours: Open daily mid-April through Nov. 1; hours vary (check Web site)
Fee: Check Web site for fee schedule (www.secretcaverns.com/)
Degree of Difficulty: Easy. The cave is a commercial attraction and has been modified to make the passageway easily negotiated.

Description: What makes the waterfall at Secret Caverns so unique is that it is located entirely underground. Approximately 1000 feet from the entrance to the caverns is a 100-foot-high waterfall, originating from a swampy area on the lands above, that plummets into the cavern through a high dome.[1] From there, the waters flow into the Lost River—the main stream forming the cave.

The waterfall, although beautiful, is not naturally formed. Its waters are controlled by the management of Secret Caverns and released from the swampy area above the dome[2-3]—one of the "secrets" of Secret Caverns.

History: Secret Caverns was developed as a commercial attraction in 1929 by Roger H. Mallery. What Mallery attempted to offer was a more natural feeling of wilderness caving than the experience afforded at Howe Caverns, Secret Cavern's nearby rival. Unlike Howe Caverns, which takes you down 160 feet into the cave by an elevator through a man-made shaft, Secret Caverns allows you to enter the cave through its natural entrance and work your way in. With its narrow passageways and less "high-tech" look, Secret Caverns is more like what you would find in a non-commercialized cave in northeastern New York State.

According to Marilyn Milow Francis: "The caverns in this area were formed largely during the last ice age, when titanic waterfalls, pouring off the glaciers, bored great holes (potholes) into the ground. Whenever these potholes were forced into a crevice, the water worked its way through that opening into the valley below, forming the caverns that exist today."[4] Those early days as the glaciers retreated must have been awesome, indeed.

Additional Point of Interest: While you are in the area, stop in at the Caverns Creek Grist Mill, which was built in 1816 and is now on the National Register of Historic Places. The gristmill provides the rare opportunity of seeing a working water-powered mill in operation—complete with a mill race, millstone, and waterwheel. The mill is open daily from Memorial Day through Labor Day; weekends only in May, September, and October.[5]

Directions: From the NYS Thruway (I-90), get off at exit 25A for Schenectady and Binghamton and proceed southwest on I-88. If you pay close attention, you will see a pretty waterfall on your left along I-88 approximately 4.5 miles from Duanesburg. Get off I-88 at Exit 23 for Central Bridge and Schoharie, and turn right onto Rt. 30A. You will immediately come to Rt. 7. Turn left onto Rt. 7 and drive west for 4.5 miles, going through the village of Central Bridge in the process. Turn right onto Cave Road and drive uphill for 1.1 miles. Then turn right and follow Caverns Road (Rt. 9) for 1.5 miles. The entrance to Secret Caverns will be directly on your left, with the site's multi-colored building clearly visible from roadside.[6] The cavern is open daily from May to October.

Don't be too concerned about missing a turn or two on the way to Secret Caverns. Once you arrive at Central Bridge, multiple billboards and signs dot the road, continuously pointing the way to both Secret Caverns and Howe Caverns.

Secret Caverns has its own waterfall. Postcard circa 1930.

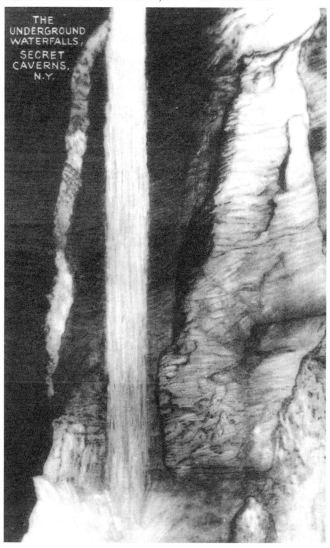

67. Cave Waterfalls

As a general rule, waterfalls above ground are not likely to form in areas where caves are plentiful. This is because caverns divert water underground, preventing surface streams from maintaining sufficient hydropower to generate waterfalls.

The question then becomes: how likely is it to find waterfalls inside caves where surface streams have been pirated underground? Generally speaking, there are few caves in eastern New York State that contain waterfalls of any significant size. Secret Caverns is an exception to this rule, but its waterfall is actually artificially created. Still, there are a number of area caves that do contain waterfalls of varying sizes, although the term "waterfall" may not always have the same meaning below ground as above. Cavers tend to use hyperbole when describing underground wonders. When they speak of underground lakes, for example, they are generally referring to cave passages filled with water, and these passages tend to be narrow. Likewise, when they talk about waterfalls, they may be referring to a drop in the streambed of only a foot or two. The only major exceptions are in vertical caves, where larger waterfalls can form as the stream drops through a pit or dome as it makes it way down into the bowels of the Earth.

Most waterfalls formed underground have a look and feel that is totally different from any on the surface of the Earth: they are entombed by rock, imprisoned in stygian darkness, and engulfed by an unearthly stillness.

Not all cave-related waterfalls form inside the cave. Some are fashioned in sinkholes—surface features created when a stream runs into a hole in the ground. The waterfall is formed as the stream plummets over the lip of the sinkhole and plunges into the darkness below.

If you're interested in exploring caves and seeking out underground waterfalls, it is important that you join a local caving club, or "grotto" as they are known. By caving under the auspices of a caving organization, you avoid the unpleasant and sometimes dangerous pitfalls that novices are subjected to as they learn through trial and error. You will also learn about the aesthetics of caving. Most importantly, you will learn where the accessible caves are. Below is contact information for two local organizations:

Helderberg-Hudson Grotto
PO Box 804
Schoharie, NY 12157

Rensselaer Outing Club
Attn: Caving Chair
RPI Student Union
Troy, NY 12180

Following is a selection of cave sites with underground waterfalls worth visiting once you have been initiated into a caving club.[1]

Onesquethaw Cave
This well-known cave is located in Albany County and contains a tiny waterfall near its entrance. Onesquethaw Cave achieved notoriety after several cavers almost drowned in 1993 when a dam two miles distant gave way and flooded the cave.

Stair Step Shafts Cave
Stair Step Shafts Cave is located in Herkimer County and consists of a series of horizontal passageways combined with vertical drops totaling 110 feet in relief. A stream runs through the cave, and the waterfalls form at various drops. Wetsuits and experience in vertical cave climbing are mandatory if you want to see these falls.

Howe Waterfall Pit
This pit can be found in the town of Howes Cave in Schoharie County and consists of a tiny stream running into a deep sinkhole. There is no real cave, but there is a waterfall.

McFail's Cave
Located in Schoharie County, McFail's Cave is a "caver's cave" and cannot be entered except by permission from the NSS (the National Speleological Society). You will need to prove that you are competent

in vertical caving, and must be accompanied by an experienced leader. There is a notable waterfall at the beginning of the cave, which drops down a 60-foot shaft.

Crane Mountain Cave

This is a good cave for intermediates. A crawl passageway leads to a drop-off point, where the initial waterfall forms. The cave contains an upper and lower waterfall, and is located in the vicinity of Warrensburg.

Benson's Cave

Benson's Cave is part of the Secret-Benson Cave system. Entrance is via one of two deep pits—Jolly Hole or Benson Pit. From there the passageway leads 800 feet to the junction with the Secret Caverns stream. One waterfall in the cave is approximately 4 feet high.

68. High Street Bridge Falls

Location: Richmondville (Schoharie County)
NYS Atlas & Gazetteer: p. 64, CD4
Accessibility: Roadside

Description: High Street Bridge Falls is formed on Bear Gulch Stream, which issues from Bear Gulch Pond southwest of Richmondville. The waterfall is 12 feet in height with a 3-foot dam at its top, which has impounded a small pond that forms just south of the bridge.[1] There is also a small cascade a short distance further downstream.

History: Bear Gulch was used as a Native American trail long before the arrival of Europeans.

Richmondville was named after George Richmond, an early settler.

At one time during the nineteenth century, as many as nine mills drew power from Bear Gulch Stream. The abandoned C. A. Bunn mill stands next to the falls, with the words "Flour, feed, seed, salt, and grain" emblazoned in big white letters on the back of the red building. This was a working mill until 1967. For 17 years prior to that, Maynard Tillapaugh used it to grind grain for his feed and grain store.[2] Hugging the east bank of the ravine are rusted pipes that once carried water from the dam to the mill. Directly under the mill are the remains of an old waterwheel (installed in 1916) and part of the sluiceway. The waterwheel was more than 21 feet in diameter and over 3 feet wide.

Directions: From I-90 (the NYS Thruway), get off at exit 25A for Schenectady and Binghamton and proceed southwest on I-88. After you have passed by Cobleskill and Warnerville, get off at Exit 20 for Richmondville. Follow the long exit ramp to a traffic light at Rt. 7, then turn right onto Rt. 7 and drive west for 0.9 mile into the village of Richmondville. Along the way, Rt. 7 becomes Main Street. At the traffic light in the center of town, turn left onto Summit Street and drive uphill, going south, for 0.1 mile. Then turn left onto High Street and drive over an old steel bridge, built in 1929, which crosses the stream near the top of the fall.

High Street Bridge Falls on Bear Gulch Stream, circa 1910.

Immediately to your left is an old deserted building. If you park in front of it, you can walk over to the northeast end of the bridge and see the cascade from the east bank. If you drive down to the bottom of the small hill next to the mill and park near the Town of Richmondville garage, you can walk up to the base of the building and see the dry, abandoned sluiceway and the old waterwheel.

In The Bear Gulf, Richmondville, N. Y.

Bear Gulch Stream, circa 1910.

69. Falls at Lasell Park

Location: Village of Schoharie (Schoharie County)
NYS Atlas & Gazetteer: p. 65, C6
Accessibility: Short hike
Hours: The park is open daily until 10 PM
Degree of Difficulty: Easy to moderate

Description: The falls in Lasell Park consist of a double ledge plunge over a high escarpment. The falls are formed on a tiny, unnamed stream that flows into Schoharie Creek in the village of Schoharie. The upper fall is 15 feet in height and the lower fall is 25 feet, dropping over a 40-foot-high limestone bluff.

Be sure to visit the falls following snowmelt or heavy rainfall; otherwise, the volume of water carried by the stream may be disappointingly small or nonexistent.

History: Lasell Park shares a common name with nearby Lasell Hall, which was built in 1795 and served at various times as a tavern, hat factory, boarding school, and the first library in Schoharie County.[1]

Additional Point of Interest: Lasell Park contains Beckers Cave, which is well known to the speleological community. The cave should be entered only if you are an experienced caver, well equipped, and accompanied by a party of three or more similarly equipped and capable cavers.

Directions: Going southwest on I-88 from the NYS Thruway (I-90), get off at Exit 23 for Schoharie and Central Bridge. Turn left onto Rt. 30A and drive south for 2.5 miles. Along the way, Rt. 30 enters from the left at 1.1 miles. When you reach the junction of Rtes. 30 and 443, just north of Schoharie, continue south on Rt. 30 for another 1.4 miles. In the village of Schoharie, turn left onto Spring Road. (If you are approaching Middleburgh from the south on Rt. 30, turn right onto Spring Road less than 0.3 mile after passing Bridge Street.) After driving uphill on Spring Road for 0.2 mile, turn left onto Warners Hill Road where the road divides, and continue northeast for less than 0.2 mile. The entrance to Lasell Park will be on your left.

Park off the road to the side and walk into the park past two stone pillars, less than 100 feet from Warners Hill Road. Follow a flight of stone stairs to your left, leading down to the base of the escarpment. At the bottom turn right and walk north along the base of the escarpment for less than 0.1 mile. Initially the walk involves

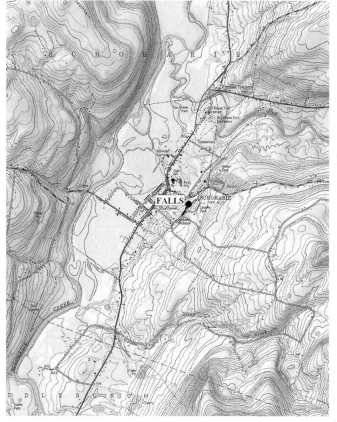

traversing across a sloping terrain. Very quickly, however, the ground levels out at a point where the bluff rises up vertically. In a moment or two you will come to the falls, directly to your right.

Lasell Park, circa 1900.

70. Falls on Little Schoharie Creek

Location: Huntersland (Schoharie County)
NYS Atlas & Gazetteer: p. 65, D6-7
Accessibility: Less than 0.1-mile walk
Fee: There is a modest day-use fee at the privately owned Waterfalls Campsite, which also offers picnicking and swimming. Campsites are available for an additional fee.
Degree of Difficulty: Easy

Description: There are two pretty waterfalls formed on Little Schoharie Creek, a medium-sized stream that rises in the hills east of Huntersland and flows into Schoharie Creek south of Middleburgh. The upper fall is 8 feet in height, but fairly flat, ending in a 3-foot plunge into a sizable swimming hole called "God's Bath Tub" by some of the locals.[1] The lower fall looks entirely different. This waterfall is very broad and clearly defined, dropping 8 feet into a lovely, deep pool.

There are small falls further upstream as well, but they are not part of the Waterfalls Campsite.

History: The area by the falls was once part of an old farm. Over the last 30 years it has been gradually converted into the campsite that you see today.

Huntersland was once a booming town, but has since declined. At one time the village had a number of businesses including a hotel (which occupied the site of the current library).

At the beginning of Huntersland Road, you will pass by a small cemetery on the side of a steep hill where the tombstone of Timothy Murphy, renowned Revolutionary War hero and frontiersman, can be seen.

Directions: From Middleburgh (junction of Rtes. 30 and 145S), drive south on Rt. 145 for 1.0 mile. Turn left onto Huntersland Road and drive east for 3.3 miles. When you reach the sign for the Waterfalls Campsite, turn right onto Waterfall Drive. The campsite office is directly to your right as you proceed downhill.

The Waterfall Campsite provides a rare opportunity to camp in a rustic area with two waterfalls and two natural swimming holes. The campsite also permits day use.

71. Bouck Falls (Historic)

Location: Near Breakabeen (Schoharie County)
Accessibility: The falls are located on private property and are not open to the public.

Description: Bouck Falls is a historically significant waterfall formed on Panther Creek, a medium-sized stream that rises from Rossman Pond and flows into Schoharie Creek near Max Shaul State Park. One author describes the waterfall as 25 feet wide and 100 feet high.[1] The fall consists of a series of nearly perpendicular drops and plunges encased in towering vertical walls of rock.[2-4] The bottom of Bouck Falls opens up into a large, deep swimming hole, still encased within the walls of the gorge.

History: The waterfall is named after former Governor William C. Bouck.[5, 6]

The Bouck Falls House is located at roadside near the top of the fall. It was built in 1856 and operated as a roadside inn.[7] Later, it was converted into a bar and then into a private residence, which it remains today. A wooden platform directly behind the house and overlooking the top of the falls speaks of times past when Bouck Falls was accessible to the public.

It is alleged that the famed "Indian fighter" Timothy Murphy once concealed himself behind the veil of the waterfall to hide from a pursuing war party.[8] This legend has been immortalized in a delightful epic poem entitled the *Ballad of Timothy Murphy*,[9] of which the following is but a small excerpt:

The foe closed in, and Murphy dashed
Beneath the shelf of Panther Falls;
Over his buckskin, water splashed
And muskrats sidled down the halls
Of sandstone where the bat wings thrashed
Against the evening's misty shawls.
Tim shivered in the damp till morn
And water soaked his powder horn.

When dawn intruded, Murphy saw
A figure shadowed in the mist;
Another climbed the Panther's jaw.
Tim picked John Johnson's royalist
As first to tumble from the maw
Of the rocky grotto, but a twist
Of the powder horn betrayed his debt
To fortune on the parapet.

You can make out what you will regarding the validity of these
stanzas, for legend also has it that Murphy once found himself
trapped in a hole so deep that he had to run back to his house to
get a shovel so that he could dig himself out of it. Still, unlike Paul
Bunyan, Murphy was a real-life, historical figure who actually *was*
a feared Indian fighter and a Morgan's Rifleman who distinguished
himself at the Battle of Saratoga by mortally wounding British General
Frasier.

Schoharie Valley was known as "the breadbasket of the American
Revolution," and sources claim that millstones used for grinding
grain by General George Washington's army were found in close
proximity to the gorge.[10]

72. Falls on Tributary to Panther Creek

Location: Near West Fulton (Schoharie County)
NYS Atlas & Gazetteer: p. 65, D5
Accessibility: 0.2-mile hike down a steeply inclined hill
Degree of Difficulty: Difficult, because of significant change in elevation and the steepness of trail

Description: There are over a dozen waterfalls of varying sizes formed on a small tributary to Panther Creek that rises from a small pond south of Rossman Hill Road and flows into Panther Creek southwest of West Fulton. Panther Creek subsequently discharges into Schoharie Creek near Max Shaul State Park.

The first cascade is 15 feet in height and encountered immediately as you start down the trail. Near the base of the waterfall is the intact stone foundation of an old gristmill. After a couple of hundred feet further, the waterfalls begin revealing themselves in seemingly unlimited numbers and continue without interruption until you have descended hundreds of vertical feet, covering a distance of well over 0.1 mile.

The first waterfall is 25 feet high, plunging vertically over a broad wall of shale. Immediately below, the stream drops again, this time down a 30-foot cascade into a deeply cut gorge. With only the slightest pause, the stream rapidly plunges another 12 feet down an overhanging ledge, and then drops 20 feet over a vertical drop. Each time you reach the next waterfall, the impression is that you are approaching the bottom of the hill, but each time the gorge continues, following the descending slope, with the aqua-blazed Long Trail paralleling the gorge close by.

The next fall is 8 feet high, followed immediately by a series of smaller falls and cascades totaling over 40 feet in height. But still the bottom has not been reached. You will encounter at least four or five more 5-foot-high ledge falls, one right after the other, ending in

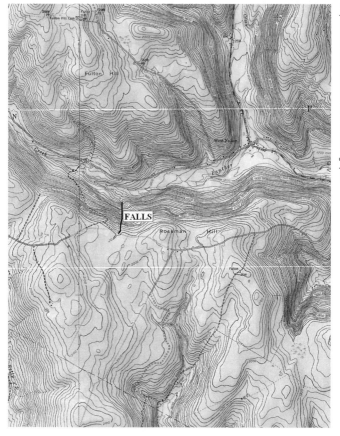

a 5-foot-high cascade. Just when you think you've finally reached the end, more falls materialize. Within another several hundred feet is a 15-foot ledge falls, finally ending in a 5-foot drop.

This really is the quintessential waterfall trail—a scaled down, miniature version of Ricketts Glen in Pennsylvania with its endless variety of waterfalls.

Directions: From Middleburgh (junction of Rtes. 30 and 145N), drive southwest on Rt. 30 for 6.3 miles. As soon as you pass by Max Shaul State Park and cross over Panther Creek, turn right onto West Fulton Road (Rt. 4) and proceed west for 2.1 miles. Then turn left onto Rossman Hill Road and continue west for roughly 2.8 miles. Look for the Long Path as it crosses Rossman Hill Road, over 0.1 mile after you pass by the Burnt-Rossman Hill State Forest sign. Park off to the right of the road close to the trail marker.

Follow the trail to your right, going north, downhill. You will immediately pass by a cascade and then the ruins of an old mill. From there, you will see one waterfall after another during a steep descent of almost 0.2 mile. The only disadvantage to this approach is that the successive waterfalls are encountered as you head downhill. The most exciting views will be as you hike back up.

If your wish is to see the waterfalls in reverse order, starting from the bottom and hiking up to the top, then an alternate route can be taken. From the intersection of Rossman Hill Road and West Fulton Road, continue straight on West Fulton Road (instead of turning left onto Rossman Hill Road) for another 1.8 miles. Then turn left onto Sawyer Hollow Road (Rt. 20) and proceed west for slightly over 1.2 miles. Turn into the small pull-off on your left for the Panther Creek Public Fishing Stream (an access point for fishermen).

Walk up the road for less than a hundred feet and you will see the aqua-blazed Long Trail. Follow the trail down a sloping hill. Within less than 0.1 mile you will reach the woods. Just before crossing over a stream, turn right onto the Long Trail. This can be easy to miss if you are not paying attention. Follow the trail, paralleling the stream, for 0.1 mile. You will come to a small footbridge that crosses over the creek. Beneath the bridge is a structure known as a "pool digger." Its purpose is to help put oxygen back into the water. A number of these can be found along the stream and were initially built in the 1940s by the Civilian Conservation Corps.[1] Continue uphill along the aqua-blazed trail for 0.3 mile until you reach the bottom of the first falls.

73. Krum's Falls

Location: Near Breakabeen (Schoharie County)
NYS Atlas & Gazetteer: p. 65, D5
Accessibility: Roadside; park at a distance from the no-parking signs and walk up to the bridge

Description: There are two midsized waterfalls that have formed in a deeply cut gorge on the Keyser Kill, a medium-sized stream that rises near Broome Center and flows into Schoharie Creek at Breakabeen. The stream is named after a family of farmers who occupied the lands in the early days.[1, 2] The falls have also been known as Butts Fall.

The tops of both waterfalls can be seen from a small bridge spanning the Keyser Kill. Each waterfall is roughly 15–20 feet high. Further downstream, nearly 0.5 mile from the upper two falls, is a third waterfall, approximately 20 feet in height. This fall is inaccessible, however.

Krum's Falls, circa 1910.

Falls on the Keyser Kill, circa 1910.

History: According to *Glacial Geology of the Catskills*, "The upper half of the valley of Keyser Kill might fairly be called The Valley of the Deltas." Eleven deltas were mapped ranging in elevation from 1,615 to 1,960 feet.[3] At one time there were five mills in operation on the Keyser Kill.[4]

The name of the small hamlet on the way to the falls, Breakabeen, is derived from the German word, *Breakaben*, meaning "covered with brakes or ferns" or "rushes that grew on the creek banks."[5, 6]

Additional Point of Interest: Max Shaul State Park is located at the foot of Toe Path Mountain and can be entered directly from Rt. 30, just a short distance north of Breakabeen. The park provides a natural setting for picnicking, and was named after Max V. Shaul, a prominent local farmer who died in 1980.

Directions: From Middleburgh (junction of Rtes. 30 and 145N) continue southwest on Rt. 30 for over 7.5 miles. Along the way you will pass by a sign on your right for the Max V. Shaul State Park. At Breakabeen turn left onto Clauverwie Road (Rt. 36). You will notice an historic marker stating: "Indian Trail: Keyserkill to Catskill Creek and Hudson River, connecting Hudson, Schoharie, Mohawk, Delaware and Susquehanna Valleys and the west." Drive east for 1.2 miles, then turn right onto Keyserkill Road (Rt. 17). After over 0.3 mile, turn right onto Guinea Road (Rt. 53). At 0.2 mile you will come to a bridge with a 15-ton weight limit, where the falls can be seen.

Park off to the side of the road before crossing over the bridge. From the west end of the bridge, you can obtain excellent views into the gorge and over the top of the two waterfalls.

Take note of the posted signs and remain on the road.

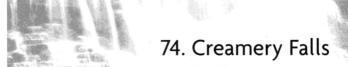

74. Creamery Falls

Location: North Blenheim (Schoharie County)
NYS Atlas & Gazetteer: p. 51, A5
Accessibility: Roadside

Description: This pretty, two-tiered waterfall is formed on Mill Creek, a small stream that rises east of Jefferson and flows into the West Kill at the base of the falls, roughly 0.1 mile upstream from the West Kill's confluence with Schoharie Creek. The falls are nearly 20 feet high and divided into two sections, with the upper section 10 feet in height and the lower 8 feet high.

History: The town of Blenheim (pronounced *blen´-him*) was named after the Battle of Blenheim in Bavaria.[1-3]

Directions: From Middleburgh (junction of Rtes. 30 and 145N) continue south on Rt. 30, heading toward the tiny hamlet of North Blenheim. At roughly 12 miles you will cross over Schoharie Creek. As soon as you come to West Kill Road on your right, continue south on Rt. 30 for another 0.1 mile and you will arrive at a bridge spanning the West Kill. Turn right onto Creamery Road just before crossing the bridge. The falls will be immediately to your left, visible from roadside, directly across the road from the Blenheim House (built in 1840), which is now a restaurant.

Additional Point of Interest: Approximately 12 miles south of the junction of Rtes. 30 and 145 in Middleburgh is the famous Blenheim Bridge, built in 1855 by Nicholas Powers.[4] At 232 feet in length, it was considered to be the longest single-span, wooden bridge of its kind in the world, containing 127 tons of wood and 5,100 pounds of bolts and washers. During its construction the bridge was known as "Powers' Folly," because skeptics were convinced that the bridge would collapse under its own weight once the supporting scaffolding was removed. Powers, however, was not dissuaded, and just to prove his point, sat on top of the bridge with his legs dangling as the false works were removed. The bridge stood, and has for another 150 years.

To get to the Blenheim Bridge: just before crossing Schoharie Creek on the way to North Blenheim and Creamery Falls, turn left onto East Side Road and drive for less than 0.1 mile to the bridge, which will be to your right.

The famous Blenheim Bridge, circa 1920.

75. Haverly Falls (Historic)

Location: North Blenheim (Schoharie County)
Accessibility: Inaccessible; located on private property

Description: Haverly Falls is a medium-sized waterfall formed on the West Kill just upstream from its confluence with Mill Creek.[1]

History: The waterfall is named after Seneca Haverly who established a gristmill at the falls around 1880.[2] Later, the mill's operation was taken over by West Haverly, Seneca's son. The building not only served as a gristmill, but also as a sawmill. Water to power the mill was carried in a 200-foot-long, 3-foot-wide wooden conduit from the top of the falls to the mill. The mill survived into the 1940s, at which time it was torn down. A private home is now located next to the fall.

Haverly Falls, circa 1910.

76. Mine Kill Falls

Location: Near North Blenheim (Schoharie County)
NYS Atlas & Gazetteer: p. 51, A5
Accessibility: 0.2-mile walk over uneven terrain, with small change in elevation
Hours: The park is open year round; closes daily at 5 PM
Degree of Difficulty: Easy to moderate

Description: Mine Kill Falls consists of three waterfalls formed on the Mine Kill, a medium-sized stream that rises in the hills north of South Jefferson and flows into Schoharie Creek a short distance downstream from the lowermost falls.[1-7]

The upper fall is 20 feet in height; the middle cascade is roughly 30 feet high; and the lower cascades are over 20 feet in height combined. Note that these are rough estimates made from the top of the gorge.

The falls are contained in the 500-acre Mine Kill State Park, which features a swimming pool and accommodations for fishing, boating, and hiking. The entrance to the main section of the park is 0.6 mile south of the Mine Kill Falls Overlook, so none of these facilities will be evident when you pull into the waterfall overlook section of the park.

According to the *New York State Museum Bulletin: Glacial Geology of the Catskills,* the "Mine Kill cascades into an older, partly drift-filled gorge"[8]—a reference to the fact that retreating glaciers 10,000 years ago filled the valley with glacial debris, in some places to a height of over 250 feet above the present level of the streambed. According to prominent Catskills geologist Robert Titus, the rocks are stratified, formed mostly out of shale and sandstone, and were deposited some 380 million years ago on the bottom of the Hamilton Sea, a fairly shallow ocean.[9]

History: Mine Kill State Park was originally built by the New York Power Authority, but is now operated under the auspices of the Saratoga Capital District State Park Commission.

An 1886 account written by one of the guests boarding in the home of Dr. Christopher Best of Broome Center provides an interesting insight into how the falls appeared nearly 150 years ago:

> We had just driven up to the Minekill bridge, that had been completed but two weeks. It is an iron bridge, and spans an abyss sixty feet deep, through which the water flows peacefully along, after rushing over rock after rock, forming in all, the picturesque Minekill Falls. As we stood on the bridge, we looked up to where a narrow stream flows over a precipice, on a ledge of rocks. Here it again falls, now surging over a descent of thirty feet, into what is known as the Devil's bedroom. It then falls again as a narrow stream, over another precipice, where the rocks seem almost to meet, there being just space enough, as you stand in the right position, to see the falls above. Here we see the most picturesque part, as the water falls over

Bridge over Upper Mine Kill Falls, circa 1900.

Lower Mine Kill Falls, circa 1900.

rocks forty feet high and thirty feet wide, making a grand foaming cataract.[10]

The stream and waterfalls derived their names from a nearby copper mine, with the Dutch word *kill*, meaning "stream," added on.

Directions: From Middleburgh (junction of Rtes. 30 and 145N), continue south on Rt. 30 for roughly 16 miles. Along the way you will see the turn-off on your left for the Blenheim-Gilboa Pump Station Storage Power Project Visitors Center. From the Power Project, set the odometer to 0.0 and continue south along Rt. 30. At 1.1 miles you will pass by a left-hand turn that leads into Mine Kill State Park. Ignore the sign and continue driving south on Rt. 30. At 1.6 miles you will cross over a bridge spanning the Mine Kill and the mouth of a gorge. Drive 0.1 mile further and turn left into the parking area indicated for Mine Kill Falls Overlook.

From the parking area proceed north on foot, following a turquoise-blazed trail, which is part of the Long Path. In less than 0.1 mile the trail bears to the right. For the moment walk straight ahead and you will quickly come to a descending wooden railed stairway that leads to several views of the Mine Kill Gorge. From the upper and lower observation decks, you can obtain good views of the fall at the mouth of the gorge, elegantly framed by the Rt. 30 stone bridge. You can also peer down at the top of the middle fall, where the stream drops into a very narrow chasm.

After enjoying these views, return to the turquoise trail and follow it downhill. In 0.2 mile the trail emerges into a clearing where spectacular 100-foot-high cliffs tower above a pool of water. It is at this point that the Mine Kill breaks through the escarpment face, producing a striking double cascade in the process.

If you stand close to the cliff wall, you can look upstream through the notch created by the Mine Kill and see the middle falls. The final cascade is formed as the stream issues from the slot canyon and spreads out in a wide fan, dropping into an inviting pool of water. Take note, however, that swimming and wading are not permitted.

During wet conditions a tiny cascade tracks down the face of the cliff, just downstream from the falls.

Views can also be obtained from the Rt. 30 bridge spanning the Mine Kill, but you will need to be watchful for traffic.

Additional Point of Interest: The Blenheim-Gilboa Pump Station Storage Power Project deserves a visit while you are in the area. A visitor center at the project is open year-round and allows you to see firsthand the power that can be generated by falling water.

This is not your typical power generating plant, however. The system consists of two reservoirs of approximately the same size: a lower reservoir intercepting Schoharie Creek and an upper reservoir over 1,200 feet higher up on Brown Mountain. When power is needed, water is released from the upper reservoir through huge vertical shafts that are five times taller than Niagara Falls. In times of peak demand, the system can generate 1,040,000 kilowatts of power, virtually instantaneously.

What's unusual is that the water is then pumped back up into the upper reservoir at night, when the power project can purchase electricity at considerably less cost, thus producing a net savings and allowing the system to stay in the black financially.

The turn-off for the power project is approximately 14.5 miles south of Middleburgh (junctions of Rtes. 30 and 145N), or 1.7 miles north of the Mine Kill Falls Overlook along Rt. 30.

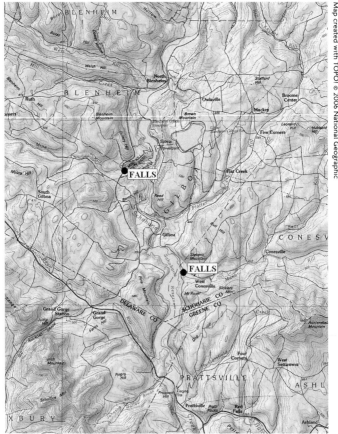

Map created with TOPO! © 2006 National Geographic

77. Manor Kill Falls

Location: Near Gilboa (Schoharie County)
NYS Atlas & Gazetteer: p. 51, AB5
Accessibility: Roadside

Description: Manor Kill Falls consists of a series of waterfalls and cascades formed on the Manor Kill, a medium-sized stream that rises in the hills northeast of Manorkill and flows into the Schoharie Reservoir just downstream from the base of the last fall.[1-4] Altogether the Manor Kill drops nearly 100 feet over a series of drops and plunges before flowing into one of the deepest sections of the Schoharie Reservoir. The falls have also been known as Stryker Falls,[5] named after Barent Stryker who built the first mill in the Town of Conesville in the narrow gorge at the top of the falls.[6]

From the high bridge spanning the Manor Kill, you can observe a good-sized cascade downstream from the bridge, as well as a series of prominent cascades upstream.

In *New York State Museum Bulletin: Glacial Geology of the Catskills*, mention is made that the "Manor Kill enters the Schoharie over a beautiful waterfall, now partly buried under the waters of Gilboa Reservoir. A buried channel of Manor Kill appears to lie a short distance south of the falls."[7] Fortunately, a significant part of Manor Kill Falls was at a high enough elevation to survive the reservoir's creation without being engulfed.

The falls are described by William E. Moore as follows:

> … entering upon the western border with the waters of the Manorkill leaping over the precipitous ledge that nature has so regularly laid as a barrier to the inundations of the Schoharie, a different impression is made. As the tumbling foam dashes from rock to rock with the deep thundering of greater falls, and sends its spray over the

path it once followed, ages upon ages ago, our genius is at once lured to admire and find beauty, grandeur and even romance in each object that surrounds us.[8]

Manor Kill Falls, circa 1900.

There are views of the falls from the bridge, but none of them are superlative, and the gorge is closed to further exploration. Posted signs along the top, stating "Private, City of New York Water Supply Property" prevent entry into the gorge below unless you have obtained a special access permit for fishing.

History: Gilboa was named after a mountain ridge in Palestine where Saul was defeated and killed. The name originally referred to "bubbling water."[9]

In 1791, Gershom Stevens, Sr., a Revolutionary War veteran, purchased a farm and soon was operating a sawmill, gristmill, tannery, and a shingle and turning factory, powered by the lower falls on the Manor Kill. In 1830, Barent and Peter Stryker built a tannery on the upper falls.

At one time a bridge made out of logs and planks spanned the top of the falls and served as the original road to Prattsville.[10]

A poem about Manor Kill Falls appeared in the *Gilboa Monitor* in 1884, written by an unidentified author.[11] The first stanza goes as follows:

> One morn in the golden October
> When our footsteps could wander at will.
> We turned them with joy to revisit
> The falls of the bright Manorkill.
> 'Tis a place of rare beauty and wildness
> Where nature still resigns undefiled.

Unfortunately, despite the sentiments expressed in the poem, nature here has been defiled. A bridge now spans the Manor Kill midway between the falls, and the reservoir has engulfed the cascades that once babbled over ledges further downstream.

Along Schoharie Creek not far from Manor Kill Falls, an autumn flood in 1869 uncovered the fossilized remains of a number of seed-bearing tree ferns named *eospermatopteris*, dating back to approximately 370 million years ago. This is one of the oldest known forests on earth. These fossils are called "cast type fossils," meaning that as the wood decayed, the space created in the mud was filled by sandstone.[12]

Lower Manor Kill Falls, circa 1920.

After more fossils were uncovered in the early 1920s, Winifred Gold-ring created a reconstruction of the Gilboa forest in 1924 at the old New York State Museum. A mural of the Manor Kill Falls vicinity was used as background scenery for the exhibit.[13]

The Schoharie Reservoir (also called the Gilboa Reservoir) was created in 1926 by impounding Schoharie Creek. In doing so, a body of water nearly 6 miles long, 0.7 mile wide, covering 1,142 acres, and containing 22 billion gallons of water was formed in a valley where only a stream had been before.[14]

Schoharie Creek is a tributary to the Mohawk River, but only half of the water carried by the Schoharie ever reaches its confluence with the Mohawk. The rest is channeled through huge underground tunnels for 18 miles, south to the Esopus Creek at Allaben. From there the waters flow into the Ashokan Reservoir, where they are again impounded and channeled downstate underground.

Directions: From Middleburgh, continue south on Rt. 30 through North Blenheim. After passing the turn-off for the Mine Kill Falls Overlook, drive 0.3 mile further south, turn left onto Stryker Road (Rt. 13), and continue southeast towards Gilboa. After over 2.3 miles you will come to Rt. 99V. Turn left, cross over a bridge spanning Schoharie Creek, and continue southeast. At 0.7 mile you will pass by a pull-off on your right for views of the Gilboa Dam. At 0.9 mile you will pass by Wyckoff Road on your left. Drive for 1.0 mile further and you will come to a point where the road divides. Bear to the right on Prattsville Road where a green sign indicates 6 miles to Prattsville, and you will immediately cross over a high bridge spanning the Manor Kill. Park off to the right at either end of the bridge.

Walk over to the top of the bridge for views of the falls, which are both upstream and downstream from the bridge.

Additional Points of Interest: *Gilboa Dam*, which impounds the Schoharie Reservoir, is worth seeing. From Manor Kill Falls, return back the way you came for 1.2 miles and park in the designated area on your left, from where excellent views of the dam can be obtained. A historic marker states: "Cotton mill 1840–1869. Tannery, church, and cemetery stood on ground now covered by NYS Water Supply." In 2006 the dam achieved considerable notoriety as villagers downstream became concerned that it might fail structurally.

The Gilboa Forest consists of the fossilized remains of a number of seed-bearing tree ferns representing one of the oldest forests on earth. An outdoor exhibition featuring these fossils can be seen nearby. As you turn left off of Stryker Road onto Rt. 99V, drive 0.3 mile, crossing over Schoharie Creek in the process. Look to your left and you will see the turn-off for the exhibit, which is at roadside.

Gilboa Dam, circa 1940.

78. Devasego Falls (Historic)

Location: Gilboa Reservoir (Delaware County)
NYS Atlas & Gazetteer: p. 51, AB5
Accessibility: The falls became inaccessible after 1926, when the valley was flooded to create the Schoharie Reservoir.

Description: According to Irma Mae Griffin, author and historian, "These falls are over 50 feet high and nearly 125 feet wide, and are almost a perfect miniature of the great Niagara Falls."[1] Other sources claim heights varying from 30 or 50 feet.[2-5] Today there is no way to confirm these estimates unless scuba gear is donned and one dives down to the bottom of the reservoir.

History: In the mid-1700s the waterfall was known as Owlflec, but how this name arose is lost to time. The later name, Devasego, supposedly came from a French Indian who resided in the area.

In the late 1700s a tannery was built near the falls by a man named Bell. Later the tannery was purchased by Charles Smedberg, a native of Sweden, who operated it until the tannery burned down in 1823. A second tannery was built and also destroyed by fire.

The Devasego Inn, built near the falls, began operating in the late 1800s, and by 1910 had grown in size to accommodate about 100 guests. People would travel to the inn by horse and buggy after departing from the train station at Grand Gorge. In 1915 a small dam was placed across the top of the falls so that electric power could be provided to the inn. The Devasego Inn came to an end in 1920, prior to the reservoir's creation.

Directions: Devasego Falls is currently—and likely forever—buried under the reservoir's deep waters. According to several sources the site of the falls is roughly 2.7 miles south from where the Manor Kill enters the reservoir, or just a little over 1.0 northwest of Prattsville. Looking east across the reservoir from Hardenbergh Falls (see *Catskill Region Waterfall Guide*), Devasego Falls is located underwater not far from the opposite shore, slightly to the north.

Devasego Falls is buried under the reservoir. Postcard circa 1900.

79. Stratton Falls

Location: Roxbury (Delaware County)
NYS Atlas & Gazetteer: p. 50, BC4
Accessibility: Roadside; somewhat obscured by trees

Description: Stratton Falls is formed on a medium-sized stream rising from the mountains north of West Settlement and flowing into the East Branch of the Delaware River not too far downstream from the falls. Stratton Falls is approximately 25 feet in height and located just downstream from an old, abandoned stone bridge that still stands parallel to the main road.[1]

History: Roxbury was named after Roxbury, Connecticut. The village of Roxbury is historically notable as the birthplace of Jay Gould and naturalist John Burroughs. In later life Burroughs maintained a summer residence just west of Roxbury on Clump Mountain, a camp that still stands today under the name of Woodchuck Lodge.

Stratton Falls was named after Samuel and Joseph Stratton, two brothers who moved to Roxbury in 1792 and set up a farm near the fall. Within a short time they also had built a fulling mill (woolen mill) just downstream from the fall. According to Irma Mae Griffin, author and historian: "In the glen of Stratton Falls there was a mill of some sort, run by water power. ... There was a cooper shop and a blacksmith shop at the falls, and also an old inn or tavern." None of these is evident today.

Directions: From Middleburgh, follow Rt. 30 down through the Schoharie Valley to Grand Gorge. (Or, from Mine Kill Falls Overlook Park, drive approximately 5.5 miles.) At Grand Gorge continue southwest on Rt. 30 for another 7.0 miles until you reach the southern end of the village of Roxbury. Turn right onto Bridge Street (County Rt. 41), following it as it bears to the left and turns into Stratton Falls Road.

Stratton Falls.

Proceed southwest for a total of 2.4 miles. As soon as you cross over a small bridge, you will reach a crossroads. The way to Meeker Hollow continues straight ahead, while the route to your right leads to West Settlement. Turn left, following the Cold Spring Road, for less than 0.05 mile. Park in a pull-off on your left. From there, walk back along the guardrail. You will have good views of the waterfall, on your right, from roadside.

What Comes Next?

Since the publication of *Adirondack Waterfall Guide* (2003), *Catskill Region Waterfall Guide* (2004), and *Hudson Valley Waterfall Guide* (2005), I have been called upon to give lectures and slideshow presentations to historical associations, hiking clubs, libraries, museums, and private organizations and groups on numerous occasions. During these presentations I would talk with great enthusiasm about waterfall preservation, detailing how humanity's appreciation of its natural resources has increased in recent years.

I would find my enthusiasm becoming tinged with melancholy, however, as I turned to the future of waterfalls and considered how the eventual depletion of fossil fuels could drive us back to exploiting waterfalls for their ability to produce natural, renewable, nonpolluting energy. I envisioned the waterfalls described in this guidebook obscured and desecrated by hydroelectric plants, with high-tension wires spanning the gorges and obstructing the view, and streams reduced to mere trickles before they could dribble over the tops of huge vertical drops that once produced thunderous waterfalls.

That was before good fortune intervened and I had the opportunity to meet Jim Besha, who offered me a decidedly more upbeat, waterfall-friendly vision of what the future could be for waterfalls as we face a world continuing to expend its fossil fuels at an accelerating pace. Mr. Besha is a hydroelectric engineer whose company, Albany Engineering Corporation, builds hydroelectric plants that are efficient, environmentally unobtrusive, and respectful of the area's surrounding history. Sound impossible?

Up until then, I had incorrectly assumed that hydroelectric plants were always erected *next* to waterfalls and were, therefore, unavoidably unsightly and intrusive. "Why not hollow out an enormous cavity inside the Earth and build the power plant there?" Besha asked. "That way, nothing is left on the surface to obstruct one's view, or diminish the waterfall's natural beauty." Was such an engineering project feasible? Not only was it possible, it has already been done at Dionondahowa Falls and Mt. Ida Falls (two falls that I had written about in *Hudson Valley Waterfall Guide* without realizing that the sites contained underground hydroelectric plants) and at French's Hollow (which I have included in this book).

Cohoes Falls serves as a present-day case study of a waterfall that could go either way in the future—either above ground or below ground. The power plant that you presently see by the falls is an antiquated facility (built in 1910), operated by Brookfield Power (a Canadian-based company), which is capable of generating 38 megawatts of power. There is little to commend the facility aesthetically. It sits next to Cohoes Falls Overlook Park, and its high-tension wires span the gorge directly in front of the falls. Presently one cannot enjoy the falls without the distraction of the intervening wires. Worse yet, the plant diverts so much water from the fall that little remains to run down its face; as a result, for most of the year Cohoes Falls looks like a large, imposing, naked cliff of shale. As if that were not bad enough, migratory species like the blueback herring and the endangered American eel suffer tremendous losses when they run through the whirling blades of the turbines while trying to negotiate the falls. If things remain the same, this plant, or one like it, will continue to operate for years to come, and the falls will remain blighted by industry. This is one possible future for Cohoes Falls.

If, on the other hand, there is the option of building a new power plant entirely underground, Cohoes Falls may return to its former splendor. The plant will not be visible and there will be no power lines spanning the gorge in front of the falls. And, because the kind of power plant that Besha proposes incorporates the latest technology, it will be able to generate 100 megawatts of power and to do so in such an efficient manner that there will always be a continuous veil of water going over the falls, night and day, 365 days a year. Also, the new system that engineers call the "FIsh Safe Hydro Intake System" will cause no loss of life to herrings, eels, and other river life that currently get caught up and mangled in the turbines. The plans also include an expanded overlook for tourists, nighttime illumination of the falls, additional park areas, and conversion of the existing plant into an educational museum with large glass windows overlooking the base of the falls to showcase electricity and hydropower.[1]

An unobtrusive power-generating facility such as this would provide Cohoes with an opportunity to again promote Cohoes Falls as the region's premier tourist attraction, just as it once was in the 1700s and 1800s when Cohoes Falls rivaled the fame and magnificence of Niagara Falls. With Cohoes Falls rightfully restored as a natural wonder and cascading continuously in all its glory, the falls could become the centerpiece for Cohoes' revitalization of its history—from the Heritage Museum to the Historic Harmony Mills District; from the original Erie Canal ("Clinton's Ditch) to the enlarged Erie Canal.

The future, of course, is always unknown, but it is reassuring to know that there is hope—that a model exists that would allow waterfalls to coexist with power plants. The deciding factor will be this: if our resolve to maintain the environment in as pristine a state as possible for future generations to enjoy will match our zeal to exploit alternative, dependable sources of energy.

List of Waterfalls

About the Author

Russell Dunn is the author of three previous guidebooks to the waterfalls of eastern New York State: *Adirondack Waterfall Guide: New York's Cool Cascades* (Black Dome Press Corp., 2003); *Catskill Region Waterfall Guide: Cool Cascades of the Catskills & Shawangunks* (Black Dome Press Corp., 2004); and *Hudson Valley Waterfall Guide: From Saratoga and the Capital Region to the Highlands and Palisades* (Black Dome Press Corp., 2005).

Dunn is also the author of *Adventures around the Great Sacandaga Lake* (Nicholas K. Burns Publishing, 2002), and co-author with his wife, Barbara Delaney, of *Trails with Tales: History Hikes through the Capital Region, Saratoga, Berkshires, Catskills and Hudson Valley* (Black Dome Press Corp., 2006). He has published many articles in regional magazines and newspapers including *Adirondack Life, Adirondac Magazine, Hudson Valley, Adirondack Sports & Fitness, Catskill Mountain Region Guide, Glens Falls Chronicle, Kaatskill Life, Northeastern Caver, Voice of the Valley, Edinburg Newsletter*, and *Sacandaga Times*.

Dunn is a New York State Licensed Guide. Together with his wife, Barbara Delaney (also a NYS Licensed Guide), he has been leading hikes to waterfalls in the Adirondacks, Catskills, and Hudson Valley, as well as to other areas of exceptional beauty and historical importance. Dunn has given numerous lecture and slideshow presentations to regional historical societies, libraries, civic groups, organizations, hiking clubs, and museums. He welcomes your comments, questions, and corrections, and can be reached by e-mail at: rdunnwaterfalls@yahoo.com.

PREFACE

1. Russell Dunn, *Hudson Valley Waterfall Guide: From Saratoga and the Capital Region to the Highlands and Palisades* (Hensonville, N.Y.: Black Dome Press Corp., 2005).

2. Russell Dunn, "Cooper's Cave: Fact and Fiction," *Glens Falls Magazine* Vol. 5, no. 5 (spring 2004), 25–30.

3. Russell Dunn, "Hiking the Waterfall Trail," *Adirondac* May/June 1998, 22–25.

WATERFALLS OF THE MOHAWK VALLEY

Introduction

1. John Grabowski and David Rhoden, *Awesome Almanac* (Walworth, Wis.: B & B Publishing, Inc., 1995), 22.

2. Yngvar W. Isachsen, *Guide Book for Geological Field Trips to the Mohawk Valley and Lake George Regions: Part Two. Albany to the Glen via Lake George. Leaflet # 18* (Albany, N.Y.: New York State Museum and Science Service, Education Building, 1966), 1.

3. Chuck Porter, retired Hudson Valley Community College geology professor.

4. Donald McLaughlin, "The Noses: Mohawk Valley Gateway," *Mohawk Valley USA* Vol. 1, no. 3 (December, 1980), 26. Talking about the barrier that once existed between the Noses, McLaughlin writes, "Either there would have been a spectacular waterfall for many centuries while the flow wore down the barrier, or if the 'blow out' took place, it would have been one of nature's cataclysmic events."

5. Isachsen, op. cit., 75. "The main tributary to the Colonie channel, the ancient Mohawk channel shown on Figure 6, has been traced as far west as the Hoffman Fault, where a 100 foot high waterfall may have existed in pre-glacial times."

6. Rachel Bliven, "Take the Thruway Cruise," *Mohawk Valley Heritage: The Magazine of the Mohawk Valley* Vol. 3, #1, 9.

7. Percy M. Van Epps, *The Van Epps Papers: A Collection of the Reports of Percy M. Van Epps on the History of the Town of Glenville* (Glenville, N.Y.: The Town Board, 1998). In the section entitled "Alplaus: Once Camping Ground of a French Army," Van Epps describes how the Mohawk River, when temporarily blocked, was channeled through Ballston and Round Lake and down the Anthony Kill to the Hudson River.

8. www.nysm.nysed.gov.

9. Isachsen, op. cit., 19.

10. Ibid., 11.

11, Ibid., 11.

12. Carl Carmer (selector), *The Tavern Lamps are Burning: Literary Journeys Through Six Regions and Four Centuries of New York State* (New York, N.Y.: David McKay Company, Inc., 1964), 242. Codman Hislop mentions that the Mohawk Valley provided the only entrance to the western plains between Georgia and the St. Lawrence Valley.

13. www.paulkeelerbooks.com, "Mohawk Discovering the Valley of the Crystal."

Additional Sources of Information:

Codman Hislop, *Rivers of America: The Mohawk* (New York/Toronto: Rinehart & Company, Inc., 1948).

Gerrard R. Megathlin, *New York Museum Bulletin: Faulting in the Mohawk Valley, New York* (Albany, N.Y.: University of the State of New York, 1938), 86.

Theodore P. Wild, "Te-Non-An-At-Che: A Mohawk Legend," *Mohawk Valley USA* Vol. 3, no. 11 (winter 1982), 33. Wild writes about the legend of how the Mohawk Valley came to be created.

Michael Gimigliano, "Middle Mohawk Images," *Mohawk Valley USA* Vol. 5, no. 4 (winter, 1984), 14–17, 46. The author writes about both the legendary and geological creation of the Mohawk Valley.

Cohoes Falls

1. A picture of Cohoes Falls can be seen in Cohoes in *'76: American Bicentennial. 1776–1976* (Cohoes, N.Y.: United States Bicentennial Commission of Cohoes, N.Y., 1976), pages unnumbered.

2. Benson J. Lossing, *The Hudson: from the Wilderness to the Sea* (1866; reprint, Hensonville, N.Y.: Black Dome Press, 2000), 110–111. "The width of the grand cataract of Cohoes is nine hundred feet, and the fall about seventy-five feet, of which about forty are perpendicular. Below the falls, the water rushes over a rocky bed, in foaming rapids, between high banks, to the plain, where the islands divide it into channels, and through these it flows into the Hudson."

3. *Mohawk River, N.Y.: Letter from the Secretary of the Army* (Washington, D.C.: Government Printing Office, 1957). The writer refers to the last few miles of the Mohawk River, "where the Mohawk River drops 169 feet over Cataract Dam, Cohoes Falls, and two power dams, and flows into the Hudson River at elevation 14.3 feet, mean sea level."

4. Several pictures of Cohoes Falls can be seen in Thomas Phelan's *Hudson Mohawk Gateway: An Illustrated History* (Northridge, Calif.: Windsor Publications, 1985): On page 143 a photograph of the fall taken

by G. Steven Draper shows the fall during the peak of the dry season with little water running over it; on page 23, a photo taken by Robert Chase presents the fall running full throttle; finally, next to the preface at the beginning of the book, can be seen an idealized engraving of Cohoes Falls.

5. *History of the Mohawk Valley: Gateway to the West. Vols. 1 & 2* (Chicago, Ill.: The S. J. Clarke Publishing Company, 1925), 1550. "The precipitous banks of the Mohawk, the falls and the rapids, the pine clad hills and deep ravines, the thunderous roar of its massive cataract, its savage and restless current masked by the spray flung mist, made it the show place of America and the goal of travelers who, surfeited with old world marvels, came here to see and be charmed." A picture of the fall can be seen on page 1553.

On page 87 mention is made that "the falls of Cohoes have cut back a distance of only about 2,000 feet. This is due to the fact that only a part of the postglacial greater Mohawk's waters came through the present channel for a long period of time and also because of the character of the rock bed of the river in the region of the falls." The author refers to the fact that a significant portion of the Mohawk River was going up through Ballston Spa until the entire stream was recaptured at Rexford.

6. Roland Van Zandt, *Chronicles of the Hudson: Three Centuries of Travel & Adventure* (1971; reprint, Hensonville, N.Y.: Black Dome Press Corp., 1992), 85. According to Charles Carroll, in 1776, "The perpendicular fall is seventy-four feet, and the breadth of the river at this place, as measured by General Schuyler, is one thousand feet." In 1780 the Marquis de Chastellux wrote (on page 112) that "This cataract is the whole breadth of the river, that is to say, nearly two hundred toises, or about 1200 English feet wide. It's a vast sheet of water, which falls 76 English feet." On page 25 a line drawing of Cohoes Falls can be seen, complete with a rainbow spanning the gorge from one bank to the other.

7. Natalie Walsh, "Falls for Spring," *The Sunday Gazette,* Lifestyles Section H, May 15, 2005, H1, H2. Walsh writes, "On a recent afternoon, the falls were magnificent. The water from all the rain roared over the rocks, mist rose from the base and several small rainbows formed in the sky directly above the falls."

8. Gilbert W. Hagerty, *Wampum, War & Trade Goods, West of the Hudson* (Interlaken, N.Y.: Heart of the Lakes Publishing, 1985), 24. "... the sources of the many streams that poured into the Mohawk to make a mighty eight foot wall of water with boiling rapids to thunder over 900 feet of rocks down into the Hudson, seventy-eight feet below at Cohoes."

9. Mary Adria Galbraith, "Cohoes" *Mohawk Valley* Vol. 1, no. 3 (Dec. 1980), 2. A Dutch settler in the 1600s writing home to the Netherlands is quoted as saying, "It is the greatest falls not only in New Netherlands but in North America and perhaps as far as known in the whole world."

On page 7 can be seen a picture of Cohoes Falls taken from the north bank.

10. Philip Lord, Jr., *The Navigators: The Journal of Passage on the Inland Waterways of New York, 1793*. Bulletin no. 498. (Albany, N.Y.: New York State Museum, 2003). A picture of Cohoes Falls can be seen on the back cover.

11. James M. Stoller, "The Falls and Gorge of the Mohawk at Cohoes," *Geological Excursions: A Guide to Localities in the Region of Schenectady and the Mohawk Valley and the Vicinity of Saratoga Springs* (Schenectady, N.Y.: Union Book Co., 1931), 29–34. On page 30 Stoller writes, "When the water is on, it does not descend in a vertical sheet, but flows over the steeply inclined face of the rocks."

12. A picture of Cohoes Falls flowing at full volume can be seen in C. R. Roseberry's *Albany: Three Centuries a County* (Albany, N.Y.: Albany County Tricentennial Commission, 1983), 33.

13. Peter Eisenstadt (editor-in-chief), *The Encyclopedia of New York State* (Syracuse, N.Y.: Syracuse University Press, 2005). 355. Cohoes Falls is described as 78 feet (23.8m) in height.

14. Spindle City Historic Society, *Harmony Mills Historic District: Self Guided Tour* (pamphlet printed by The Rickman Press, Inc.)

15. Joel Munsell, *The History of Cohoes, New York: From Its Earliest Settlement to the Present Time* (1877; reprint, Salem, Mass.: Higginson Book Company, n.d.), 2–3.

16. Van Zandt, op. cit., 112.

17. Carl Carmer (selector), *The Tavern Lamps are Burning: Literary Journeys Through Six Regions and Four Centuries of New York State* (New York, N.Y.: David McKay Company, Inc., 1964). On pages 278–279 can be found a piece entitled "To the Falls of the Mohawk," written in 1804 by Thomas Moore while at Cohoes

18. Codman Hislop, *Rivers of America: The Mohawk* (New York/Toronto: Rinehart & Company, Inc., 1848), 5. "The once-renowned falls at Cohoes, which the canal bypasses, are now for most part of the year a poor trickle of water, for the river here is drained into power flumes for the benefit of the factories that crowd around the last few miles of the Mohawk's course."

19. Jim Besha, hydroelectric engineer.

20. Miriam Axel-Lute, "Falls Guys," *Metroland* Vol. 28, no. 23 (June 9, 2005), 19.

21. John R. Fitzgerald, *The New Erie Canal: A Recreational Guide* (Saratoga Springs, N.Y.: Quest Press, 1993), 37. "Cohoes Falls must be the original 'thundering cataract.' This was the first block to westward navigation. ... In the late eighteenth and early nineteenth centuries, many who looked at these falls thought the idea of a canal around them foolhardy."

22. John G. Waite and Diana S. Waite, *Industrial Archeology in Troy, Waterford, Cohoes, Green Island, and Watervliet* (Troy, N.Y.: Hudson-Mohawk Industrial Gateway, 1973), 40. A fair amount of detail on the Harmony Mills complex is provided.

23. *Cohoes in '76: American Bicentennial. 1776–1976* (Cohoes, N.Y.: United States Bicentennial Commission of Cohoes, N.Y., 1976), pages unnumbered.

24. Spindle City Historic Society, op. cit., 20.

25. Roseberry, op. cit. The history of daredevil Bobby Leach, who pulled off some stunts at the fall, is touched upon briefly.

26. Jordan Carleo-Evangelist, "Firefighters Pull Pair from Brink of Disaster" *Times Union,* Wednesday, July 28, 2004. A thrilling account of the rescue of a man and boy is depicted on pages B1 and B5.

27. Wallace Bruce, *The Hudson* (New York: Bryant Union, 1913), 186.

28. Hagerty, op. cit., 3. The impact of Cohoes Falls on salmon fishing is discussed.

29. Axel-Lute, op. cit., 14.

Falls near Lock 7

1. *Along the Bike Trail* (Schenectady, N.Y.: The Environmental Clearinghouse of Schenectady, Inc., 1986), 14. Information is provided concerning the lock and dam.

2. *Environmental Trip Tips in and around Schenectady, New York* (Schenectady, N.Y.: The Environmental Clearinghouse of Schenectady, Inc., 1976), 42. "The influence of the eastern Taconic and Appalachian mountain building can be seen in the tilted rock layers of shale at Lock 7."

3. *Along the Bike Trail,* op. cit., 7.

4. Lloyd M. Brinkman and Members of the Niskayuna Historical Society. *A History of Niskayuna, New York: 1809, Volume One* (Niskayuna, N.Y.: n.p., 1976), 59.

Additional Information:

Brinkman, etc., op. cit., 4. In Chapter 1, "Geology of the Town of Niskayuna," the authors suggest that another waterfall existed between Cohoes Falls and Lock 7: "A gorge, 140 feet in depth, was cut through these shales and extended to the falls at Vischer Ferry. Here another broad basin was formed which extended nearly to Crescent."

Falls between Lock 7 and Rexford

1. Chris W. Brown, *Guide to New York Waterways and Lake Champlain* (Gretna, La.: Pelican Publishing Company, Inc., 1998), 257. A 15-foot-high falls on a tributary to the Mohawk River can be found along the south side between the dam and Rexford Bridge.

2. Rich Macha, "Mohawk and Hudson Rivers: A Variety of Experiences in the Capital Region," *Adirondack Sports & Fitness* Issue # 50 (July 2004), 7. "After about a mile, the river is lined with cliffs and there are several waterfalls, the best one of which, especially when it rains, is about three miles from the start near a power line on the south shore." Here, the author is talking about the waterfall near Rexford.

3. James H. Stoller, *Geological Excursions: A Guide to Localities in the Region of Schenectady and the Mohawk Valley and the Vicinity of Saratoga Springs* (Schenectady, N.Y.: Union Book Company, 1931), 26.

Waterfall near Bike Path in Rexford

1. Natalie Walsh, "Falls for Spring," *The Sunday Gazette,* Lifestyles Section H, May 15, 2005, H1 and H2. On H1 Walsh writes, "The stream itself is a pretty sight with several little falls over slabs of shale."

Falls on Indian Kill

1. *The Indian Kill Study: January 1998 to October of 1999,* conducted by the Environmental Study Team and prepared by J. Kelly Nolan. A picture of one of the falls on the Indian Kill, taken by Susan Hayes, can be seen on the cover of the study.

2. Maureen Cary, "Information Comes Naturally," *Schenectady Magazine* Vol. 1, no. 3 (winter 1998). A picture by Claire Schmitt of Fall #2 can be seen on pages 32–33.

3. Pictures of the various cascades can be seen on www.anglefire.com/ny4/waterfalls/newyork.html.

4. Claire K. Schmitt, *Natural Areas of Schenectady County* (Schenectady, N.Y.: The Environmental Clearinghouse of Schenectady and The Schenectady County Environmental Advisory Council, 1986). A map of the Indian Kill Preserve, prepared by Pierre M. Lanoue, can be found on page 15.

5. www.schenectadycounty.com/index.php?page-id = 273 gives the size of the preserve as 100 acres.

6. Percy M. Van Epps, "The Mills & Other Industries of Early Glenville, New York (1930)," *The Van Epps Papers: A Collection of the Reports of Percy M. Van Epps on the History of the Town of Glenville, 3rd Edition* (Glenville, N.Y.: The Town Board, 1998), 55.

Krystal Falls

1. James H. Stoller, *Museum Bulletin # 154: Glacial Geology of the Schenectady Quadrangle* (Albany, N.Y.: University of the State of New York, 1911), 26. "At High Mills the creek enters a rocky gorge from which, after a descent of 40 feet in the course of a mile, it emerges on the floor of the Ballston channel." On page 27 Stroller writes, "... while below High Mills the gorge with vertical walls of rock in places 60 feet high, has been eroded out."

2. Kathie Armstrong and Chet Harvey (editors), *Canoe and Kayak Guide. East Central New York State: Includes Selected Waterways of Western New England,* first edition (Lake George, N.Y.: Adirondack Mountain Club 2003), 228 and 230. The author describes a "4-foot ledge extending across the creek just upstream of the NY 50 bridge."

3. Percy M. Van Epps, "The Mills & Other Industries of Early Glenville, New York (1930)," *The Van Epps Papers: A Collection of the Reports of Percy M. Van Epps on the History of the Town of Glenville,* third edition (Glenville, N.Y.: The Town Board, 1998), 54.

4. *History of the County of Schenectady, N.Y. From 1662–1866* (New York: W. W. Munsell & Co., 1886), 187. High Mills is described as "a small place, containing a grist-mill and saw-mill, a blacksmith shop, wagon shop, and a few other small shops." Mention is made that the iron bridge spanning Alplaus Creek had replaced an earlier wooden bridge.

5. W. Bronson Taylor, Levi Packard and Percy Van Epps, *Stories and Pictures of Charlton, New York* (Middle Grove, N.Y.: W. Bronson Taylor, 1959). On page 70 can be seen a 1913 photo of the High Mills Grist Mill, located just below Rt. 50.

Additional Sources of Information:

Austin A. Yates, *Schenectady County, New York: Its History to the Close of the Nineteenth Century* (N.p: New York History Company, 1902), 414. "High Mills is situated in the northeastern part of the town. At this place the town built a fine iron bridge across the Alplaat Creek." Yates continues by mentioning that the underlying rock in Glenville tends to be shale of the Hudson River group, covered with a thick layer of clay.

James D. Livingston (editor), *Glenville—Past and Present. Sesquicentennial Celebration* (Glenville, N.Y.: Sesquicentennial Committee, 1970), 1 and 26.

Kathie Armstrong and Chet Harvey (editors), op. cit., 231. "Below the falls, the stream flows through a wilderness gorge with walls rising 20 to 50 feet above the creek. ... A tributary drops over the cliff on river left as a lovely waterfall."

Percy M. Van Epps, "Stories and Legends of our Indian Paths"

(1940), *The Van Epps Papers: A Collection of the Reports of Percy M. Van Epps on the History of the Town of Glenville,* third edition (Glenville, N.Y.: The Town Board, 1998). Section 5 presents information on the Aalplaats on pages 323–343.

Plotter Kill Falls

1. Claire K. Schmitt, *Natural Areas of Schenectady County,* third edition (Schenectady, N.Y.: The Environmental Clearinghouse of Schenectady and The Schenectady County Environmental Advisory Council, 1986). A map of the preserve can be seen on pages 33–34.

2. Austin A. Yates, *Schenectady County New York: Its History to the Close of the Nineteenth Century* (New York: New York History Company, 1902), 415. "The streams are Norman's Kill in the south, Platt's Kill in the center, and Zantzee Kill in the northwest. Upon this stream is a cascade sixty feet high, and from this point to the Mohawk are numerous falls and cascades." Presumably, Yates is referring to the falls on the Plotter Kill. The only other stream that might fit this description would be Sandsea Creek, which is slightly northwest of the Plotter Kill and which contains a number of impressive cascades.

3. Nelson Greene, *The Old Turnpike Book* (Fort Plain, N.Y.: n.p., 1924). A picture of the main fall, identified as "Platterkill Falls," can be seen on page 62.

4. Natalie Walsh, "Falls for Spring," *The Sunday Gazette,* Lifestyles Section H, May 15, 2005, pages H1 and H2. A picture of what is possibly the main fall is featured on page H1.

5. www.angelfire.com/ny4/waterfalls/newyork.html contains a picture of the lower falls on the Plotter Kill.

6. Larry Hart, *Steinmetz in Schenectady: A Picture Story of Three Memorable Decades* (Scotia, New York: Old Dorp Books, 1978). A picture of the lowermost ledge falls, taken in 1896, is shown on page 48 (plate #23); a photograph of one of the large main falls, taken in 1897, can be seen on page 50 (plate #24).

On page 51, Hart writes, "An environment of unusual setting, such as imposing rock formations or a falls or a deep gorge with a fast-moving stream, also was a magnet to this man [Charles Proteus Stenimetz] who was awed by nature's wonders."

7. Schenectady County Historical Society, *Images of America: Rotterdam* (Charleston, S.C.: Arcadia Publishing, 2004). On page 18 is shown a picture of the upper fall on the Plotter Kill, ca. 1890. Page 19 contains a picture of the lower fall on the Plotter Kill, also ca. 1890.

8. Irma Mastrean (compiler), *Princetown: Portrait of a Town* (Princetown, N.Y.: Princetown Historical Society, 1990). The heights of the falls are listed as 60 for the upper, and 40 for the lower.

9. Almy and Anne Coggeshall, *25 Ski Tours in the Adirondacks* (Somersworth, N.H.: New Hampshire Publishing Company, 1979), p. 43.

10. Schmitt, op. cit. A picture of the main falls is displayed on the front of the book.

11. Donald W. Fisher, *Bedrock Geology of the Central Mohawk Valley* (Albany, N.Y.: The State Education Department, 1980), 42. Fisher states that the gorge of the Plotter Kill is a "continuous sequence of sandstones, siltstones, and shales of the Schenectady formation."

Cascades on Moccasin Kill

1. Francis P. Kimball, *The Capital Region of New York State: Crossroads of Empire. Vol. II* (New York: Lewis Historical Publishing Company, Inc., 1942), 408.

2. Jackson Davis, etc. (compilers and editors), *Guide to Natural Areas of the Eastern New York Chapter of the Nature Conservancy*, seventh edition (Albany, N.Y.: Eastern New York Chapter, 1980), 45.

3. Ibid. A map of the sanctuary can be seen on page 44.

4. Claire K. Schmitt, *Natural Areas of Schenectady* (Schenectady, N.Y.: The Environmental Clearinghouse of Schenectady and The Schenectady County Environmental Advisory Council, 1986). A map of the preserve is presented on page 29.

Falls on Washout Creek

1. *Environmental Trip Tips in and around Schenectady, New York* (Schenectady, N.Y.: The Environmental Clearinghouse of Schenectady, Inc., 1976), 53. "There are two waterfalls within 1/2 mile."

2. www.townofglenville.org/public_documents/glenvilleny mentions that the preserve contains 370 acres.

3. Rachel Bliven, "Take the Thruway Cruise," *Mohawk Valley Heritage: The Magazine of the Mohawk Valley,* Vol. 3, no. 1, 9.

4. James D. Livingston (editor), *Glenville—Past and Present 1820–1970 Sesquicentennial Celebration* (Glenville, N.Y.: Glenville Sesquicentennial Committee, 1970). On page 25 mention is made that Washout Creek and Washout Road were named after the Great Washout of 1885, in which a railroad bridge several miles east of Hoffman was destroyed by raging waters, leaving the train track dangling. A passenger train and a freight train narrowly missed being swallowed up by the gulf.

5. Percy Van Epps, "The Place Names of Glenville (1926)," *The Van Epps Papers: A Collection of the Reports of Percy M. Van Epps on the History of the Town of Glenville* (Glenville, N.Y.: The Town Board, 1998), 4.

6. Claire K. Schmitt, *Natural Areas of Schenectady County* (Schenectady, N.Y.: The Environmental Clearinghouse of Schenectady and The

Schenectady County Environmental Advisory Council). A map of the preserve can be found on page 19.

Adriutha Falls (Historic)

1. W. Max Reid, *The Mohawk Valley: Its Legends and Its History. 1609–1780* (Harrison, N.Y.: Harbor Hill Books, 1979), 357. On page 355, Reid describes the fall as a "sheer precipice of perhaps fifty feet" and then goes on to say that "we find that about fifty feet from the brink is another fall, about ten feet high, that cannot be seen from the bed of the creek below."

2. Katherine M. Strobeck, *Mohawk Valley Happenings* (Montgomery County, N.Y.: Montgomery County Historical Society, 1990), 45. "He then goes on to describe the falls about 50 feet in height, where the stream comes in from the north." A picture of the fall is also presented.

3. Nelson Greene, *The Old Turnpike Book* (Fort Plain, N.Y.: n.p., 1924). A picture of the waterfall can be seen on page 78. On page 79, Greene states, "About 400 feet north of the Turnpike are the pretty little falls of the Adriutha, accessible by footpath and one of the few cascades close to the highway."

4. www.neuswaterfalls.com.

Fall at Cliffside Restaurant

1. Hugh P. Donlon, *Amsterdam New York: Annals of a Mill Town in the Mohawk Valley* (Amsterdam, N.Y.: Donlon Associates, 1980), 49. "The Tepee Restaurant is located in a picturesque setting with waterfall that was once an East Main St. quarry that was operated by Baid Bros., a major contracting firm at the beginning of the century. From this side hill excavation were taken many tons of stones used in resurfacing local streets."

Falls at Kirk Douglas Park

1. *History of Montgomery and Fulton Counties, N. Y.* (reprint: Interlaken, N.Y.: Heart of the Lakes Publishing, 1979), 85. Chuctanunda means "twin sister," which sounds sensible enough since the North Chuctanunda comes into the Mohawk River directly opposite the South Chuctanunda.

2. Percy M Van Epps, *The Van Epps Papers: A Collection of the Reports of Percy M. Van Epps on the History of the Town of Glenville* (Glenville, N.Y.: The Town Board, 1998).

3. Nelson Greene, *The Old Turnpike Book* (Fort Plain, N.Y.: n.p.,1924). The name Chuctanunda refers to either a "rocky point or overhanging rocky ledge" (page 132), or "stony creek" (page 82).

4. Katherine M. Strobeck, "Amsterdam. USA: Centennial Celebration," *Mohawk Valley USA,* Vol. 6, no. 2 (summer 1985), 5. The author

refs to the Albert Vedder and Joseph Hagaman mills around which the settlement of Veddersburg sprang up. Veddersburg was later renamed Amsterdam.

5. Carl Carmer (selector), *The Tavern Lamps are Burning: Literary Journeys through Six Regions and Four Centuries of New York State* (New York: David McKay Company, Inc., 1964), 244. In the chapter by Codman Hislop, entitled "Upstream," the author provides statistics on the river's change in height between Cohoes and Amsterdam.

6. Max W. Reid, *The Mohawk Valley: Its Legends and Its History* (Harrison, N.Y.: Harbor Hill Books, 1979), 321. Reverend John Taylor's 1802 journal gives the following account of Amsterdam's early appearance: "Near the centre of this town the Ouctanunda Creek empties into the Mohawk—a very fertile and useful stream. On this stream and in this town there stand 4 grist mills, 2 oil mills, 1 iron forge and 3 saw mills."

7. Hugh P. Donlon, *Amsterdam New York: Annals of a Mill Town in the Mohawk Valley* (Amsterdam, N.Y.: Donlon Associates, 1980). Information is provided on the history of Amsterdam. The section on "Carpets and Rugs," pages 87–96, is most relevant to Amsterdam's industrial past.

Additional Sources of Information:
Katherine M. Strobeck, "The Chuctanunda Hills," *Mohawk Valley Happenings* (Montgomery County, N.Y.: Montgomery County Historical Society, 1990), 24–25.

Albert Perry Brigham, *New York State Museum Bulletin: Glacial Geology and Geographic Conditions of the Lower Mohawk Valley* (Albany, N.Y.: University of the State of New York, 1929), 121.

Little Chuctanunda Falls

1. Max Reid, *The Mohawk Valley: Its Legends and Its History. 1609–1780* (Harrison, N.Y.: Harbor Hill Books, 1979), 101. An interesting photo in the book refers to the cascade as "Falls on the South Chuctanunda." (In actuality, it is on a tributary of the South Chuctanunda.)

Cider Mill Falls

1. Katherine M. Strobeck, *Port Jackson: An Erie Canal Village* (Port Jackson, N.Y.: Port Jackson Publishing Company, 1989). Page 22 shows a picture of "Mudge Hollow Falls."

2. Hugh P. Donlon, *Amsterdam New York: Annals of a Mill Town in the Mohawk Valley* (Amsterdam, N.Y.: Donlon Associates, 1980), 183. "On the fifth ward site, the South Chuctanunda had some popular water holes as the placid stream wound beneath the steep cliffs of Mudge Hollow at the end of Florida Ave. South Siders were joined in plunging near

the old cider mill by swimmers from far away sections, like Reid Hall."

3. Ibid. "The rocky projection that to some resembled a lion's head gave name to the pool area, but the identification has been greatly eroded."

4. threerivershms.com.

5. Donlon, op. cit., 9. Mention is made of the variety of mills that once populated the South Chuctanunda at Mudge Hollow.

Yatesville Falls

1. Donald W. Fisher, *Bedrock Geology of the Central Mohawk Valley, New York* (Albany, N.Y.: The State Education Department, 1980), 42. The author calls the fall "Buttermilk Falls," and describes the fall as formed out of "Schenectady sandstone resting abruptly on Utica black shale." A photograph of Yatesville Falls looking very dry is displayed on the same page.

2. Hugh P. Donlon, *Outlines of History: Montgomery County. State of New York. 1772–1972. Bicentennial Edition* (Amsterdam, N.Y.: Printed by Noteworthy Co., 1973), 82. "Yatesville Creek attracted the pioneers who built near Vrooman's Falls," which suggests that Yatesville Falls was at one time known as Vrooman's Falls (a prominent name in Schoharie Valley). Donlon goes on to say, on the same page, that "An enterprising start was continued until Yatesville Creek with its drop of 25 feet went on a rampage in 1813."

3. www.dec.state.ny.us/website/dlf/publiclands/stateforests/reg4/ruralgrove.html indicates that the fall has also been called Buttermilk Falls.

4. Ibid. The size of the park is stated as being 714 acres.

5. Gilbert W. Hagerty, *Wampum, War & Trade Goods West of the Hudson* (Interlaken, N.Y.: Heart of the Lakes Publishing, 1985), 41. "... the first castle of Onekagonckan would fall somewhere above Caughnawaga Rapids near Yatesville Creek."

6. *History of Montgomery and Fulton Counties, N. Y.* (reprint: Interlaken, N.Y.: Heart of the Lakes Publishing, 1979), 165. "Yatesville is a hamlet on the Erie Canal, in the northeastern part of the town, important chiefly as a point for the shipment of hay."

Flat Creek Falls (Historic)

1. Donald W. Fisher, *Bedrock Geology of the Central Mohawk Valley* (Albany, N.Y.: University of the State of New York, The State Education Department, 1980). A picture of the waterfall can be seen on page 36.

2. Nelson Greene, *The Old Mohawk Turnpike Book* (Fort Plain, N.Y.: n.p., 1924), 137. "The Onagerea, also known as Plattekill or Flat Creek, enters the Mohawk at Sprakers. In the creek about a mile south is a fall about 60 feet high, the highest cascade along the course of the Mohawk, close to the river."

3. Hugh P. Donlon, *Outlines of History: Montgomery County. State of New York. 1772–1972 Bicentennial Edition* (Amsterdam, N.Y.: Printed by Noteworthy, 1973). Donlon compares Yatesville Falls with Flat Creek Falls. On page 82 he writes, "Another falls with a drop of 65 feet on Flat Creek about a mile above Sprakers was more picturesque than the Yatesville site, but with less economic value."

4. Douglas Ayres, "Sculptured Rocks," *Mohawk Valley USA*, Vol. 1, no. 4 (March 1981). On page 11 can be seen two photos of Flat Creek Falls. On page 8, the author states: "In approximately three-fourths of a mile, the stream flow abruptly changes from a west to east course, as it plunges over a 40 foot drop to a deep plunge pool and then veers almost due north on its way to the river. This is the famous high falls. The rock here is singularly hard and massive in quite thick, dense sedimentary beds"

5. www.geocites.com.

6. Greene, op. cit. The author mentions that the fall was also known as Plattkill.

7. www.paulkeeslerbooks.com.

8. www.nysm.nysed.gov/research/history/canajohary/canjo3.html.

9. Greene, op. cit., 137. "Traces of lead and silver have been found along the Onagerea."

10. *History of Montgomery and Fulton Counties, N.Y.* (reprint: Interlaken, N. Y.: Heart of the Lakes Publishing, 1979), 164. "Sutphen's Hollow is a hamlet at the high falls on Flat Creek. ... It was originally called Hamilton's Hollow from Solomon Hamilton. ... In its best days the place had a flouring-mill, a saw-mill, a carding-mill, works for a cloth-dressing, a distillery and a number of dwellings."

11. Donlon, op. cit., 83. The author makes reference to the Flat Creek Cheese Factory.

12. Louis Rossi, *Cycling Along the Canals of New York: 500 Miles of Bike Riding along the Erie, Champlain, Cayugaseneca, and Oswego Canals* (College Park, Md.: Vitesse Press, 1999), 31.

13. Rachel Bliven, "Take the Thruway Cruise," *Mohawk Valley Heritage: The Magazine of the Mohawk Valley,* Vol. 3, no. 1, 9–10.

Canajoharie Falls: Upper Gorge

1. *Encyclopedia of New York*, Vol. 2 (New York: Somerset Publishers, Inc., 1996), 58. "About a mile up the creek is a waterfall which drops 45 feet into the gorge."

2. Mary Lynn Blanks, *Fun with the Family in New York: Hundreds of Ideas for Day Trips with the Kids*, third edition (Guilford, Conn.: The Globe Pequot Press, 2001), 102. "Canajoharie Falls is "a spectacular waterfall rushing over geological potholes."

3. Walter F. Burmeister, *Appalachian Waters 2: The Hudson River*

and Its Tributaries (Oakton, Va.: Appalachian Books, 1974), 277. "About one and three-fourths miles upstream Canajoharie Falls drops 30 feet from the upper level of the gorge into the lower chasm."

4. *History of the Mohawk Valley: Gateway to the West, 1614–1925* (Chicago, Ill.: S. J. Clarke Publishing Company, 1925), 1678. "About one and one-half miles south of its outlet into the Mohawk, the creek makes a forty-five-foot drop into a deep pool, which forms the picturesque Canajoharie Falls."

5. *History of the Mohawk Valley: Gateway to the West*, op. cit. On page 1687 can be seen a winter shot of Canajoharie Falls by M. J. Bucklin, showing the gorge encased in ice; on page 1681 can be seen a photograph of Canajoharie Falls as well as a photograph of the Canajoharie Pothole.

6. Hugh P. Donlon, *Outlines of History: Montgomery County. State of New York. 1772–1972 Bicentennial Edition* (Amsterdam, N.Y.: Printed by Noteworthy Co., 1973), 63. "About a mile and a half south of its outlet into the Mohawk River there is a sheer drop of 45 feet that creates a picturesque falls with miniature canyon walls 100 feet high."

7. Dennis Savoie, *Cranks from Cooperstown: 50 Bike Rides in Upstate New York.* (Cooperstown, N.Y.: Tourmaster Publications, L.L.C., 1998), 84. Canajoharie Falls is described as being "60-foot high."

8. *History of the Mohawk Valley: Gateway to the West,* op. cit., 1678. According to the author, "Simms, the historian, says the Mohawks here did their courting." The man referred to is Jeptha R. Simms, Mohawk Valley historian who lived from 1807–1883.

Canajoharie Falls: Lower Gorge

1. Frederick G. Vosburgh, *Drums to Dynamos on the Mohawk* (Washington, D.C.: National Geographic Society, 1947). A marvelous picture of the Canajoharie Pothole, complete with skinny-dipper, can be seen on Plate VII.

2. Gilbert W. Hagerty, *Wampum, War & Trade Goods West of the Hudson* (Interlaken, N.Y.: Heart of the Lakes Publishing, 1985). A picture of the Canajoharie Pothole is shown on page 46.

3. Donald W. Fisher, *Bedrock Geology of the Central Mohawk Valley, New York* (Albany, N.Y.: The University of the State of New York, The State Education Department, 1980). On page 14 can be seen a picture of the famed Canajoharie Pothole.

4. Hagerty, op. cit., 46. The author goes into extensive detail about how Canajoharie was named.

5. Phyllis Lake, "Canajoharie Gorge," *Mohawk Valley Magazine,* Vol. 1, no. 1 (June 1980). Lake relates the industrial history of the gorge.

Falls on Tributaries to Nowadaga Creek

1. Gilbert W. Hagerty, *Wampum, War & Trade Goods West of the Hudson* (Interlaken, N.Y.: Heart of the Lakes Publishing, 1985), 47.

Scudders Falls

1. *History of the Mohawk Valley: Gateway to the West* (Chicago, Ill.: S. J. Clarke Publishing Company, 1925), 1741. "Picturesque Zimmerman Creek here enters the Mohawk, its water power being the cause of the original settlement made here by Jacob Timmerman, who located a mill on its bank." Mention is made that the name Timmerman and Zimmerman are one and the same, being different spellings of the same first settler.

2. Richard Triumpho, "Cases's Mill," *Mohawk Valley USA*, Vol. 4, no. 9 (summer, 1982), 6.

3. www.innbythemill.com

Falls at "Inn by the Mill"

1. *History of Montgomery and Fulton Counties, N.Y.* (1887, reprint; Interlaken, N.Y.: Heart of the Lakes Publishing, 1979), 171. "Upper St. Johnsville, situated on Klock's Creek, about one mile west of St. Johnsville, contains the three story stone flouring and custom mill of Beekman brothers."

2. Much of the information in this chapter was obtained from Ronald and Judith Hezel (innkeepers at The Inn by the Mill).

Fall on Timmerman Creek

1. Ronald and Judith Hezel (innkeepers at The Inn by the Mill)

Beardslee Falls (Historic)

1. Hugh P. Donlon, *Outlines of History: Montgomery County. State of New York. 1772–1972 Bicentennial Edition* (Amsterdam, N.Y.: Printed by Noteworthy Co., 1973), 85. Reference is made to the waterpower of nearby streams coming into the Mohawk River, "particularly the 75-foot drop about one mile north of the mouth of East Canada Creek."

2. Linda Cuda, "Beardslee Manor: Fact and Fantasy," *Mohawk Valley USA*, Vol. 3, no. 10 (fall 1982), 37–39, 46. Cuda provides relevant information on the life and times of John Beardslee, the community called "Beardslee City," and how the waterfall was used to generate power.

Faville Falls

1. H. P. Cushing, *New York State Bulletin 77. Geology 6: Geology of the Vicinity of Little Falls, Herkimer County* (Albany, N.Y.: State Education Department, 1905). A picture of the waterfall is shown on plate #11, next to page 72. Cushing talks about a "Fall in creek over the pre-

Cambrian at the Little Falls fault line 2 miles west of Dolgeville. The creek is in a postglacial valley, and has only cut back its fall 100 yards from the fault plane, the volume being slight and the rocks very resistant. The perpendicular walls of the gorge below are due to the joint planes, and the large loose blocks are disclosed mainly by frost."

2. www.dolgeville.info/sights.html provides a picture of the falls.

3. Nelson Greene, *Old Mohawk Turnpike Book* (Fort Plain, N.Y.: n.p., 1924), 186. "John Faville settled on Ransom creek in 1795, where he built a grist mill and saw mill." Around these mills grew up a tiny settlement, consisting of a blacksmith shop, tannery, and school house. Greene's quote also appeared in *History of the Mohawk Valley: Gateway to the West. 1614–1925.*

4. Cushing, op. cit. Mention is made of the Little Falls Fault.

Falls by Old Dolgeville Mill

1. Historic Marker.

High Falls

1. Walter F. Burmeister, *Appalachian Waters 2: The Hudson River and Its Tributaries* (Oakton, Va.: Appalachian Books, 1974). On page 221, Burmeister talks about the height of the dam and falls.

2. Lucinda M. Parker, *The Little Falls & Dolgeville Railroad: 72 Years of Shortline* (Brookfield, N.Y.: Worden Press, 1986), 22. The author quotes Charles Sullivan (president of the LF&D) from an advertising booklet, undated, but written circa 1894: "The waters dash over great boulders in myriads of cascades, which merge themselves as they fall into a seething, foamy mass. Below the falls are deep, cool canyons, while on every side are lovers' walls and lanes in deeply shaded groves." On page 20, Parker displays two photos of High Falls under fairly dry conditions. For those interested in the former High Falls Park, a map is included on page 19.

3. Burmeister, op. cit., 222. East Canada Creek is briefly discussed.

4. *History of the Mohawk Valley: Gateway to the West, 1614–1925* Vol. II (Chicago, Ill.: The S. J. Clarke Publishing Company, 1925), 1754. "In 1887 Mr. Dolge bought the Reuben Faville farm on the east side of the creek, including picturesque High Falls of the East Canada. Dolge laid out 500 acres of this land as a park and presented this picturesque and beautiful place to the people of Dolgeville."

5. Eleanor Franz, "The Town that Dolge Built," *Adirondack Life, Vol. V., no. 4 (fall, 1974). A picture of Alfred Dodge & Son's Felt & Sound*ing Board Company (which now serves as an antique center) can be seen on page 23. The dimensions of the building are 300 feet by 70 feet, and its limestone rocks were quarried from nearby Inghams Mills. Another picture shows the High Falls Dam under construction.

Falls on Spruce Creek

1. www.nycoveredbridges.org/page17.html shows a picture of the covered bridge from below the falls.

2. ifhistoricalsociety.org/storepostm.html contains a picture of the cascade downstream from the covered bridge.

3. www.nycoveredbridges.org/page17.html provides significant information about the covered bridge.

Little Falls

1. Nelson Greene, *Old Mohawk Turnpike Book* (Fort Plain, N.Y.: n.p., 1942), 211. "The river here has a fall of 42 feet in half a mile, affording great water power."

2. Walter F. Burmeister, *Appalachian Waters 2: The Hudson River and Its Tributaries* (Oakton, Va.: Appalachian Books, 1974), 275. "At this point an ancient fall of immense proportions eroded the deep gorge." Burmeister goes on to say that, "The river drops 40 feet within these rocky narrows."

3. *History of the County of Schenectady, N.Y. From 1662–1886* (New York, N.Y.: W. W. Munsell & Co., 1886), 46. "At Little Falls there is a descent in the river of forty feet in the distance of half a mile, up the current of which no boats could be forced; so it became a portage."

4. Roland Van Zandt, *Chronicles of the Hudson: Three Centuries of Travel & Adventure* (1971, reprint; Hensonville, N.Y.: Black Dome Press Corp., 1992), 179. According to William L. Stone, "Through this chasm the Mohawk tumbles over a rocky bed, and falls, in the distance of half a mile to the depth of forty feet."

5. Gilbert W. Hagerty, *Wampum, War & Trade Goods West of the Hudson* (Interlaken, N.Y.: Heart of the Lakes Publishing, 1985), 11. "In ancient geological times the massive glacial waters, impounded above present Little Falls, were released by cutting towards the Little Falls gorge, forming the shortest and more realistic water level route from the Atlantic to the Great Lakes." Also, "At the gorge a waterfall surged wildly down over and around 3/4 of a mile of rocks in a 39 foot drop."

6. Codman Hislop, *Rivers of America: The Mohawk* (New York/Toronto: Rinehart & Company, Inc., 1948), 8. "Here, in strange contrast to the town's name, once roared the vast falls of the prehistoric Mohawk."

7. Nelson Greene, *The Mohawk Valley: Gateway to the West*, Vol. 1 (Chicago, Ill.: The S. J. Clarke Publishing Company, 1925), 80. The fossil imprint of the once-mighty cataract at Little Falls is sited: "The largest of the potholes of the Little Falls Gorge is the basin just below the lower falls, with the water over 150 feet deep." On page 77, the author writes that "the volume of water which flowed ... must have been greater than that which now goes over Niagara Falls."

8. Herkimer County Historical Society, *Herkimer County at 200* (Herkimer, N.Y.: Herkimer County Historical Society, 1992), 19. "The enormous volume of water finally broke down the Precambrian divide at Little Falls, and a mighty river was born: the Iro-Mohawk. It swept over the divide in a waterfall greater than Niagara."

9. Nelson, op. cit., 211.

10. Max W. Reid, *The Mohawk Valley: Its Legends and Its History. 1609–1780* (Harrison, N.Y.: Harbor Hill Books, 1979), 364.

11. Louis Rossi, *Cycling along the Canals of New York: 500 Miles of Bike Riding along the Erie, Champlain, Cayugaseneca, and Oswego Canals* (College Park, Md.: Vitesse Press, 1999), 35.

WATERFALLS ALONG ROUTE 20

Introduction

1. *I Love NY: Map and guide to Scenic Route 20,* 2005, Official publication of the Route 20 Association of New York State Inc.

Additional Source of Information:

Irma Mastrean (compiler), *Princetown: Portrait of a Town* (Princetown, N.Y.: Princetown Historical Society, 1990), 98.

French's Falls

1. C. R. Roseberry, *Albany: Three Centuries a County* (Albany, N.Y.: Albany County Tricentennial Commission, 1983), 22. "There the Normans Kill had cut a gorge, with a waterfall, in an outcropping of shale bedrock."

2. A picture of the fall is displayed on the cover of the Guilderland Historical Society's 2005 calendar.

3. Roseberry, op. cit. On page 22, Roseberry writes that Abel French was the first settler to establish a gristmill and sawmill at the falls.

4. Arthur B. Gregg, *Old Hellebergh* (Guilderland, N.Y.: Guilderland Historical Society, 1975), 3. An early photograph of French's Hollow is shown, depicting a mill and covered bridge. The perspective suggests that the picture was taken by a photographer positioned at the top of the upper falls.

5. Alice G. Begley and Mary Ellen Johnson, *Images of America: Guilderland, New York* (Charleston, S.C.: Arcadia Publishing, 1999). The authors present a series of photographs of French's Hollow, with historically interesting captions. On page 79 is a fascinating picture of an old mill on the west bank, complete with a covered bridge, train trestle, and French's Falls in the distance. Perhaps one of the most interesting photographs is an aerial shot of French's Hollow (page 83), taken in more recent times.

6. Alice C. Begley, *Historic Markers in the Town of Guilderland, Albany County, New York* (Altamont, N.Y.: The Altamont Enterprise, 1994), 17. Begley writes that "A button factory, a grist mill, and employee housing all congregated near the necessary water supply."

7. Begley and Johnson, op. cit. On page 80 can be seen a photograph of French's Woolen Mill, which was used for multiple purposes after it was abandoned as a mill before 1860.

8. Ibid. The present bridge, now restricted to pedestrian traffic only, crosses the Normanskill at the same spot as the old covered bridge.

9. Jim Besha, hydroelectric engineer

10. Dennis Sullivan, *Voorheesville, New York: A Sketch of the Beginnings of a Nineteenth Century Railroad Town* (Voorheesville, N.Y.: The Village of Voorheesville, n.d.). A picture of LaGrange Falls can be seen on page 71.

11. New Scotland Historical Association, *Images of America: New Scotland Township* (Charleston, S.C.: Arcadia Publishing, 2000). A picture of LaGrange Falls can be seen on page 70. According to the accompanying text, a sawmill was built in 1720 by the LaGrange family, which is how the fall came to be named. Later, in 1831, a gristmill was erected.

12. Howell and Tenney, *History of the County of Albany, New York. From 1609 to 1886 with Portraits, Biographies and Illustrations* (1886, reprint; Salem, Mass.: Higginson Book Company, n.d.). "There are a few natural falls upon several of these kills or creeks, and facilities for increasing greatly their hydraulic power. Vly Kill has a remarkable cascade of 60 feet." This is a reference to LaGrange Falls.

Additional Source of information:

Warren Liddle, *Days Before Yesteryear* (Duanesburg, N.Y.: V. O. D. Communications, Inc., 1978). Information on the Normans Kill and its mills (particularly the Liddle Mill) is presented on pages 2 and 3.

Bozen Kill Falls

1. Carl Carmer (selector), *The Tavern Lamps Are Burning: Literary Journeys through Six Regions and Four Centuries of New York State* (New York, N. Y.: David McKay Company, Inc., 1964), 534. Under Lansing Christman in the section entitled "Biographies," mention is made of the Bozen Kill "whose foaming waters stagger through the slanting acres of the old Christman farm."

2. Ibid., 534.

3. Natalie Walsh, "Falls for Spring," *The Sunday Gazette*, Lifestyles Section H, May 15, 2005, H1 and H2. A Picture of the fall (taken from near the lean-to) is displayed on H2.

4. *Environmental Trip Tips in and around Schenectady, New York*

(Schenectady, N.Y.: The Environmental Clearinghouse of Schenectady, 1976), 38. "The sandstone layers form the ledges and waterfalls; the shale crumbles and erodes easily. Fossils are rare in these four hundred and fifty million year old Schenectady beds."

5. Walsh, op. cit., H2. The "30-foot falls themselves are powerful and as lovely in the dead of winter as they are now."

6. Jackson Davis, etc. (compilers and editors), *Guide to Natural Areas of the Eastern New York Chapter of the Nature Conservancy*, seventh edition (Albany, N.Y.: Eastern New York Chapter, 1980), 21. A "30-foot high upper falls" is mentioned. A map of the preserve is displayed on page 20.

7. www.localhikes.com gives a height of 30 feet for the main fall.

8. *History of the County of Schenectady, N.Y. From 1662–1886* (New York, N.Y.: W. W. Munsell & Co., 1886), 161. "The Bozen Kill, or Mad Creek, one of the branches of the Normans Kill, is a picturesque stream on which is a fall of seventy feet."

9. Ibid., 304–307. Samples of W. W. Christman's poetry are offered in the section on "Song of the Western Gateway."

10. Background information on William Christman is displayed inside the lean-to by the waterfall.

11. Davis, op. cit., 21.

12. Warren Liddle, *Duanesburg: Land of Mills* (n.p.,: n.p, 1984), 1.

13. Ibid., 2.

14. Claire K. Schmitt, *Natural Areas of Schenectady County*, third edition (Schenectady, N.Y.: The Environmental Clearinghouse of Schenectady and The Schenectady County Environmental Advisory Council, 1986), 9. A map of the Christman Sanctuary is included with the text.

Dugway Falls

1. Sandra Manko and Jean Bakkom (editors), *A Touch of Nostalgia: Sharon Springs Spa* (Sharon Springs, N.Y.: Sharon Historical Society, 2000). A picture of the fall can be seen on page 2. The waterfall is identified as Ravine Falls.

2. Marian S. Lynes, *Water-Powered Grist Mills of Schoharie County* (Cobleskill, New York: Printed by the *Times-Journal*, 1981). On page 146, Lynes quotes Thomas F. Gordon from his 1836 *Gazetteer of the State of New York*, in which the waters of Dugway Falls are referred to as "a ledge of rocks over which they fall perpendicularly 60 feet, and have volume sufficient to drive a grist mill." To clarify her point, Lynes continues by saying that, "Here Gordon is describing the Brimstone Creek and Falls which flow down a gorge of exceptional interest and beauty, onward toward the Mohawk Valley." Lynes also provides background information on the mills that were earlier built near the falls.

3. Sandra Manko, Katina Manko and Jean Makkom, *Reflections on Sharon: 1797–1997. A Pictorial History* (Sharon Springs, N.Y.: Sharon Historical Society, 1997). A picture of the fall is shown on page 71.

4. Stuart M. Blumin (text) and Hans Durlach (photos), *The Short Season of Sharon Springs: Portrait of Another New York* (Ithaca, N.Y.: Cornell University Press, 1980). The book provides a detailed history of Sharon Springs and the sulfur springs.

5. *The Encyclopedia of New York*, Vol. 2 (New York: Somerset Publishers, Inc., 1996), 212. Information is provided on the town's history. On page 213, the author writes, "The village and the springs lie in a ravine. They are nine hundred feet above the Mohawk Valley, with pure air, magnificent views, natural scenery, and a variety of rural life."

6. Lynes, op cit., 146.

Judd Falls

1. www.cherryvalleymuseum.org/tekahar.htm.

2. Donald W. Fisher, *Bedrock Geology of the Central Mohawk Valley, New York* (Albany, N.Y.: University of the State of New York, The State Education Department, 1980), 20. A picture of the fall, looking rather dry, can be seen in Fisher's book.

3. Brian and Becky Nielsen, *Around Cooperstown in Vintage Postcards* (Postcard History Series) (Charleston, S.C.: Arcadia Publishing, 2000). A beautiful photograph of Tekaharawa (Judd) Falls is shown on page 123.

4. Dennis Savoie, *Cranks from Cooperstown: 50 Bike Rides in Upstate New York*. (Cooperstown, N.Y.: Tourmaster Publications, L.L.C., 1998), 80. "The Mohawk Indians named this beautiful 135 foot waterfall 'Tekaharawa, The Place of High Waters.'"

5. www.cherryvalleymuseum.org.

6. Ibid.

Leatherstocking Falls

1. www.bluemingoinn.com.

2. Brian and Becky Nielsen, *Around Cooperstown in Vintage Postcards* (Postcard History Series) (Charleston, S.C.: Arcadia Publishing, 2000). On page 21 can be seen a postcard reproduction of Leatherstocking Falls.

3. Ralph Birdsall, *Story of Cooperstown* (Cooperstown, N.Y.: The Arthur H. Christ Co., 1917). A photograph of the waterfall can be seen on page 352. On page 351 Birdsall writes: "for here the water comes tumbling down from the height in the beautiful Leatherstocking Falls. A shady glen is here, a favorite resort of small picnic parties."

4. Star Brunmeler and Heidi Miller, in conjunction with Hugh C.

MacDougall, "The Allure of Lake Otsego," *Kaatskill Life,* Vol. 12, no. 2 (summer 1997). A picture of the fall can be seen on page 40.

5. Nielsen, op. cit., 33.

6. www.bluemingoinn.com.

7. Walter R. Littell, *A History of Cooperstown including "The Chronicles of Cooperstown" by James Fenimore Cooper, "The History of Cooperstown 1839–1886" by Samuel M. Shaw and "The History of Cooperstown 1886–1929" by Walter R. Littell* (Cooperstown, N.Y.: The Freeman's Journal Company, 1929). Background historical information on Leatherstocking Falls is provided on pages 139 and 178.

8. Ibid., 37.

9. Dennis Savoie, *Cranks from Cooperstown: 50 Bike Rides in Upstate New York.* (Cooperstown, N.Y.: Tourmaster Publications, L.L.C., 1998), 82. "Leatherstocking Falls ... is easy to see during the spring runoff, before the leaves sprout."

Falls at Van Hornsville

1. Frank Oppel (compiler), "Richfield Springs," *New York State: Tales of the Empire State* (Secaucus, N.J.: Castle, 1988). A line drawing of the fall can be seen on page 168.

2. A picture of Sawmill Falls can be seen on www.paulkeelerbooks. com.

3. Douglas Ayres, Jr., "Van Hornsville Caves," *Mohawk Valley USA*, Vol. 7, no. 1 (spring 1986), 37–39.

Additional Sources of Information:

Cris Young, "The School That Was Owen Young's Dream," *Route 20 Pulse: The Heartbeat of the Highway of Dreams*, Vol. 2, no. 9, 7 and 9. Young provides background on Owen Young and the school that he helped establish.

Herkimer County Historical Society, *Herkimer County at 200* (Herkimer, N.Y.: Herkimer County Historical Society, 1992). A picture of the Tufa Caves can be seen on page 14.

Button Falls

1. Rich and Sue Freeman, *200 Waterfalls in Central & Western New York: A Finder's Guide* (Fishers, N.Y.: Footprint Press, 2002), 352.

2. Mrs. L. M. Hammond, *History of Madison County, State of New York, Book One* (Syracuse, N.Y.: Truair, Smith & Co., Book and Job Printers, 1872), 176. Button Falls is described as "a very pretty cataract some seventy feet in height."

3. Ibid., 173. "The first saw mill built in the town was erected by Captain Brown, in the year 1792, and the same year John Button built a

grist mill on the same stream some distance south of the saw mill, which gave the stream the name of 'Buttons Mill Creek.' A short time after, Jabez Brown built the second saw mill on the same stream."

Rexford Falls

1. Rich and Sue Freeman, *200 Waterfalls in Central & Western New York: A Finder's Guide* (Fishers, N.Y.: Footprint Press, 2002), 308.

2. John P. Gomph, *Sherburne Illustrated: A History of the Village of Sherburne, New York. Its Scenery, Development, and Business Enterprises* (Utica, N.Y: John P. Gomph, 1896). A picture of the fall can be seen on page 7. Gomph goes on to mention, on the same page: "The first saw-mill was located about a mile below Rexford Falls, in the gulf."

3. Joel Hatch, Jr., *Reminiscences, Anecdotes, and Statistics of the Early Settlers and the 'Olden Time' in the Town of Sherburne, Chenango County, New York* (Utica, N.Y.: Curtiss & White Printers, 1862). On page 67 Hatch includes a quote from Lardner Van Vexem's 1842 *Geological Report of the State:* "The next point is the falls and banks of Handsome Creek [Sulphur Springs Creek], north of Sherburne. The water falls for sixty or more feet, and the sides of the Creek expose about one hundred feet of the finer kind of shale." Also on page 67: "A Sulphur Spring issues from the slate of the Hamilton group, at the foot of the falls, on Handsome Brook near Sherburne."

4. David O'Connor, *Old Chenango County in Postcards* (New Berlin, N.Y.: Molly Yes Press, 1983), 58. "The height of the falls is about 75 feet, and the rocky gorge is nearly 100 feet deep."

5. James H. Smith, *History of Chenango and Madison Counties, New York, with Illustrations and Biographical Sketches of Some of Its Prominent Men and Pioneers* (Syracuse, N.Y.: D. Mason & Co., 1880). The frontispiece for Book I is a full-page illustration of the fall.

6. www.rootsweb.com.

7. Ibid. The Web site provides information on how the fall came to be named, and its early industrial history.

8. O'Connor, op. cit., 58.

9. Hatch, op. cit., 30. Other names of the brook are given as well.

10. O'Connor, op. cit., 58.

11. Peter Eisenstadt (editor-in-chief), *The Encyclopedia of New York State* (Syracuse, N.Y.: Syracuse University Press, 2005), 1409. According to Dale C. Storms, "At Rexford Falls, site of Sulfur Springs and the Spring House hotel (1883), a 78 ft. (238m) Whipple arch-type truss bridge by Sheldon and Ross of Norwich remains a landmark after more than a century."

Oriskany Falls

1. www.paulkeelerbooks.com.

2. Rich and Sue Freeman, *200 Waterfalls in Central & Western New York: A Finder's Guide* (Fishers, N.Y.: Footprint Press, 2002), 349.

3. Peter Eisenstadt (editor-in-chief), *The Encyclopedia of New York State* (Syracuse, N.Y.: Syracuse University Press, 2005), 1158. Mention is made of the following industries: tannery (1816); distillery (circa 1825); foundry and machine shop (1853); woolen factory (1865).

Stockbridge Falls

1. Rich and Sue Freeman, *200 Waterfalls in Central & Western New York: A Finder's Guide* (Fishers, N.Y.: Footprint Press, 2002), 347.

2. Mrs. L. M. Hammond, *History of Madison County, State of New York. Book Two* (Syracuse, N.Y.: Truair, Smith & Co., Book and Job Printers, 1872). On pages 729–730, Oneida Creek is mentioned: "The chief branch of this creek has its source in Smithfield, and enters the valley in the southeast corner of the town. Its course is marked by the wildest scenery. Before entering the valley it pours down a series of cascades, low falls and rapids, which for beauty are not surpassed by anything in this part of the country."

3. James H. Smith, *History of Chenango and Madison Counties, New York, with Illustrations and Biographical Sketches of Some of Its Prominent Men and Pioneers* (Syracuse, N.Y.: D. Mason & Co., 1880). In Book II, page 706, the author writes about Oneida Creek, stating, "Its course down the west hill to the valley and the junction with its confluent is marked by a succession of rapids and low falls, presenting a series of varied and beautiful cascades amidst highly picturesque scenery, and furnishing numerous mill sites."

4. Ibid., 707.

5. Hammond, op. cit., 729–730.

Chittenango Falls

1. Rich and Sue Freeman, *200 Waterfalls in Central & Western New York: A Finder's Guide* (Fishers, N.Y.: Footprint Press, 2002), 343–345.

2. Mrs. L. M. Hammond, *History of Madison County, State of New York Book One* (Syracuse, N.Y.: Truair, Smith & Co., Book and Job Printers, 1872). On page 198, Hammond writes, "the water plunges in a beautiful cascade, perpendicularly, over a ledge of limestone rock, 136 feet in height." On the same page, mention is also made that, "It is a singularly romantic, wild and awe inspiring spot, at the foot of the fall, as one stands in the deep shadows of overhanging rocks, perpendicular hills and thick forest, the gloom increased by rising spray, the changing and uncertain light and shades glancing on the falling, foaming forest, the

rush, the roar, the boiling, trembling basin, the quivering earth with its apparently unstable footing."

3. Ibid., 197.

4. Richard Palmer, "State Park is Nationally Recognized," *Route 20 Pulse: The Heartbeat of the Highway of Dreams,* Vol. 2, no. 10, 13.

5. Hammond, op. cit., 197.

6. Freeman, op. cit., 344.

7. Palmer, op. cit., 13.

8. Ibid., 13.

9. myhome.sunyocc.edu/ ~ mcanincb/es-pages/trips.html.

Pratt Falls

1. Rich and Sue Freeman, *200 Waterfalls in Central & Western New York: A Finder's Guide* (Fishers, N.Y.: Footprint Press, 2002), 340–342.

2. www.geocities.com/yosemite/rapids/8910/highestfalls.html, a site that ranks the "50 Highest Waterfalls in Western New York," gives the height of Pratt Falls as being 137 feet.

3. Professor W. W. Clayton, *History of Onondaga County, New York, with Illustrations and Biographical Sketches of Some of Its Prominent Men and Pioneers* (Syracuse, N.Y.: D. Mason & Co., 1878). Next to the title page of Clayton's book can be seen a full-page illustration of Pratt Falls (referred to as "Pratt's Falls, Pompey, N.Y.") The illustration shows two separate chutes of water coming over the top and then joining as one, two-thirds of the way down from the top. On page 395, Clayton writes: "Pratt's Falls, upon the west branch of the Limestone Creek, are one hundred and thirty-seven feet in perpendicular height; and within a few rods of them are several other fine cascades. Near the north line, upon the same creek, is a cascade of seventy feet tall. Just east of the county line, near Delphi, on the east branch of the Limestone, are two other fine cascades."

4. Hammond, op. cit., 198.

5. Clayton, op. cit., 395.

6. Freeman, op. cit., 341.

Clark Reservation

1. nysparks.state.ny.us/parks.

WATERFALLS OF THE HELDERBERGS

Outlet Falls

1. James H. Stoller, *Geological Excursions: a Guide to Localities in the Region of Schenectady and the Mohawk Valley, and the Vicinity of Saratoga Springs* (Schenectady, N.Y.: Union Book Co., 1932), 82. The author writes about "where a stream [Outlet Creek] falls from the summit of the cliff to its base, a drop of about 100 feet."

2. Frank Oppel (compiler) "The Helderbergs," *New York State: Tales of the Empire State* (Secaucus, N.J.: Castle, 1988), 265.

3. James Cullen, John Mylroie and Art Palmer, *Karst Hydrogeology of Eastern New York: a Guidebook to the Geology Field Trip* (Pittsfield, Mass.: National Speleological Society Annual Convention, 1979), 47. "Outlet Creek and Outlet Falls were, at one time, much larger than they are now. At the present time, the drainage in this region is primarily underground, consequently Outlet Creek is quite small."

4. Oppel, op. cit., 265. Verplanck Colvin is quoted as saying: "This is the Small Fall, sometimes called the 'Dry Falls.' The latter name you will hardly appreciate should you visit it when swollen by recent rains. Here you may enjoy an unequaled shower-bath; but the stream carries pebbles, and the dashing water itself stings like a shower of shot."

Minelot Falls

1. Frank Oppel (compiler), "The Helderbergs," *New York State: Tales of the Empire State* (Secaucus, N.J.: Castle, 1988). On page 266 mention is made that the waterfall has also been known as "Big Falls" and "Indian Ladder Falls." Page 269 contains more description of Minelot Falls. On page 274 is a line drawing of Minelot Falls in the winter, shaped like an inverted cone.

2. Mary Lynn Blanks, *Fun with the Family in New York: Hundreds of Ideas for Day Trips with the Kids*, third edition (Guilford, Conn.: The Globe Pequot Press, 2001), 88. The author mentions that the park contains 2,300 acres of land.

3. Gary L. Donhardt, *Indian Ladder: A History of Life in the Helderbergs* (Collierville, Tenn.: Donhardt and Daughters Publishers, 2001), 123. "At Minelot Falls, water flows over Coeymans limestone and pours 100 feet onto the Indian Ladder beds below."

4. C. R. Roseberry, *From Niagara to Montauk: the Scenic Pleasures of New York State* (Albany, N.Y.: The State University of New York Press, 1982), 188. "The escarpment has two large reentrants, the Indian Ladder Gulf and the Cave Gulf. In former times, perhaps interglacially, streams pouring over the cliffs eroded these notches with high waterfalls." A few sentences later Roseberry writes that, "Only one cataract of any size comes

over the cliff today. This is the Indian Ladder Falls, 116 feet high."

5. Stella Green and H. Neil Zimmerman, *50 Hikes in the Lower Hudson Valley* (Woodstock, Vt.: Backcountry Guides, 2002), 277. Barbara McMartin is quoted as saying "When the water table is high these two creeks form spectacular falls that you can walk behind on the trail."

6. Herb Chong (editor), *The Long Path Guide*, fifth edition (Mahwah, N.J.: The New York-New Jersey Trail Conference, 2002). A picture of the fall, with overhanging ice, can be seen on page 206.

7. Oppel, op. cit., 266.

8. Bradford B. Van Diver, *Upstate New York* (Dubuque, Iowa: Kendall/Hunt Publishing Company, 1980), 182. "... the Lower Bear Path passes by Outlet and Minelot Creeks. ... They once carried much more water than they do now, but today, because of extensive solution of the host limestone, most of the flow is lost to underground conduits."

9. Barbara McMartin and Peter Kick, *Fifty Hikes in the Hudson Valley: From the Catskills to the Taconics, and from the Ramapos to the Helderbergs* (Woodstock, Vt.: Backcountry Publications, 1985), 221. "Once in the large amphitheater, which is called Indian Ladder Gulf, you will see Outley [*sic*] and Minelot Creeks. Together they have been responsible for the erosion of this impressive embayment. When the water table is high, these two creeks form spectacular falls that you can walk behind on the trail."

10. Bill Bailey, *New York State Parks: a Complete Outdoor Recreation Guide for Campers, Boaters, Anglers, Hikers, Beach and Outdoor Lovers* (Saginaw, Mich.: Glovebox Guidebooks of America, 1997). A map of John Boyd Thacher Park can be found on page 302.

Onesquethaw Falls (Historic)

1. Howell and Tenney, *History of the County of Albany, NY. From 1609 to 1886 with Portraits, Biographies and Illustrations* (1886, reprint; Salem, Mass.: Higginson Book Company, n.d.), 14. "There are a few natural falls upon several of these kills or creeks, and facilities for increasing greatly their hydraulic power. Vly Kill has a remarkable cascade of 60 feet, and another of 40 feet is the Oneskethau."

2. New Scotland Historical Association, *Images of America: New Scotland Township* (Charleston, S.C.: Arcadia Publishing, 2000). On page 112 can be seen a picture of the waterfall. According to the accompanying text, Teunis Slingerlands built a gristmill at the 40-foot-high fall in 1755.

Cascade at Hannacroix Ravine Preserve

1. Claire K. Schmitt and Mary S. Brennan, *Natural Areas of Albany County* (Niskayuna, N.Y.: Environmental Clearinghouse of Schenectady, 1991), 55.

2. Jackson Davis, etc. (compilers and editors), *Guide to Natural Areas*

of the Eastern New York Chapter of the Nature Conservancy, seventh edition (Albany, N.Y.: Eastern New York Chapter, 1980), 28.

3. Ibid., 33. In addition, the authors go on to say that, "There are many waterfalls where the stream tumbles over the more resistant sandstone layers."

4. C. R. Roseberry, *Albany: Three Centuries a County* (Albany, N.Y.: Albany County Tricentennial Commission, 1983), 13.

5. J. Van Vechten Vedder, *History of Greene County, New York* (1927, reprint; Cornwallville, N.Y.: Hope Farm Press, 1985), 110. "Hannacroix creek is the principal stream and called in early days Haanekraai-kill (Cock crowing creek)."

Fall at Alcove

1. According to www.catskillcenter.org/programs/edu/csp/h2o/lesson4.htm, the Alcove Reservoir holds 13.5 billion gallons of water.

Dickinson Falls

1. Edward D. Gidding, *Coeymans and the Past* (Coeymans, N.Y.: Tricentennial Committee of the Town of Coeymans, 1973). The book contains a picture of the falls, identified as "Falls of the Hannacroix."

Lobdell Mill Falls

1. C. R. Roseberry, *Albany: Three Centuries a County* (Albany, N.Y.: Tricentennial Commission, 1983). The text on page 24 tells how Basic Creek came to be named, as well as presenting some of the mill-related history of Westerlo.

Falls #1 at Partridge Run: Partridge Run Road

1. Claire K. Schmitt and Mary S. Brennan, *Natural Areas of Albany County* (Niskayuna, N.Y.: The Environmental Clearinghouse of Schenectady, 1991). A map of Partridge Run is included on page 62.

2. Robert M. Toole, *A Look at Metroland* (Saratoga Springs, N.Y.: Office of R. M. Toole, Landscape Architect, 1976). On page 66, Toole mentions a 1,000-foot drop in elevation from the Helderberg Plateau to Berne.

3. C. R. Roseberry, *Albany: Three Centuries a County* (Albany, N.Y.: Albany County Tricentennial Commission, 1983), 18. Rosenberry writes that Henry Hill is the highest point in the Helderbergs.

Rensselaerville Falls

1. C. R. Rosenberry, *Albany: Three Centuries a County* (Albany, N.Y.: Albany County Tricentennial Commission, 1983), 11. According to Rosenberry, the mills benefited from "excellent waterpower provided by a drop of 100 feet in Tenmile Creek."

2. Howard Stone, *25 Bicycle Tours in the Hudson Valley: Scenic Rides from Saratoga to West Point* (Woodstock, Vt.: Backcountry Publications, The Countryman Press, Inc., 1989). A picture of Rensselaerville Falls can be seen on page 62.

3. *People Made It Happen Here: History of the Town of Rensselaerville ca. 1788–1950* (Rensselaerville, N.Y.: The Rensselaerville Historical Society, 1977). A picture of the falls can be seen on page 46.

4. Claire K. Schmitt and Mary S. Brennan, *Natural Areas of Albany County* (Niskayuna, N.Y.: The Environmental Clearinghouse of Schenectady, 1991), 59.

Falls at Berne

1. Arthur B. Gregg, *Old Hellebergh* (Guilderland, N.Y.: Guilderland Historical Society, 1975). A picture of the falls, entitled "Mill site of Malachi Whippe," can be seen on page 123.

2. Robert M. Toole, *A Look at Metroland* (Saratoga Springs, N.Y.: Office of R. M. Toole, Landscape Architect, 1976), 67. Toole mentions how the town was named, and includes the history of the flour mill.

WATERFALLS OF THE SCHOHARIE VALLEY

Introduction

1. Gilbert W. Hagerty, *Wampum, War & Trade Goods West of the Hudson* (Interlaken, N.Y.: Heart of the Lakes Publishing, 1985), 63.

2. Walter F. Burmeister, *Appalachian Waters 2: The Hudson River and Its Tributaries* (Oakton, Va.: Appalachian Books, 1974), 324.

3. Thelma P. Stone, *Thumbnail Sketches of the Schoharie Valley* (Pattersonville, N.Y.: Unicorn Publications, 1981), 3.

4. John P. D. Wilkinson, "The Timothy Murphy Trail: A Scenic Route through History," *Kaatskill Life*, Vol. 10, no. 2 (summer 1995), 18–25.

Falls on Wilsey Creek

1. *1991 National Speleological Society Convention Program* (Cobleskill, N.Y.: NSS, 1991), 81. Wilsey Creek is described as "a minor creek (as opposed to stream) that falls about 25' into a plunge pool right beside the road."

2. www.albanylandtrust.org mentions the height of the fall as 30 feet.

3. www.mohawkhudson.org.

4. Ibid.

5. Ibid.

6. Albert Perry Brigham, *New York State Museum Bulletin: Glacial Geology and Geographic Conditions of the Lower Mohawk Valley* (Albany, N.Y.: University of the State of New York, 1929), 126.

7. Walter F. Burmeister, *Appalachian Waters 2: The Hudson River and Its Tributaries* (Oakton, Va.: Appalachian Books, 1974), 330.

Waterfall at Secret Caverns

1. Marilyn Milow Francis, "Beneath Rolling Hills: New York State's Best Kept Secret," *Kaatskill Life*, Vol. 9, no. 2 (summer 1994). A picture of the fall can be seen on page 106.

2. John Evans, Peter Quick, and Bruce Sloane (editors), *An Introduction to Caves of the Northeast: Guidebook for the 1979 National Speleological Society Convention* (Pittsfield, Mass.: National Speleological Society, 1979). The secret behind Secret Cavern's enormous waterfall is revealed on page 54: "At the extreme end of the tourist route, there is a room 30 feet in diameter. A vertical dome soars up about 100 feet from the west side of the room. This chimney is open to the surface through a small passage at the top about 15 feet long. The passage is a watercourse that connects with a swampy pond on the surface. The cavern owners have installed a valve to control the flow of the water. Thus when tourists enter, an impressive 100 foot waterfall is made to fall into a deep rocky pool below."

3. Clay Perry, *Underground Empire: Wonders and Tales of New York Caves* (New York: Stephen Daye Press, 1948), 82. According to Perry, Secret Caverns is "furnished with a waterfall at the far end, which is brought into play by turning an electric switch that opens the gate to a dam across a small surface stream."

4. Francis, op. cit., 105.

5. Mary Robinson Sive, "Highways and Byways of Schoharie County," *Catskill Mountain Region Guide*, Vol. 18, no. 7 (July 2003), 40.

6. Joe Maher, "Funky Billboards Tell Secret," *Daily Gazette*, August 27, 2000. The writer captures the funky quality of Secret Caverns that distinguishes it from its more famous and frequented cousin, Howe Caverns.

Cave Waterfalls

1. Michael Nardacci, ed., *Guide to the Caves and Karst of the Northeast: 50th Anniversary NSS Convention* (Huntsville, Ala.: The National Speleological Society, 1991). A picture of the waterfall in the downstream end of Benson's cave can be seen on page 58; one of the waterfall in McFail's Cave is on page 49; and a 70-foot-high waterfall in the Hell's Hole entrance to McFail's Cave is shown on page 133.

High Street Bridge Falls

1. Marian S. Lynes, *Water-Powered Grist Mills of Schoharie County* (Cobleskill, New York: Printed by the *Times-Journal*, 1981). An early postcard of the waterfall can be seen on page 117.

2. Ibid., 150. Lynes provides valuable information on the fall and its history.

Falls at Lasell Park

1. The Daily Star Online Edition, October 9, 2001, www.thedailys-tar.com.

Falls on Little Schoharie Creek

1. Background information obtained from Bertha Lawyer, owner of Waterfall Campgrounds.

Bouck Falls

1. Dorwin W. Bulson, *To-Wos-Scho-Hor: The Land of the Unforgotten Indian. A True Story of the Schoharie Creek* (n.p., 1961), 13. "Here a twenty-five-foot-wide waterfall of around one hundred feet pours loudly between very acutely rising hill sides, which later attain an altitude of nineteen hundred feet on either side." A picture of Bouck Falls, facing the falls and from above, can be seen on the insert between pages 13 and 14.

2. Walter F. Burmeister, *Appalachian Waters 2: The Hudson River and Its Tributaries* (Oakton, Va.: Appalachian Books, 1974), 329. "Bouck Falls, enclosed by a wild ravine, drops 80 feet within one-fifth mile."

3. Thelma P. Stone, *Thumbnail Sketches of the Schoharie Valley* (Pattersonville, N.Y.: Unicorn Publications, 1981), 2. Bouck Falls is "a magnificent natural cataract which falls over solid rock cliffs."

4. Marian S. Lynes, *Water-Powered Grist Mills of Schoharie County* (Cobleskill, New York: Printed by the *Times-Journal*, 1981), 77. Catherine Lawyer is quoted as describing the "falls where water dashes down in a twisted descent over 120 feet into a pool it has excavated at its base."

5. Jill Dail (editor), *Folklore and Folk Names of Schoharie County* (Cobleskill, N.Y.: State University of New York, Agricultural and Technology College, 1976), 25. Bouck Falls was named in honor of Governor Bouck.

6. Stone, op. cit., 2. The author mentions that Bouck Island is the ancestral home of former governor William C. Bouck.

7. nywaterfallhouse.com.

8. Barbara Delaney, "Timothy Murphy: The Making of a Legend," *Mohawk Valley Heritage*, Vol. 2, no. 2, 46. "If you visit Bouck Falls, you will note there isn't room behind the falling waters for even a small child, let alone an adult."

9. A. M. Sullivan, *Tim Murphy Morgan Rifleman and other Ballads* (New York: The Declan X. McMullen Company, Inc., 1947), 101.

10. Lynes, op. cit., 77.

Falls on Tributary to Panther Creek

1. Herb Chong (editor), *The Long Path Guide*, fifth edition (Mahwah, N.J.: The New York-New Jersey Trail Conference, 2002), 176.

Krum's Falls

1. Information provided by Elizabeth Sweet, one of the earlier generation of the Keyser family.

2. Marian S. Lynes, *Water-Powered Grist Mills of Schoharie County* (Cobleskill, New York. Printed by the *Times-Journal,* 1981), 72. The Keyser Kill was named after the grandfather of Barent Keyser.

3. John Lyon Rich, *New York State Museum Bulletin: Glacial Geology of the Catskills* (Albany, N.Y.: University of the State of New York, 1934), 108.

4. Mrs. Kenneth C. Bouck, "Hometown—Breakabeen," *Schoharie County Historical Review*, Vol. 46, no. 2 (fall–winter, 1982), 25. On page 26, Bouck mentions, "There was a dam over the Keyserkill just west of the bridge atop the natural waterfall and millraces built to each mill."

5. Dorwin W. Bulson, *To-Wos-Scho-Hor: The Land of the Unforgotten Indian. A True Story of the Schoharie Creek* (n.p., 1961), 14.

6. Edward R. Gazda, *Place Names in New York* (Schenectady, N.Y.: Gazda Associates, Inc., 1997), 12.

Creamery Falls

1. Edward R. Gazda, *Place Names in New York* (Schenectady, N. Y.: Gazda Associates, Inc., 1997), 10.

2. Jill Dail (editor), *Folklore and Folk Names of Schoharie County* (Cobleskill, N.Y.: State University of New York, Agricultural and Technology College, 1976), 2. Dail mentions that Blenheim was originally known as Patchin Hollow, after General Freegift Patchin. The name was later changed to that of the famous battlefield in Europe.

3. Dorwin W. Bulson, *To-Wos-Scho-Hor: The Land of the Unforgotten Indian. A True Story of the Schoharie Creek* (n.p., 1961), 14. The author mentions how the name Blenheim arose.

4. Ibid., 14. The author provides details on the dimensions and construction of the Blenheim Bridge.

Haverly Falls (Historic)

1. Helen Patchin, *History of the Town of Blenheim, Schoharie County, New York. 1797–1959* (Schoharie County, N.Y.: Town of Blenheim, 1959), 6. "Westkill Creek—runs by the creamery—outlet of Summit Lake—West Haverly owned the Haverly Falls—it was used as a millsite—flows into Schoharie Creek, almost opposite the Westkill Road turn off the village road." A photo of Haverly Falls can be seen on page 190.

2. Marian S. Lynes, *Water-Powered Grist Mills of Schoharie County* (Cobleskill, New York: Printed by the *Times-Journal*, 1981), 23–24. Background historical information on Haverly Falls is provided.

Mine Kill Falls

1. Cynthia Lewis and Thomas Lewis, *Best Hikes with Children in the Catskills & Hudson River Valley* (Seattle: The Mountaineers, 1992). A picture of the falls can be seen near the title page.

2. The *1995 I Love New York Travel Guide* contains a picture of Mine Kill Falls on page 24.

3. Herb Chong, "The Attraction of Falling Water" *Catskill Mountain Region Guide*, Vol. 18, no. 5 (May 2003), 41. "Mine Kill Falls in Mine Kill Falls State Park near Blenheim is typical of waterfalls that are in the western portion, cutting through layered gray rock over modest drops." Referring to the lower fall, Chong writes on page 42: "The waterfall slices downward through a narrow opening into a wide and shallow basin. At times of high water, a brown flood roars through, obliterating all other sounds from the vantage points that allow you to see up the gorge. Much of the rest of the time, it's a steady flow of white water spilling out."

4. "County Roads," *Schenectady & Upstate New York*, Vol. III, no. 1 (summer 1990), 60. A photo by Jo-Ellen Matusik shows a rather intrepid visitor standing inside the narrowly cut chasm just above the lower cascade.

5. Herb Chong (editor), *The Long Path Guide*, fifth edition (Mahwah, N.J.: The New York-New Jersey Trail Conference, 2002). A picture of the lower falls can be seen on page 170. On page 169 Chong writes, "The falls come out of a deep gorge and plummet into a pool where swimming is restricted."

6. Thelma P. Stone, *Thumbnail Sketches of the Schoharie Valley* (Pattersonville, N.Y.: Unicorn Publications, 1981), 2. "... a small bridge crosses a beautiful gorge and its stream which tumbles towards the Schoharie Creek below; this spot is locally known as the Minekill."

7. "Floods and Dams on Schoharie Creek at Gilboa," *Schoharie County Historical Review*, Vol. XXXIX, no. 1 (summer–spring, 1975). A photograph of Mine Kill Falls can be seen on page 4. On page 3, Mine Kill Falls is described as being between 100–110 feet in height.

8. John Lyon Rich, *New York State Museum Bulletin: Glacial Geology of the Catskills* (Albany, N.Y.: University of the State of New York, 1934), 94.

9. Robert Titus, "Rising Out of the Sea," *Kaatskill Life*, Vol. 16, no. 4 (winter 2001). Titus's article also includes pictures of Mine Kill Falls, on pages 44 and 45.

10. "Summersett House," *Schoharie County Historical Review*, Vol. 62 (spring–summer, 1998), 2–6.

Manor Kill Falls

1. John Lyon Rich, *New York State Museum Bulletin: Glacial Geology of the Catskills* (Albany, N.Y.: University of the State of New York, 1934). A picture of the falls is displayed on page 147.

2. Derek Doeffinger and Keith Boas, *Waterfalls of the Adirondacks and Catskills* (Ithaca, N.Y.: McBooks Press, 2000). A picture of the falls can be seen on page 101.

3. Herb Chong (editor), *The Long Path Guide*, fifth edition (Mahwah, N.J.: The New York-New Jersey Trail Conference, 2002). A picture of the upper fall can be seen on page 163.

4. Mildred Bailey, "Floods and Dams on Schoharie Creek at Gilboa," *Schoharie County Historical Review*, Vol. 39, no. 1 (summer–spring, 1975). The height of the falls is described as being 200 feet.

5. www.thecatskillsvintageviews.com.

6. Beatrice M. Mattice, *They Walked These Hills before Me: An Early History of the Town of Conesville* (Cornwallville, N.Y.: Hope Farm Press, 1980), 86.

7. Rich, op. cit., 94.

8. William E. Roscoe, *The History of Schoharie County* (Syracuse, N.Y.: D. Mason & Co., 1882), 129.

9. Russ Patton, Jr., "Historic Highlights: The Gilboa Town Museum," *Kaatskill Life*, Vol. 20, no. 2 (summer 2005), 24.

10. Mattice, op. cit., 86.

11. Ibid., 156.

12. Patton, op. cit., 25.

13. Robert Titus, "The Gilboa Forest," *Kaatskill Life*, Vol. 8, no. 1 (spring 1991).

14. Patton, op. cit., 25.

Devasego Falls

1. Irma Mae Griffin, *History of the Town of Roxbury* (Roxbury, N.Y.: by author, 1975), 25–26. Here, the flow of water went over the top of the wheel; hence its name.

2. Arthur G. Adam, *The Catskills: An Illustrated Historical Guide with Gazetteer* (New York: Fordham University Press, 1990). A picture of the fall can be seen on page 247.

3. R. Lionel De Lisser, *Picturesque Catskills: Greene County* (reprint; Cornwallville, N.Y: Hope Farm Press, 1971), 148. "Although but fifty feet high, it is a beautiful sheet of water, and has been many times called a miniature Niagara. It is one hundred and twenty-five feet wide, and the water below is flanked by high ledges. ... It was named after a French Indian who once lived in this vicinity."

4. Dowin Bulson, *To-was-scho-hor: The Land of the Unforgotten*

Indian (n.p, 1961). A picture of the falls can be seen on one of the plates between pages 15 and 16. There is also a plate containing a picture of the Gilboa Forest exhibit in the New York State Museum, Albany.

5. "Floods and Dams on Schoharie Creek at Gilboa," *Schoharie County Historical Review,* Vol. XXXIX, no. 1 (summer–spring, 1975). A photograph of Devasego Falls can be seen on page 4. On page 3, the waterfall is described as being 30 feet high.

Stratton Falls

1. A picture of the fall can be seen at www.strattonfalls.com.

Bibliography

Adams, Arthur G. *The Catskills: An Illustrated Historical Guide with Gazetteer*. New York: Fordham University Press, 1990.

Armstrong, Kathie and Chet Harvey, eds. *Canoe and Kayak Guide. East Central New York State: Includes Selected Waterways of Western New England*, first edition. Lake George, N.Y.: Adirondack Mountain Club, 2003.

Axel-Lute, Miriam. "Falls Guys." *Metroland*, Vol. 28, no. 23 (June 9, 2005).

Ayres, Douglas, Jr. "Sculptured Rocks." *Mohawk Valley USA*, Vol. 1, no. 4 (March 1981).

———. "Van Hornsville Caves." *Mohawk Valley USA*, Vol. 7, no. 1 (spring 1986).

Bailey, Bill. *New York State Parks: A Complete Outdoor Recreational Guide for Campers, Boaters, Anglers, Hikers, Beach and Outdoor Lovers*. Saginaw, Mich.: Glovebox Guidebooks of America, 1997.

Bailey, Mildred. "Floods and Dams on Schoharie Creek at Gilboa." *Schoharie County Historical Review*, Vol. 39, no. 1 (spring–summer, 1975).

Begley, Alice C. *Historic Markers in the Town of Guilderland, Albany County, New York*. Altamont, N.Y.: The Altamont Enterprises, 1994.

Begley, Alice and Mary Ellen Johnson. *Images of America: Guilderland, New York*. Charleston, S.C.: Arcadia Publishing, 1999.

Birdsall, Ralph. *Story of Cooperstown*. Cooperstown, N.Y.: The Arthur H. Christ Co., 1917.

Blanks, Mary Lynn. *Fun with the Family in New York: Hundreds of Ideas for Day Trips with the Kids*, third edition. Guilford, Conn.: The Globe Pequot Press, 2001.

Bliven, Rachel. "Take the Thruway Cruise." *Mohawk Valley Heritage: The Magazine of the Mohawk Valley*, Vol. 3, # 1.

Blumin, Stuart M. (text) and Hans Durlach (photos). *The Short Season of Sharon Springs: Portrait of Another New York*. Ithaca, N.Y.: Cornell University Press, 1980.

Bornt, Evelyn, Beryl Harrington and Ellen L. Wiley (editors and compilers). *Pittstown through the Years.* Pittstown, N.Y.: Pittstown Historical Society, 1989.

Bouck, Mrs. Kenneth C. "Hometown—Breakabeen." *Schoharie County Historical Review*, Vol. 46, no. 2 (fall–winter, 1982).

Brigham, Albert Perry. *New York State Museum Bulletin: Glacial Geology and Geographic Conditions of the Lower Mohawk Valley.* Albany, N.Y.: The University of the State of New York, 1929.

Brinkman, Lloyd M. and Members of the Niskayuna Historical Society. *A History of Niskayuna, New York: 1809,* Volume One. Niskayuna, N.Y.: n.p., 1976.

Brown, Chris W., III. *Guide to New York Waterways and Lake Champlain.* Gretna, La.: Pelican Publishing Company, Inc., 1998.

Bruce, Wallace. *The Hudson.* New York: Bryant Union, 1913.

Bulson, Dorwin W. *To-Wos-Scho-Hor: The Land of the Unforgotten Indian. A True Story of the Schoharie Creek.* n.p., 1961.

Burmeister, Walter F. *Appalachian Waters 2: The Hudson River and Its Tributaries.* Oakton, Va.: Appalachian Books, 1974.

Campbell, Malcolm W. *Play Hard. Rest Easy. New England: The Ultimate Getaway Guide.* Charlotte, N.C.: Walkabout Press, Inc., 2001.

Carleo-Evangelist, Jordan. "Firefighters Pull Pair from Brink of Disaster." Albany *Times Union.* July 28, 2004.

Carmer, Carl (selector). *The Tavern Lamps Are Burning: Literary Journeys through Six Regions and Four Centuries of New York State.* New York: David McKay Company, Inc., 1964.

Cary, Maureen. "Information Comes Naturally." *Schenectady Magazine*, Vol. 1, no. 3 (winter 1998).

Chong, Herb. "The Attraction of Falling Water." *Catskill Mountain Region Guide*, Vol. 18, no. 5 (May 2003).

———, ed. *The Long Path Guide*, fifth edition. Mahwah, N.J.: The New York-New Jersey Trail Conference, 2002

Clayton, W. W. *History of Onondaga County, New York, with Illustrations and Biographical Sketches of Some of Its Prominent Men and Pioneers.* Syracuse, N.Y.: D. Mason & Co., 1878.

Conroy, Dennis with Shirley Matzke. *Adirondack Cross-County Skiing: A Guide to Seventy Trails*. Woodstock, Vt.: Backcountry Publications, 1992.

"County Roads." *Schenectady & Upstate New York*. Vol. III, no. 1 (Summer 1990).

Cuda, Linda. "Beardslee Manor: Fact and Fantasy." *Mohawk Valley USA*, Vol. 3, no. 10 (fall 1982).

Cullen, Jim, John Mylroie and Art Palmer. *Karst Hydrogeology and Geomorphology of Eastern New York: a Guidebook to the Geology Field Trip*. Pittsfield, Mass.: National Speleological Society Annual Convention, 1979.

Cushing, H. P. *NYS Museum Bulletin 77. Geology 6: Geology of the Vicinity of Little Falls, Herkimer County*. Albany, N.Y.: New York State Education Department, 1905.

Dail, Jill, ed. *Folklore and Folk Names of Schoharie County*. Cobleskill, N.Y.: State University of New York Agricultural and Technology College, 1976.

Davis, Jackson, Anne Williams and Carol Winchester (compilers and editors). *Guide to Natural Areas of the Eastern New York Chapter of the Nature Conservancy*, seventh edition. Albany, N.Y.: Eastern New York Chapter, 1980.

Delaney, Barbara, "Timothy Murphy: The Making of a Legend." *Mohawk Valley Heritage*, Vol. 2, issue 2.

De Lisser, R. Lionel. *Picturesque Catskills: Greene County*. Reprint; Cornwallville, N.Y.: Hope Farm Press, 1971.

Doeffinger, Derek and Keith Boas. *Waterfalls of the Adirondacks and Catskills*. Ithaca, N.Y.: McBooks Press, 2000.

Donhardt, Gary L. *Indian Ladder: A History of Life in the Helderbergs*. Collierville, Tenn.: Donhardt and Daughters Publishers, 2001.

Donlon, Hugh P. *Amsterdam New York: Annals of a Mill Town in the Mohawk Valley*. Amsterdam, N.Y.: Donlon Associates, 1980.

———. *Outlines of History: Montgomery County. State of New York. 1772–1972. Bicentennial Edition*. Amsterdam, N.Y.: Printed by Noteworthy, 1973.

Driscoll, Daniel A., and Lindsay N. Childs, eds. *Helderberg Escarpment Planning Guide*. Albany, N.Y.: Albany County Land Conservancy, 2002.

Dunn, Russell. *Adirondack Waterfall Guide: New York's Cool Cascades*. Hensonville, N.Y.: Black Dome Press Corp., 2003.

———. *Catskill Region Waterfall Guide: Cool Cascades of the Catskills & Shawangunks*. Hensonville, N.Y.: Black Dome Press Corp., 2004.

———. *Hudson Valley Waterfall Guide: From Saratoga and the Capital Region to the Highlands and Palisades*. Hensonville, N.Y.: Black Dome Press Corp., 2005.

———. "Cooper's Cave: Fact and Fiction" *Glens Falls Magazine*, Vol. 5, no. 5 (spring 2004).

———. "Hiking the Waterfall Trail." *Adirondac*, May/June 1998.

Dunn, Shirley W. *The Mohicans and Their Land. 1609–1730*. Fleischmanns, N.Y.: Purple Mountain Press, 1994.

Eisenstadt, Peter, ed. *The Encyclopedia of New York State*. Syracuse, N.Y.: Syracuse University Press, 2005.

Encyclopedia of New York, Vol. 2. New York: Somerset Publishing, Inc., 1996.

Environmental Clearinghouse of Schenectady, Inc. *Along the Bike Hike Trail: A Guide to the Mohawk-Hudson Bikeway in Schenectady County*. Schenectady, N.Y.: The Environmental Clearinghouse of Schenectady, Incorporated and The Schenectady County Environmental Advisory Council, 1986.

———. *Environmental Trip Tips in and around Schenectady, New York*. Schenectady, N.Y.: The Environmental Clearinghouse of Schenectady, Inc., 1976.

Evans, John, Peter Quick and Bruce Sloane, eds. *An Introduction to Caves of the Northeast: Guidebook for the 1979 National Speleological Convention*. Pittsfield, Mass.: National Speleological Society, 1979.

Fisher, Donald W. *Bedrock Geology of the Central Mohawk Valley, New York*. Albany, N.Y.: The University of the State of New York, The State Education Department, 1980.

Fitzgerald, John R. *The New Erie Canal: A Recreational Guide*. Saratoga Springs, N.Y.: Quest Press, 1993.

Francis, Marilyn Milow. "Beneath Rolling Hills: New York State's Best Kept Secret." *Kaatskill Life*, Vol. 9, no. 2 (summer 1994).

Franz, Eleanor. "The Town that Dolge Built." *Adirondack Life*, Vol. 5, no.4 (fall, 1974).

Freeman, Rich and Sue Freeman. *200 Waterfalls in Central & Western New York: A Finder's Guide.* Fishers, N.Y.: Footprint Press, 2002.

Galbraith, Mary Adria. "Cohoes." *Mohawk Valley*, Vol. 1, no. 3 (Dec. 1980).

Gazda, Edward R. *Place Names in New York*. Schenectady, N. Y.: Gazda Associates, Inc., 1997.

Gibson, Chuck. *Forty Falls*. Ticonderoga, N.Y.: RA Press, 2003.

Gimigliano, Michael. "Middle Mohawk Images." *Mohawk Valley USA*, Vol. 5, no. 4 (winter, 1984).

Gomph, John P. *Sherburne Illustrated: A History of the Village of Sherburne, New York. Its Scenery, Development, and Business Enterprises*. Utica, N.Y.: John P. Gomph, 1896.

Grabowski, John and David Rhoden. *Awesome Almanac*. Walworth, Wisconsin: B & B Publishing, Inc., 1995.

Green, Stella and H. Neil Zimmerman. *50 Hikes in the Lower Hudson Valley*. Woodstock, Vt.: Backcountry Guides, 2002.

Greene, Nelson. *Old Mohawk Turnpike Book*. Fort Plain, N.Y.: n.p., 1924.

———, ed. *The Mohawk Valley: Gateway to the West, 1614–1925*. Vols. 1 and 2. Chicago, Ill.: The S. J. Clarke Publishing Company, 1925.

Gregg, Arthur B. *Old Hellebergh*. Guilderland, N.Y.: Guilderland Historical Society, 1975.

Griffin, Irma Mae. *History of the Town of Roxbury*. Roxbury, N.Y.: Irma Mae Griffin, 1975.

Grinnell, Lawrence I. *Canoeable Waterways of New York State and Vicinity*. New York: Pageant Press, 1956.

Hagerty, Gilbert W. *Wampum, War & Trade Goods, West of the Hudson*. Interlaken, N.Y.: Heart of the Lakes Publishing, 1985.

Hammond, Mrs. L. M. *History of Madison County, State of New York*. Syracuse, N.Y.: Truair, Smith & Co., Book and Job Printers, 1872.

Hart, Larry. *Schenectady: Facts and Stuff*. Scotia, N.Y.: Old Dorp Books, n.d.

————. *Steinmetz in Schenectady: A Picture Story of Three Memorable Decades*. Scotia, N.Y.: Old Dorp Books, 1978.

Hatch, Joel, Jr. *Reminiscences, Anecdotes, and Statistics of the Early Settlers and the 'Olden Time' in the Town of Sherburne, Chenango County, New York*. Utica, N.Y.: Curtiss & White Printers, 1862.

Herkimer County Historical Society. *Herkimer County at 200*. Herkimer, N.Y.: Herkimer County Historical Society, 1992.

Hislop, Codman. *Rivers of America: The Mohawk*. New York/Toronto: Rinehart & Company, Inc., 1948.

History of Montgomery and Fulton Counties, N.Y. 1887. Reprint; Interlaken, N.Y.: Heart of the Lakes Publishing, 1979.

Houghton, Raymond C. *A Revolutionary War Road Trip on NY Route 5*. Delmar, N.Y: Cyber Haus, 2005.

Howell, George Rogers, ed. *History of the County of Schenectady, N.Y. From 1662–1886*. New York: W. W. Munsell & Co., 1886.

Howell and Tenney. *History of the County of Albany, NY. From 1609 to 1886 with Portraits, Biographies and Illustrations*.1886. Reprint; Salem, Mass.: Higginson Book Company, n.d.,

I Love NY: Map and Guide to Scenic Route 20. 2005 map. Official publication of the Route 20 Association of New York State Inc.

Isachsen, Yngvar W. *Guide Book for Geological Field Trips to the Mohawk Valley and Lake George Regions: Part Two. Albany to the Glen via Lake George. Leaflet # 18*. Albany, N.Y.: New York State Museum and Science Service, Education Building, 1966.

Kenney, Alice P. *Stubborn for Liberty: The Dutch in New York*. Syracuse, N.Y.: Syracuse University Press, 1975.

Kimball, Francis P. *The Capital Region of New York State: Crossroads of Empire*, Vol. 2. New York: Lewis Historical Publishing Company, Inc., 1942.

Lake, Phyllis. "Canajoharie Gorge." *Mohawk Valley Magazine*, Vol. 1, no. 1 (June 1980).

Lanza, Michael. *New England Hiking: the Complete Guide to More Than 350 of the Best Hikes in New England*. San Francisco.: Foghorn Press, 1997.

Lewis, Cynthia and Thomas Lewis. *Best Hikes with Children in the Catskills & Hudson River Valley*. Seattle, Wash.: The Mountaineers, 1992.

Liddle, Warren. *Days before Yesterday*. Duanesburg, N.Y.: V.O.D. Communications, Inc., 1978.

Littell, Walter R. *A History of Cooperstown: including "The Chronicles of Cooperstown" by James Fenimore Cooper, "The History of Cooperstown 1839–1886" by Samuel M. Shaw, and "The History of Cooperstown 1886–1929" by Walter R. Littell*. Cooperstown, N.Y.: The *Freeman's Journal* Company, 1929.

Livingtston, James D., ed. *Glenville— Past and Present. 1829–1970. Sesquicentennial Celebration*. Glenville, N.Y.: Glenville Sesquicentennial Committee, 1970.

Lord, Philip, Jr. *The Navigators: The Journal of Passage on the Inland Waterways of New York, 1793*. Bulletin no. 498. Albany, N.Y.: NYS Museum, 2003.

Lossing, Benson J. *The Hudson: from the Wilderness to the Sea*. 1866. Reprint; Hensonville, N.Y.: Black Dome Press Corp., 1998.

Lynes, Marian S. *Water-Powered Grist Mills of Schoharie County*. Cobleskill, N.Y.: Printed by the *Times-Journal*, 1981.

Macha, Rich. "Mohawk and Hudson Rivers: A Variety of Experiences in the Capital Region." *Adirondack Sports & Fitness*, Issue #50 (July 2004).

Maher, Joe. "Funky Billboards Tell Secret" Schenectady *Daily Gazette*, August 27, 2000.

Manko, Sandra and Jean Bakkom, eds. *A Touch of Nostalgia: Sharon Springs Spa*. Sharon Springs, N.Y.: Sharon Historical Society, 2000.

Manko, Sandra, Katina Manko and Jean Bakkom, eds. *Reflections on Sharon: 1797–1997. A Pictorial History*. Sharon Springs, N.Y.: Sharon Historical Society, 1997.

Mastrean, Irma. *Princetown: Portrait of a Town*. Princetown, N.Y.: Princetown Historical Society, 1990.

Mattice, Beatrice M. *They Walked These Hills Before Me: An Early History of the Town of Conesville*. Cornwallville, N.Y.: Hope Farm Press, 1980.

McLaughlin, Donald. "The Noses: Mohawk Valley Gateway." *Mohawk Valley USA*, Vol. 1, no. 3 (December 1980).

McMartin, Barbara and Peter Kick. *Fifty Hikes in the Hudson Valley: From the Catskills to the Taconics, and from the Ramapos to the Helderbergs*. Woodstock, Vt.: Backcountry Publications, 1985.

Megathlin, Gerrard R. *New York State Museum Bulletin: Faulting in the Mohawk Valley, New York*. Albany, N.Y.: University of the State of New York, 1938.

Mohawk River, N.Y.: Letter from the Secretary of the Army. Washington, D.C.: Government Printing Office, 1957.

The Mohawk Trail. Brookline, Me.: Muddy River Press, 2003.

Mundow, Anna. *Southern New England*. Oakland, Calif.: Compass American Guides, 1999.

Munsell, Joel. *The History of Cohoes, New York: From Its Earliest Settlement to the Present Time*. 1877. Reprint; Salem, Mass.: Higginson Book Company, n.d.

Nardacci, Michael, ed. *Guide to the Caves and Karst of the Northeast: 50th Anniversary NSS Convention*. Huntsville, Ala.: The National Speleological Society, 1991.

1991 National Speleological Society Convention Program. Cobleskill, N.Y.: NSS, 1991.

New Scotland Historical Association. *Images of America: New Scotland Township*. Charleston, S.C.: Arcadia Publishing, 2000.

Nielsen, Brian and Becky Nielsen. *Around Cooperstown in Vintage Postcards (Postcard History Series)*. Charleston, S.C.: Arcadia Publishing, 2000.

Nolan, J. Kelly (preparer). *The Indian Kill Study: January of 1998–October 1999*. Conducted by the Environmental Study Team.

Nutting, Wallace. *New York Beautiful*. Garden City, N.Y.: Garden City Publishing Co., Inc. in cooperation with Old America Company, 1936.

O'Connor, David. *Old Chenango County in Postcards*. New Berlin, N.Y.: Molly Yes Press, 1983.

Oppel, Frank (compiler). *New York State: Tales of the Empire State*. Secaucus, N.J.: Castle, 1988.

Palmer, Richard. "State Park is Nationally Recognized." *Route 20 Pulse: The Heartbeat of the Highway of Dreams*, Vol. 2, no. 10.

Parker, Lucinda M. *The Little Falls & Dolgeville Railroad: 72 Years of Shortline*. Brookfield, N.Y.: Worden Press, 1986.

Parsons, Greg and Kate B. Watson. *New England Waterfalls: A Guide to More Than 200 Cascades and Waterfalls*. Woodstock, Vt.: The Countryman Press, 2003.

Patchin, Helen. *History of the Town of Blenheim, Schoharie County, New York. 1797–1959*. Schoharie County, N.Y.: Town of Blenheim, 1959.

Patton, Russ Jr. "Historic Highlights: The Gilboa Town Museum." *Kaatskill Life*, Vol. 20. no. 2 (summer 2005).

Perry, Clay. *Underground Empire: Wonders and Tales of New York Caves*. New York: Stephen Daye Press, 1948.

Phelan, Thomas. *The Hudson Mohawk Gateway: An Illustrated History*. Northridge, Calif.: Windsor Publications, Inc., 1985.

Reid, Max. *The Mohawk Valley: Its Legends and Its History. 1609–1780*. Harrison, N.Y.: Harbor Hill Books, 1979.

Rensselaerville Historical Society. *People Made It Happen Here: History of the Town of Rensselaerville ca. 1788–1950*. Rensselaerville, N.Y.: The Rensselaerville Historical Society, 1977.

Rich, John Lyon. *New York State Museum Bulletin: Glacial Geology of the Catskills*. Albany, N.Y.: University of the State of New York, 1934.

Roscoe, William E. *The History of Schoharie County*. Syracuse, N.Y.: D. Mason & Co., 1882.

Roseberry, C. R. *From Niagara to Montauk: the Scenic Pleasures of New York State*. Albany, N.Y.: State University of New York Press, 1982.

Rossi, Louis. *Cycling along the Canals of New York: 500 Miles of Bike Riding along the Erie, Champlain, Cayugaseneca, and Oswego Canals*. College Park, Md.: Vitesse Press, 1999.

Savoie, Dennis. *Cranks from Cooperstown: 50 Bike Rides in Upstate New York*. Cooperstown, N.Y.: Tourmaster Publications, L.L.C., 1998.

Schenectady County Historical Society. *Images of America: Rotterdam*. Charleston, S.C.: Arcadia Publishing, 2004.

Schmitt, Claire K. *Natural Areas of Schenectady*. Schenectady, N.Y.: The Environmental Clearinghouse of Schenectady and The Schenectady County Environmental Advisory Council, 1986.

Schmitt, Claire K. and Mary S. Brennan. *Natural Areas of Albany County*. Niskayuna, N.Y.: Environmental Clearinghouse of Schenectady, 1991.

Sive, Mary Robinson. "Highways and Byways of Schoharie County." *Catskill Mountain Region Guide*, Vol. 18, no. 7 (July 2003).

Smith, James H. *History of Chenango and Madison Counties, New York, with Illustrations and Biographical Sketches of Some of Its Prominent Men and Pioneers*. Syracuse, N.Y.: D. Mason & Co, 1880.

Spindle City Historic Society. *Harmony Mills Historic District: Self Guided Tour*. Pamphlet. Printed by The Rickman Press, Inc.

Stiles, Fred Tracy. *From Then till Now: History and Tales of the Adirondack Foothills*. Washington County, N.Y.: Washington County Historical Society, 1978.

Stoller, James H. *Geological Excursions: a Guide to Localities in the Region of Schenectady and the Mohawk Valley, and the Vicinity of Saratoga Springs*. Schenectady, N.Y.: Union Book Co., 1932.

———. *Museum Bulletin # 154: Glacial Geology of the Schenectady Quadrangle*. New York: University of the State of New York, 1911.

Stone, Thelma P. *Thumbnail Sketches of the Schoharie Valley*. Pattersonville, N.Y.: Unicorn Publications, 1981.

Strobeck, Katherine M. *Port Jackson: An Erie Canal Village*. Port Jackson, N.Y.: Port Jackson Publishing Company, 1989.

———. "Amsterdam. USA: Centennial Celebration." *Mohawk Valley USA*, Vol. 6, no. 2 (summer 1985).

———."The Chuctanunda Hills." *Mohawk Valley Happenings*. Montgomery County, N.Y.: Montgomery County Historical Society, 1990.

Sullivan, A. M. *Tim Murphy Morgan Rifleman and Other Ballads*. New York: The Declan X., McMullen Company, Inc., 1947.

Sullivan, Dennis. *Voorheesville, New York: A Sketch of the Beginnings of a Nineteenth Century Railroad Town*. Voorheesville, N.Y.: The Village of Voorheesville, n.d.

Taylor, W. Bronson, Levi Packard and Percy Van Epps. *Stories and Pictures of Charlton, New York*. Middle Grove, N.Y.: W. Bronson Taylor, 1959.

Titus, Robert. "Rising Out of the Sea." *Kaatskill Life*, Vol. 16, no. 4 (winter 2001–02).

———. "The Gilboa Forest." *Kaatskill Life*, Vol. 8, no. 1 (spring 1991).

Toole, Robert M. *A Look at Metroland: A New Guide to Its History and Heritage*. Saratoga Springs, N.Y.: Office of R. M. Toole,

Landscape Architects, 1976.

Triumpho, Richard. "Case's Mill." *Mohawk Valley USA*, Vol. 3, no. 9 (summer, 1982).

"Two Faces of the Mohawk River." *Explore Natural New England*, Issue # 26 (winter, 2006).

United States Bicentennial Commission of Cohoes. *Cohoes in 76: American Bicentennial. 1776–1976*. Cohoes, N.Y.: United States Bicentennial Commission of Cohoes, N.Y., 1976.

Van Diver, Bradford B. *Roadside Geology of New York*. Missoula, Mont.: Mountain Press Publishing Company, 1985.

———. *Upstate New York*. Dubuque, Iowa: Kendall/Hunt Publishing Company, 1980.

Van Epps, Percy M. *The Van Epps Papers: A Collection of the Reports of Percy M. Van Epps on the History of the Town of Glenville*, third edition. Glenville, N.Y.: The Town Board, 1998.

Van Zandt, Roland. *Chronicles of the Hudson: Three Centuries of Travel & Adventure*. 1971. Reprint; Hensonville, N.Y.: Black Dome Press Corp., 1992.

Vedder, J. Van Vechten. *History of Greene County, New York*. 1929. Reprint; Cornwallville, N.Y.: Hope Farm Press, 1985.

Vosburgh, Frederick G. *Drums to Dynamos on the Mohawk*. Washington, D.C.: National Geographic Society, 1947.

Vrooman, John J. *Forts and Firesides of the Mohawk Country, New York: Stories and Pictures of Landmarks of the pre-Revolutionary War Period throughout the Mohawk Valley and Surrounding Countryside, including Some Historical and Genealogical Mention during the Post-War Period*. Johnstown, N.Y.: Baronet Litho Co., 1951.

Waite, John G. and Diana S. Waite. *Industrial Archeology in Troy, Waterford, Cohoes, Green Island, and Watervliet*. Troy, N.Y.: Hudson-Mohawk Industrial Gateway, 1973,

Walsh, Natalie. "Falls for Spring." Schenectady *Sunday Gazette*, Lifestyles Section H, May 15, 2005.

Welcome to McArthur Park and the Gateway Gallery. Brochure.

Wild, Theodore P. "Te-Non-An-At-Che: A Mohawk Legend." *Mohawk Valley USA*, Vol. 3, no. 11 (winter 1982).

Wilkinson, John P. D. "The Timothy Murphy Trail: A Scenic Route through History." *Kaatskill Life*, Vol. 10, no. 2 (summer 1995).

Yates, Austin A. *Schenectady County, New York: Its History to the Close of the Nineteenth Century*. n.p.: The New York History Company, 1902.

Young, Cris. "The School That Was Owen Young's Dream." *Route 20 Pulse: The Heartbeat of the Highway of Dreams*, Volume 2, no. 9.

Index